A World of Polities

This collection of essays reflects the long-time collaboration of two of the world's leading international relations theorists, Yale H. Ferguson and Richard W. Mansbach. Following an introduction that traces the evolution of their ideas, the essays span the period from 1975 to the present, including selections from some of their major books and articles, as well as several previously unpublished essays.

Subjects covered include:

- theory and method in global politics;
- the role of values and the postmodern challenge;
- the complex roles of actors in global politics;
- 9/11 and its aftermath;
- the changing nature of political space and declining role of territoriality;
- US unilateralism, hegemony and empire.

A World of Polities will be essential reading for all advanced students and scholars in international relations.

Yale H. Ferguson is Co-Director and Professor, Division of Global Affairs, Rutgers University-Newark and Honorary Professor, University of Salzburg, Austria. He is a Member of the European Academy of Sciences and Arts and has been a Visiting Fellow at the University of Cambridge, the Norwegian Nobel Institute, and the University of Padova, as well as Fulbright Professor at Salzburg.
Richard W. Mansbach served as political science chair at Rutgers University-New Brunswick and Iowa State University and is currently Professor of Political Science at ISU. Formerly a Marshall Scholar, he has received three Fulbright fellowships–to Singapore, Seoul, and Vienna.

Books Ferguson and Mansbach have co-authored are *The Web of Global Politics: Nonstate Actors in the Global System* (1976), *The Elusive Quest: Theory and International Politics* (1989), *The State, Conceptual Chaos, and the Future of International Relations Theory* (1989), *Polities: Authority, Identities, and Change* (1996), *The Elusive Quest Continues: Theory and Global Politics* (2003), and *Remapping Global Politics: History's Revenge and Future Shock* (2004).

A World of Polities

Essays on global politics

**Yale H. Ferguson and
Richard W. Mansbach**

Routledge
Taylor & Francis Group

LONDON AND NEW YORK

First published 2008
by Routledge
2 Park Square, Milton Park, Abingdon, Oxon OX14 4RN

Simultaneously published in the USA and Canada
by Routledge
270 Madison Avenue, New York, NY 10016

Routledge is an imprint of the Taylor & Francis Group, an informa business

© 2008 Yale H. Ferguson and Richard W. Mansbach

Typeset in Times New Roman
Taylor & Francis Books
Printed and bound in Great Britain by
TJ International Ltd, Padstow

British Library Cataloguing in Publication Data
A catalogue record for this book is available from the British Library

Library of Congress Cataloging in Publication Data
Ferguson, Yale H.
A world of polities: essays on global politics / Yale H. Ferguson and
Richard W. Mansbach.
p. cm.
Includes bibliographical references and index.
1. International relations. I. Mansbach, Richard W., 1943- II. Title.
JZ1242.F474 2007
327.1–dc22
2007011522

ISBN13: 978-0-415-77217-4 (hbk)
ISBN13: 978-0-415-77218-1 (pbk)
ISBN13: 978-0-203-93905-5 (ebk)

Contents

Acknowledgements

We are grateful to the following journals and publishers for permission to reprint essays in this collection:

Yale H. Ferguson and Richard W. Mansbach, "Between Celebration and Despair: Constructive Suggestions for Future International Theory, *International Studies Quarterly*, volume 35, no. 4 published in December 1991 (pp. 363–86), Willey-Blackwell.

"Reconstructing Theory in Global Politics: Beyond the Postmodern Challenge", Yale H. Ferguson, Richard W. Mansbach in *International Relations and the "Third Debate": Postmodernism and Its Critics*, Darryl S. L Jervis (eds) © (2002) by Darryl S. L Jervis. Reproduced with permission of Greenwood Publishing Group, Inc., Westport, CT.

Yale H. Ferguson and Richard W. Mansbach, *Polities: Authority, Identities, and Change* (1996). Reprinted with permission of the University of South Carolina Press.

The Return on Culture and Identity in IR Theory, edited by Josef Lapid and Fredrich Kratochwil. Copyright © 1996 by Lynne Rienner Publishers, Inc.

Yale H. Ferguson, Richard W. Mansbach, "Postinternationalism and IR Theory", *Millennium: Journal of International Studies*, vol. 35, no. 3 published in September 2007.

Pearson Higher Education for Yale H. Ferguson and Richard W. Mansbach, "Values and Paradigm Change in International Relations," in *The Elusive Quest: Theory and International Politics,* © (2003) and "The Growing Irrelevance of the State-Centric Model" and "Towards a New Conceptualization of Global Politics," from Richard W. Mansbach, Yale H. Ferguson, and Donald E. Lampert, *The Web of World Politics: Nonstate Actors in the Global System* © (1976).

Part I
Introduction

The Principal Puzzle (2008)

Our three decades of collaboration began with the observation that the world depicted in the headlines of the day seemed curiously removed from the theories of international politics that we had learned in graduate school and to which, as young academics, we were introducing our students. For international relations (IR) scholars the early 1970s were heady years. 'Scientists' were enjoying what eventually proved to be a pyrrhic victory over 'traditionalists', and, as they had for centuries, theorists remained focused almost exclusively on the interstate system. Although realism remained firmly entrenched, there was increasing discussion of 'interdependence'. The war in Vietnam was drawing down, the Sino-Soviet split had ended the myth of monolithic communism, the Cold War had become ritualized, the global economy was recovering from an oil shock, and the Bretton Woods arrangements were beginning to unravel.

The media of that time were filled with stories featuring Vietnamese guerrillas and Arab *fedayeen*, giant oil companies, the Organization of the Petroleum Exporting Countries (OPEC), and the Palestine Liberation Organization (PLO). The tidy world of interstate theory, central to realism, seemed a far cry from messy reality. That idealized world was one of territorial states enjoying exclusive control of a defined territory, yoked together in an anarchic global system that featured competition for power and unrelieved conflict. We saw, instead, innumerable political entities, including many that lacked sovereignty, but nevertheless had significant influence and shared political space. Empiricists, whom a later generation of scholars would disparage as 'positivists', bolstered the interstate model of reality because it facilitated data collection and comparison. For their part, realists insisted that nothing had changed since Thucydides (as they read him) and ignored the cooperative dimension of global politics. They also used history selectively or, along with many 'scientists', ignored it entirely. For their part, 'scientists' ignored values, culture, and other subjective factors that we perceived as essential. In sum, the world of our textbooks and the world we were actually living in were poles apart.

Since its inception, the territorial state has been central to conceptions of *international* politics, and during our long collaboration the state – its

origins, theoretical utility, evolution, and future – has also been an important part of our research agenda. Over time we have explored and emphasized the full range of polities, identities, and loyalties that have been shaped
by, and have shaped, political outcomes, past and present. We have tried to
address the key question: Who or what have influenced the various outcomes in global politics – and how and why? Our search has been for the
genuine sources of effective influence, as distinct from nominal, legal, or
even legitimate authority. 'Authority' for us has been synonymous with
effectiveness, and it is constantly undergoing redistribution.

Our first collaboration, *The Web of World Politics* (Mansbach, Ferguson,
Lampert 1976), investigated what seemed to us, even then, to be the prominent role of nonstate actors in global politics. The book combined factor
analysis of an event data set with case studies of the role of transnational
corporations in Latin America, terrorists in the Middle East, and Europe's
emerging economic community. As these cases suggest, we were already
aware that the territorial state that had been constituted and legitimated by
sovereignty was being pulled from above into larger communities and was
also facing growing challenges from other transnational and subnational
entities. We urged scholars to abandon the static theories that dominated
the field. It was important to recognize that the territorial state had evolved
under specific historical conditions and, in any event, had never been the
only significant type of actor in global politics. Moreover, change was
apparently accelerating. Various types of actors formed 'complex conglomerates' and interacted around specific issues-areas that both transcended
and penetrated sovereign state boundaries.

Over a decade later we undertook a more comprehensive evaluation of
the condition of IR theory in *The Elusive Quest* (1988). The so-called Great
Debates – pitting realism against idealism and science against traditionalism – that supposedly advanced theoretical growth in the field appeared to
us to be caricatures of the way theory had really evolved, confused theory
and method, and implied quite wrongly that theory construction is a progressive enterprise. Antedating in some way the post-positivist wave, we
concluded that theoretical arguments in the field were as much normative
and political contests as they were disputes over hypothesized realities.

Realism and liberalism, far from affording serious explanations or predictions about our political universe, were two normative ideals at the ends
of four related continua concerning, respectively, the degree of mutability in
human affairs, optimism about the future, competitiveness among actors,
and elitism regarding decision-making (Ferguson and Mansbach 1988: 40–
47). The seesaw variation in the relative popularity of these schools of
thought reflected the 'normative temper of a society and an era' (Ferguson
and Mansbach 1988: 38). Indeed, we argued that relatively prolonged normative shifts lay behind the evolution of theory and policy. Thus, realists
were less interested in dispassionately describing and explaining the world
around them than in propounding a highly conservative vision of global

politics. They feared change as a threat to the status quo, in contrast to traditional liberals who sought change as the path to a better world.

Realist dominance of theorizing and analysis was perhaps to be expected in the post-World War II era. The United States sought to adjust to and cement a global position atop the status hierarchy, and counter the threat posed by Soviet efforts to share that status or oust the US from its position of primacy. Even while lamenting the loss of control over policy-making to an electorate that responded to ideological appeals and mood swings, theorists like Hans Morgenthau and practitioners like George Kennan advocated 'prudent' policies based on positions of strength in a competitive world in which the United States enjoyed significant military, economic, and technological advantages over its foe. Their nostrums remained highly state-centric, in part because any alternative threatened a loss of control for the United States and for territorial states in general. Even though dynastic sovereignty had become popular sovereignty, it remained as much a legitimacy principle for modern realists as it had for defenders of the Bourbons, Habsburgs, Romanovs, and Hohenzollerns in earlier centuries.

We insisted that, to the contrary, an overemphasis on the state and sovereignty remained an impediment to the growth and flourishing of theory and helped to preserve the 'international' (state to state) vocabulary and conceptual baggage that made it difficult to construct an alternative map of political reality. In *The State, Conceptual Chaos, and the Future of International Relations Theory* (1989) we pointed out that the many different usages of 'the state' concept itself actually masked very different interpretations of the character and significance of the state. Anarchy is another part of realist and neo-realist baggage and a justification for unilateralism in foreign policy. By contrast, we concluded that 'this central metaphor of anarchy turns attention away from describing and explaining the *dominant* patterns of peace and cooperation in international relations, as well as from the fact that the threat of violence is probably greater within many societies than among them' (Ferguson and Mansbach 1988: 188). Realists had consistently overstated the incidence of violence and cheating in global politics, while ignoring the vast areas of cooperation that existed under anarchy, and in doing so helped produce the conditions to which they claimed to be reacting. For their part, liberals, while recognizing the potential for cooperation inherent in transnational flows and international institutions such as regimes, had themselves consistently overstated the pacific nature of the domestic arena, invoked the domestic analogy on logical rather than empirical grounds, assiduously fostered the increasingly insupportable dichotomy between foreign and domestic policy, and assumed history to be 'progressive'. Only belatedly, with the introduction of 'governance' as a central concept, did theorists begin to recognize and consider the degree of 'world order' that actually exists on many levels and is by no means exclusively attributable to national governments (see, for example, Rosenau and Czempiel 1992).

We were profoundly discouraged by the apparent stagnation of theory in the field when *The Elusive Quest* appeared in 1988. 'In recent years', we concluded, 'the quest for theory in international relations has become, if any thing increasingly elusive. Those embarked on that quest stand today as in the midst of a maze, with the paths they have elected to pursue quite probably leading nowhere' (Ferguson and Mansbach 1988: 212). IR theorists seemed increasingly prone to brushing off and renaming old concepts and reinventing old ideas. '*Often it is not even that the world has changed,*' we wrote, '*as much as it is that theorists have noticed something that had always been there or have rediscovered something that is not new at all*' (Ferguson and Mansbach 1988: 221). Unexamined assumptions of rationality continued to govern claims about elite and mass behaviour, even as real behaviour – whether dealing with specific problems like the Vietnam War and nuclear proliferation or more general challenges like environmental degradation – illustrated the blinkered quality of human perceptions and the thus grave constraints on rational action in any meaningful sense.

We should not imagine that shifts and cycles in theoretical fashion are merely fads. Rather, they reflect a combination of changing global conditions and the policies advanced by political practitioners. In this respect, at least, theory construction is a far cry from the ivory tower; it is a thoroughly political enterprise, rewarding the fortunate and depriving others of tenure and funding.

The Elusive Quest also expressed our growing disenchantment with inductive empiricism and the hubris of the discipline's 'scientists'. Like later post-positivists, we were convinced that the effort to separate facts and values not only ignored much of what was genuinely 'political' in our field, but also was an impossible distinction to sustain. Even the effort to do so 'privileged' facts over values, and we concluded that all research, like practice, was infused by explicit or implicit normative biases. Scientists might use apparently value-neutral language, but were merely hiding their normative preferences. For example, more recently, research on the 'democratic peace', commonly cited (we believe, wrongly) as among the most impressive of the field's achievements, has reflected a cultural bias in favour of democracy among those doing supposedly empirical 'value-free' research. Perhaps for that very reason, research in the 'democratic peace' has also involved very shaky definitions of the central concept and a perilously small 'n' of test cases to support findings. Such dubious 'results' then, of course, seem to provide intellectual justification for practitioners' dangerously naive pro-democracy policies in places like Afghanistan and Iraq. We, too, prefer democracy as a political system, but we are not convinced that it can flourish everywhere or has anything much to do with peace.

Even before the 'democratic peace' became popular with the end of the Cold War, it seemed to us that too much intellectual firepower (as well too much government funding) had been directed by the field's scientists at great cost and with little to show for it. With few exceptions, the findings of scientists have been limited to those which are measurable and largely correlative in nature rather than genuinely explanatory. Unfortunately, faith in 'science' too often allowed methodology to drive theory rather than the reverse.

In the 1990s, we greeted the 'Third Debate' with cautious optimism because it was apparent that this new wave of theorizing would take us beyond the stale confrontation between the latest contenders for paradigmatic dominance—the two 'neos', neo-realism and neo-liberal institutionalism—and their shared assumptions of utilitarian egoism in a static universe largely drained of politics because of the dominance of structural givens. Indeed, we had ended *The Elusive Quest* by suggesting that theoretical progress in the field was only possible if we abandoned 'explicit and implicit analogies to the natural sciences', sought to understand the way 'humanists approach their materials', confronted 'squarely the political and normative environments that shape our consciousness and infuse our theories', and retreated 'from reductionism and correlative analysis' (Ferguson and Mansbach 1988: 222). Post-positivists – from constructivists across the spectrum to critical theorists and postmodernists – had begun to make similar demands.

Although some participants in the Third Debate were inclined to throw out the baby with the bath water by embracing extreme relativism and writing in riddles, the discussion served to legitimize and revitalize normative analysis and highlight the power relations inherent in social science discourse. Thus, we praised the 'refreshing appreciation of the role of "ideas" and "rules" and how these shape structures' and the renewed focus on 'the loyalties, identities, and other key attitudes of individuals' and the distribution of those attitudes (Ferguson and Mansbach 1988: 365). We remained positivists ourselves, though of a flexible variety, arguing that subjective factors, once constituted, could be examined empirically. Five conditions, we had argued in *The Elusive Quest*, were necessary for theoretical progress: (1) overcoming historical selectivity, (2) de-emphasizing strict empiricism, (3) liberating ourselves from state-centric realism, (4) erasing the boundary between the 'international' and 'domestic' arenas, and (5) moving freely among levels of analysis (Ferguson and Mansbach 1988: 367–75). A decade and a half later, the willingness of young scholars to break away from old routines and realize some or all of these conditions kindled a new sense of optimism on our part in *The Elusive Quest Continues* (Ferguson and Mansbach 2003: 224–5).

A further encouraging development was that students of global politics were again turning their attention to history in an effort to focus on change. The return to history was evident in the work of historical sociologists like Michael Mann (1986 and 1993), constructivists like Rodney Bruce Hall (1999), and even structural realists such as Barry Buzan, Charles Jones, and Richard Little (1993). Historical analyses, of course, have their own pitfalls. They reflect the normative lenses of their analysts; they are routinely revised to reflect the changing needs and conditions of the present and the perceptions of each new generation; and they inevitably focus on selected facts and events while ignoring others. Thus, 'objectivity is no easier for an historian than for a social scientist' (Ferguson and Mansbach, 2004: 63), and control of the historical archives provides control over meaning and, therefore, power. Nevertheless, historical scholarship is imperative for those seeking to explain changes in institutional and normative structures, and in political identities, loyalties, expectations, and perceived interests.

Our own growing conviction of the need for a long historical perspective with due regard for historical contingency and context found expression in *Polities: Authority, Identities, and Change* (1996). The central theoretical claim of the book was that changing authority patterns were the institutional counterpart of changing identities and loyalties and that focusing on the interaction between these was essential to making sense of shifts in the nature of global politics. The propensity of IR scholars to universalize the state and, in structural terms, to regard as significant only the distribution of power among states had prevented serious consideration of other political forms and changing authority patterns. Instead of an unchanging state-centric world, we envisioned 'a seamless web, encompassing numerous layered, overlapping, and interacting political authorities' (Ferguson and Mansbach 1996: 33–34). Returning for inspiration to David Easton's classic definition of politics as the authoritative allocation of values, we conceived of global politics 'in terms of the relationships and evolution of many polities of different types': empires, cities, corporations, religious entities, criminal organizations, families, and so on. Polities typically share some of the same 'political space'; they co-exist, cooperate, and compete with one another for the loyalties and resources of individuals and sub-groups with multiple identities. As a result, 'individuals are enmeshed in a complex web of relationships, inextricably intertwined with a large number of politically active entities' (Ferguson and Mansbach 1996: 43).

Only by a conceptual leap to a world of polities – we argued and continue to argue – can we overcome the artificial impediment posed by the levels-of-analysis 'problem', begin to break down the barriers between the traditional social science disciplines and their sub-fields, and move towards a theory or at least unified approach to understanding of 'politics' (Ferguson and Mansbach 1996: 34). Like states, all polities have their own boundaries and constitute moral communities in which members have obligations to one another that they do not have to those 'outside'.

Polities analyzed authority patterns in six historical systems that antedated the post-Westphalian era that represents the traditional scope of the IR field. However, the goal was a generic understanding of politics and hence a means of establishing the degree to which contemporary global politics is both the same as and different from the past. Each historical case reviewed shifting systemic trends as well as structural features and a variety of polity types. All six clearly illustrated that polities and their relationships continued to evolve and that such evolution was rarely, if ever, unidirectional.

Among other things, the analysis highlighted the role played by 'nested polities'. Nesting refers to the partial or complete incorporation of one polity or polity type by another in which the subordinate polity continues to influence and modify the dominant polity. 'The impact of nested polities', we concluded, 'will be felt in the unique attributes of the successor polity and show up in significant variations among institutions, ideologies, and behavior in each type of polity', and 'each polity reflects the impact of its origins and the nesting of other polity types that are the bases of its history' (Ferguson and Mansbach 1996: 395). Thus, contemporary states, far from showing the functional similarity often claimed for them, in fact exhibit profound differences owing in part to their different ancestries.

Polities examined historical systems that came before the Westphalian State. That European invention was consolidated over the course of several centuries and was exported via imperial expansion to the rest of the world. However, history did not end, and, just as authority patterns evolved in earlier centuries, they continue to evolve. Post-international global politics seems to us to exhibit a volatile combination of 'history's revenge' and 'future shock', which provided the subtitle for *Remapping Global Politics* (Ferguson and Mansbach 2004). Given the legacies from the past and accelerating change, including powerful globalising trends, we returned to the fundamental issue about how best to think about world politics and its likely course over the coming decades and centuries.

The chapters that follow suggest the paths that we have traced in our collaboration. Five of the essays and, of course, this Introduction are new, while the other seven are somewhat abbreviated versions of essays we have previously published. Our intellectual journey revealed to us a very different world than that which had been sketched for us by our own teachers and mentors. We have come a long way from a static state-centric world populated only by unitary sovereign states dominated by the exigencies of anarchy and, therefore, doomed to perpetual conflict by structural factors that determine political behaviour.

Our vision of global reality entails a fundamentally different ontological perspective. A world of polities is a dynamic one in which people, though constrained by structural factors, can and will significantly shape their own destiny. Political forms, identities, and loyalties continue to evolve at an accelerating pace. Sovereign states, though still important actors in global politics, bear little resemblance to the territorial goliaths of realist fantasy and share the stage with a multitude of other actors. Nationality shares pride of place with religion, ethnicity, tribe, race, profession, gender, and civilisation, and a host of other identities. As the role of territoriality and geography declines, the importance of psychological distance grows, and historical, normative, and cultural factors come to the fore.

Some might insist that our vision is insufficiently parsimonious. For better or worse, global politics is extraordinarily complex, and we can either deal with the world of polities as it is or achieve parsimony at the expense of understanding.

Part II

Making the Quest Less Elusive: Theory and Global Politics

1 Between Celebration and Despair

Constructive suggestions for future international theory (1991)

From Beijing to Berlin, throughout Eastern Europe and in the Soviet Union, 1989 was the year the world turned upside down. We are witnessing revolutionary change, a period in which ideologies are reordered, boundaries are redrawn, alliances are reshuffled, new symbols of identity arise, and old loyalties are resurrected.

Unfortunately, even as we urgently need to make sense of this new world of ours, theories of international relations are similarly in a condition of unprecedented disarray. Like the walls that kept peoples apart, those separating schools of thought are also tumbling down, but, as a result, there may today be less anarchy in world politics than in theories about it. Classical realism is in retreat, although it still has able defenders and has been reincarnated in modified form as neo-realism and rational choice theory. Cognitive theory has compounded the difficulty in assuming rational decision-making. Faith in strict empiricism, shared by so many in past decades, has dwindled to a few 'orphans of the scientific revolution' (Puchala 1991).

NeoMarxists and feminists clash with neo-realists, and none of these schools agree among themselves. 'Structuration' theorists pose and seek to resolve a central actor-structure problem.[1] Gramscian Critical Theory contends with Habermasian Critical Theory. Self-styled 'post-structuralists' recognize the power relations inherent in theory and reject the possibility of theoretical growth by incorporating perspectives from literary 'deconstruction'.[2] There is also a renewed emphasis among many on 'problem-solving', and a call in some quarters to postpone epistemological debates in order to concentrate upon political action.

The reason for such fragmentation is that, although there are widespread doubts about the crude, often ahistorical, empiricism that has dominated scholarship in our field for over three decades, there is little consensus about what to substitute for empiricism. Some theorists will continue the practices of the past and merely attempt to refine their tools. Some, including the authors, believe that, though it will be difficult, we can adapt empiricism to the task of making sense of the world around us. Finally, a variety of scholars have emerged who, however different their roots and modes of analysis, reject almost entirely the promise of 'positivism', which they view as a subtle means of maintaining the existing political order.

The purpose of this essay is to assess briefly the extent to which relatively 'mainstream' theorists of international relations can share assumptions with the self-proclaimed 'dissidents', and still construct a research agenda that will not abandon empirical analysis entirely.

It is equally clear to us and to those who call themselves 'dissidents' that few really important issues can be addressed by the scientific method in its strictest sense. In proposing that scholars focus their analysis of world politics upon the historically continuous competition for human loyalties, the authors believe that the discipline can take seriously the claims of its 'dissidents' while continuing to be precise in setting forth values and assumptions, defining terms, clarifying variables, and collecting evidence for generalizations. Rather than emulating natural scientists, social scientists can free themselves to develop methodologies that are appropriate to the tasks and materials at hand.

Constructive, Destructive, and Deconstructive Responses

A key part of the Third Debate is about what our fundamental attitude should be toward the prevailing condition of uncertainty. Yosef Lapid (1989) identifies and rejects two contrary judgments – 'celebration' and 'despair'. The celebratory position regards theoretical anarchy and consequent relativism in the field as a sign of vitality and exhorts us to remain faithful to the vision of future advances, perhaps even a new synthesis. Despair, by contrast, leads us either to give up 'the elusive quest' entirely or to proceed self-indulgently to 'do one's own thing' in the current extremely permissive context. Lapid defines his own middle ground, that is, continuing to pursue a less absolute standard of truth through 'science' with a recognition that there are no 'guarantees' of pay-offs.

Lapid incorrectly (though understandably) characterizes the authors' position as an example of 'despair', and we expect that the present essay will dispel that characterization. We share, for instance, Lapid's view that there is still a role for empiricism to play, but that it must be a less rigid empiricism – one that recognizes the distorting role of norms. We subscribe, also, to our interpretation of the first three of Richard K. Ashley's and R. B. J. Walker's assumptions about the contemporary world: that individuals have multiple identities and conflicting loyalties, that the struggle among competing authorities entails power, and that ultimate truth may be unknowable. Yet, in accepting these claims, we do not regard ourselves as 'dissidents', nor do we perceive ourselves at the margins of the field.

In other words, there are important insights to be culled from recent theoretical initiatives emerging from such disparate sources of inspiration as sociology of knowledge, philosophy of science, and literary criticism. By highlighting the intersubjective nature and normative foundations of concepts and theories and, therefore, our 'knowledge' of the external world, post-modernists open the door to a reinvigoration of the prescriptive, ethical dimension of theory and shift attention away from 'givens' like the nation-state to the micro-level – the authentic repository of human loyalties and affections.

There is also a refreshing appreciation of the role of 'ideas' and 'rules' and how these shape structures. Realists still focus on resources at the expense of attitudes. The assumption in such formulations that distributions of attitudes – identities, ideologies, goals, and expectations – are somehow derivative is a dubious one. More likely, resource and attitude distributions are reciprocally related, the former defining the realm of the possible, and the latter the realm of the probable.

The presence of effective rules obviously undermines the traditional stereotype of international relations as defined by anarchy, but then it always was a stereotype.

Although theorists continue to wrestle with how much can be explained by micro-level 'agents' and how much by macro-level 'structures' (a balance that we suspect is always in flux), inherent in this micro-/macro-debate is a salutary blurring of the customary intellectual boundary between domestic and international (internal/external) politics (Walker 1989: esp. 180).

Finally, some post-modernists properly argue that much of contemporary theory in international relations is ahistorical. Happily, they direct our attention once again to the 'genealogy' of concepts and the 'other worlds' that exploration of the past can reveal.

Genuinely Procrustean barriers continue to exist to transforming the field of international relations into a scientific discipline. We should not, however, rush to reject empiricism completely, but rather review our methods to sensitize them to the subjective dimension of issues that are ever lurking in research. Our view that theory reflects the dominant political and social norms of its time and place and that international relations research unavoidably reflects the norms of scholarly communities and the particular societies in which they are enmeshed, for example, has much in common with the post-modernist claim that 'the orthodoxies of our social and political worlds are recreated in the process of writing' (Shapiro 1989: 18). This does *not* mean, however, that we are unable to penetrate the 'external reality' behind the 'texts' that describe that reality. Instead, it means that empiricism must be informed by greater self-consciousness. Aware of the pitfalls highlighted by the 'dissidents', we should be getting on with trying to be as precise as possible in setting forth values and assumptions, defining concepts, and citing evidence for generalizations.

The recognition that theory is inherently subjective – even 'politicized' – is not novel. The manipulation of symbols has long been seen as central to politics, and theorists and practitioners have traditionally understood the power that flows from being able to spotlight only the facets of reality they wish, while leaving the remainder in shadow. Practitioners routinely cite 'snippets' from political theorists to buttress their position on issues. Just as Soviet Marxists for many years 'saw' only the determinist side of Karl Marx, so realists carefully embraced 'their' versions of Thucydides and Machiavelli. The recognition of such practices does not require retreat into the methodology of 'deconstruction'.

'Facts' tell us little outside of context, and context has a critical historical dimension. Things do change, and it is critical to be sensitive to variation and avoid overgeneralizing across time and space. Historians regularly remind us that it is necessary to challenge dominant interpretations of events and that it is often less important to uncover 'new' facts than to reinterpret the meaning of older ones in light of changing sociopolitical norms. Such important caveats do not, however, entail concluding that 'structure' and 'history' are necessarily antithetical to one another. Indeed, even while remaining sensitive to change, it is important to persist in seeking to identify aspects of structure(s) that are constant. And, even in the absence of homologies across time, suitable analogies have practical value in dangerous times.

In sum, students of international relations should recognize the modest progress that has been made on the long road to theory, as well as admit frankly that a much longer road still lies ahead. Now is a time for quiet reflection – and certainly for tolerance. There are many prisms through which to view reality, and the uncomfortable difficulty in achieving 'truth' does not entitle us to abandon the quest. The 'dissidents' have been accused – whether fairly or unfairly – of preaching a doctrine of stark relativism as part of their effort to achieve a social agenda. In reality, their work may help provoke a closer relationship between theory and practice. This desirable objective does not require a relativism that makes it difficult to justify one reality at the expense of another.

Thus far we have been focusing on the 'dissidents', but it is equally incumbent upon students of international relations to consolidate what is already apparent about the shortcomings of 'mainstream' approaches. Happily, we know enough to perceive some of the requirements – if not for better 'theory' in the strictest sense, at least for a better understanding of the world of politics across boundaries, which is our primary concern.

Some Guidelines for Progress in Theory

Overcome Ethnocentricity and Historical Selectivity

Most theorists of world politics remain stubbornly ethnocentric and strikingly ahistorical in their outlooks, and these two failings are related. The model of an international system of states is drawn primarily from European experience. Indeed, although the European outward thrust and 'triumph' produced a world divided into territorial states, many, especially but not exclusively in the developing world, obviously have little in common with the 'sovereign' entities that evolved in the West after Westphalia. Loyalty patterns over vast areas of the globe have less to do with frontiers arbitrarily laid down by colonial authorities than with earlier tribal authority and with ethnic and kinship patterns.

Why study the past? There is an urgent need to overcome our Eurocentric and time-bound tunnel vision and make sense of what is – and what is not – unique about the present. Looking backward can help to trace the origins of our familiar theories and concepts and to reveal how and why particular normative emphases in theory reappear century after century. It is also crucial to see whether contemporary models stand up against the litmus test of the past. Are there enduring 'laws' of politics and timeless concepts, or is everything contextual? We cannot begin to know until we have exhaustively examined the historical record.

What we mean by an exhaustive view of the past goes beyond the limited 'historicity' now becoming fashionable in some regime-theory and deconstructionist circles, focusing, respectively, upon specific 'understandings' of states and concepts.

Traditional historians and various philosophers of history stand in the wings with dire warnings about macro-history. In sum, we have to proceed as best we can, accepting lesser standards for the production of 'knowledge', if necessary.

De-emphasize Strict Empiricism

One consequence of strict empiricism has been largely to ignore the normative underpinnings of what we say and do, and theory that legitimizes behaviour and language. With this in mind, we have suggested elsewhere that theorists of global politics should pay more attention to the way in which humanists approach their material. This was not a brief for 'art' over 'science'. Raymond Martin's (1989) claim that, for historians, 'modest empirical subjectivism' is a reasonable substitute for often-unattainable certainty in understanding the past might serve as a model for our own field. Indeed, this may be what James N. Rosenau (1990: 27) has in mind when observing that to be 'short on evidence is not to be inattentive to the need for evidence'. In examining controversial cases like the collapse of Mayan civilization, Martin points out that although there are competing explanations, some are more empirically persuasive than others. In the absence of 'more reliable' ways of acquiring knowledge, Martin argues, 'it makes sense to acknowledge openly the critical role of historical judgments'. This is a constructive position, far removed from wholesale rejection of empiricism.

Not everything of theoretical significance in world politics can be *directly* 'observed' or precisely 'measured'. Scientific realism seems almost an oxymoron – a palliative for those who have given up on empiricism but who still wish to be called 'scientists' – but this school of thought makes the important point that 'unobservables' may be 'real'. Regime theorists

Kratochwil and Ruggie (1986: 763–7), for example, stress the need to address 'norms' and the 'inescapable intersubjective quality' of regimes, which means that they are known primarily 'by their principled and shared understandings of desirable and acceptable forms of social behavior'. While this is correct, it is critical to be shown that evidence for regime rules have, in Rosenau's words (1990: 27) *'potential observability'*.

Scholars in the field should be more imaginative and eclectic methodologically and adopt a less demanding view of the character of 'good theory', including the 'proofs' required to validate it. In the language of J. David Singer (1969), but antithetical to his argument, we may be 'incompleat theorists' if we have 'insight without evidence', but when evidence without insight is the only alternative, insight alone may be preferred. In many instances, 'understanding' may be the most that can be attained. Although 'impressionistic' work will fall short of the standards enshrined in the canons of science for 'causation', 'explanation', and 'laws', it can 'inform' in ways that empirical studies have, to date, largely failed to do.

A corollary is the need to downplay the virtue of parsimony in our models. All of us yearn for an elegant model that can explain everything. Regrettably, the world refuses to oblige by being – or revealing itself to be – as simple as we long for it to be. The determination to be parsimonious has repeatedly led to dangerous reductionism, with the result that most present models are caricatures of 'reality'. Imre Lakatos (1989: 35, cited in Dessler 1989: 24) has wisely suggested that we evaluate a theory not only on the basis of parsimony, but also on the grounds of the comprehensiveness of the explanation it advances and the extent to which it provides a promising foundation for future research. Of course, controversy will continue over how much any theory actually explains and how much it can be refined through future work.

Liberate Ourselves from Realist Mythology, or Pseudorealism

What we have said about loosening the bonds of empiricism is not meant to imply that 'traditionalists' had the whole truth during the debates of the 1960s. Most were as intolerant of competing visions as the then-upstart prophets of the scientific revolution because they were supremely confident of their own 'tradition', which essentially was realism. Even those venturesome traditionalists like Hedley Bull (1977), who insisted that there was something worthwhile in the notion of 'international society' and thereby tapped into a competing nonrealist tradition, remained comfortable with the realist assumption that sovereign states are the building blocks of global society.

In fact, 'the state' has so many different and value-laden meanings for analysts that it is virtually useless for theory building – a residual category. *It is at least essential that we recognize the degree to which the state concept and other concepts in the field do – and do not – contribute to understanding.*

To what extent is 'the state' observable – directly or indirectly? A major part of the problem is deciding what it is we are looking for. Is 'the state' a Hegelian symbol of collectivist identity, the highest realization of self? A 'nation', connoting ethnic identity? A 'government', that is, political institutions? A legal system? A 'country', with both territorial and perhaps some ethnic overtones? Some combination of all of these things – and more? There are, of course, many other definitions.

At best, the state as 'government' is a primary symbol of identity that competes with other symbols of identity for the loyalties of citizens. To the degree that governments can link themselves with other symbols like ethnicity, they may enhance their legitimacy and secure additional resources. Governments typically have standing military forces (of varying reliability) and tax revenues at their disposal; there is some concentration of resources at the 'centre', whether given willingly or not. The state symbol also has both normative and legal dimensions. Politicians and bureaucrats *claim* a monopoly of the legitimate exercise of violence and other 'sovereign' powers within state boundaries. They attempt to establish an effective legal system, which, among other things, assures stable property rights. They act in the name of the state, assuring all that their policies embody 'the national interest'.

From the vantage point of the global system, sovereignty 'signifies a form of *legitimation* that pertains to a *system* of relations' based on 'possessive individualist states' (Ruggie 1983: 276ff).

All this notwithstanding, it is clear that the realist/neo-realist, normative/legal conception of a world of sovereign states presents only about as accurate a vision of the 'real world' as a Hollywood western stage-set does of the old American West or as a Potemkin village did of Tsarist Russia. It is not *entirely* a fiction, but it is *primarily* a fiction. It is no more than *pseudorealism*. Norms and laws are part of the total environment that conditions behaviour, but we must go behind the normative/legal facade to see who or what is actually 'behaving' and the factors that influence behaviour.

There is no escaping three essential points: first, the state is only one of many group symbols with which people identify, and it is a tribute to the ahistorical and Eurocentric nature of the field to overestimate the extent to which loyalty to states always comes first. Virtually all individuals are subject to cross-cutting pressures arising from different identities. Loyalties to self and such extensions of self as family, clan, village, tribe, city, 'nation', 'homeland', church, profession, labour union, business corporation, political party, or ideology regularly undermine the political stability of states and everywhere limit support for government policies.

Second, states do not 'behave' – they are not actors. Individuals and a wide variety of groups within, without, and extending across state boundaries act. Given adequate information, the source(s) of *every* 'state' policy can be traced elsewhere. We can and should study the interplay of official policies of 'states' in the global arena, but if we wish to explain why such policics exist or speculate about their likelihood of continuity or change, we have to educe their genuine wellsprings.

Third, sovereignty as a normative/legal concept has modest practical consequences. There are always more interesting and significant things to comprehend about any state than its sovereign status.[3] Even if it could be decided where sovereignty actually resides, no government enjoys the degree of absolute control that the concept implies. Classic democratic theorists who held that only 'the people' are sovereign may have been closest to the mark; this apparent contradiction in terms at least embodied a recognition that shifts in ideology forced leaders to become more responsive to popular demands.

Numerous governments, in fact, face a breakdown in law and order because there is no normative consensus in their societies. They are routinely challenged by restive military establishments, street demonstrations, guerrillas in the hills, urban terrorists, ethnic hatreds, drug cartels, and so on. Control of violence is a major preoccupation even for many popular governments. In all cases, surely the existence of the violence itself is as significant as its 'illegitimate' or 'outlaw' nature.

Moreover, virtually all governments are confronted by growing challenges to their control arising from such micro and macro factors as the technological revolution, a better informed and less passive citizenry, and the international transaction flows 'managed' by transnational firms and banks. The hegemony of the superpowers and the autonomy of the governments of 'states' generally are diminishing; they are buffeted from outside and from below/within. There is a proliferation of relatively autonomous transnational and subnational groups (economic, functional, regional, ethnic) that enjoy a considerable say on the outcome of issues significant to them. *What we are witnessing appears to be nothing less than a widespread revolt against the prerogatives-and pretensions of 'the state'.* In other words, we may be approaching one of those historical sea changes (such as the conquest of tribal forms in the New World by bureaucratic European states) in which one form of political organization yields pride of place to others.

Political groups of many shapes and stripes have seduced the loyalties of citizens away from the 'centre' and have made governments everywhere increasingly responsive to official and unofficial demagogues, narrowly defined interests, public demonstrations, and opinion polls. What may be evolving is a global version of what William Kornhauser (1959: 227) described as 'the politics of mass society': 'Mass politics occurs when large numbers of people engage in political activity outside of the procedures and rules instituted by a society to govern political action.' The metaphor of unattached and atomized groups is an apt one for emerging world politics.

In the neo-realist view, anarchy is mitigated only by the widely accepted rights and duties of states that are enshrined in international law, by the existence of specific 'regimes', and by the exchange of certain considerations among states. *In reality*, governments at every turn find themselves increasingly constrained by structural interdependencies. Anarchy is not the dominant condition, unless one is referring solely to the absence of a full-fledged world government (though it repeatedly serves to justify self-help). Actually, situations vary by issue; some are characterized by greater mistrust and less coordination than others. The potential for anarchy may be growing under the 'atomized' conditions we have been describing, ironically even as the realists' state-centric world seems more remote than ever. Nevertheless, generally speaking, widespread cooperation and coordination of behaviour exist and are likely to persist, not because the idealists were right in believing that there is necessarily a broad harmony of interests, but because most participants regard the alternatives to be both undesirable and avoidable. Some policy goals clash and must be reconciled, but countless routine transactions and dependable consultative mechanisms involving a variety of actors – gloomy media headlines and precedent-breaking events notwithstanding – testify to the almost ho-hum regularity of day-to-day life in the global community. As for violence, there is a great deal more 'intrastate' than 'interstate'.

Neo-realist regime theorists and others do recognize that much of international behaviour is placidly patterned, ranging from an amorphous recognition of rules of the competitive game to more formal agreements. Agreements either codify obligations of conduct assumed by participants or create specific institutions that may themselves be the source of future rules. Yet neo-realists mar this vision with their devotion to the idea of a unified and rational state and their unnecessary and misguided fascination with the legal near-fiction of state sovereignty at the global level. Consider Keohane (1988: 385):' ... [Sovereignty] does not imply that the sovereign entity possesses de facto independence, although as a political matter, the fact that an entity is sovereign can be expected to have implications for its power and its autonomy.' Those 'implications' are not trivial, but a continued overemphasis upon them diverts us from the more important empirical question: how much autonomy do 'sovereign states' actually enjoy?

Before leaving realism, we must turn briefly to the related myths of objective state interests and rational decision making. Conceptions of 'national interest', however widely shared and parroted, are inherently subjective, and expressions of such shared subjectivities as ideology, ruling-elite beliefs, and shared foreign-policy consensus are too amorphous and often internally contradictory to explain particular policies. Actual decision-making requires participants to debate which policies will serve even the most widely shared goals and, regularly, to choose among contradictory goals. Of course, many participants seek to maximize personal, partisan, or institutional interests or those of other narrow groups.

Insights from cognitive theory suggest that Rosenau (1986: 862–3) is correct when he argues that 'the rational actor ... is an ideal type'. Happily, few decision-makers are 'irrational' in the sense of engaging in 'impetuous, erratic, spontaneous', or 'inconsistent' behaviour. On the other hand, however much individuals desire to use a cost–benefit 'rational' calculus, the result is almost always 'bounded' rationality, with uncertain bounds and consequences. They are also influenced by the adequacy of information, the press of time, idiosyncrasies of memory, personality quirks, prejudices, role constraints, competing tasks, emotional stress, and other factors.

Theorists seeking to salvage the assumption of rationality may take refuge in the claim that rationality only requires that decision-makers *attempt* to make cost–benefit calculations and, by extension, that decision-making systems are rational if they allow for interplay among participants with potentially different points of view. Theorists of this mind should ponder the wisdom of old adages like the camel being a horse designed by a committee. No attention is given to outcomes – that is, how parochial, mistaken, or even 'crazy' decisions might appear to observers. Rational decision-making theorists, like the actors they describe, are habit-driven, refusing (irrationally?) to surrender a comforting realist assumption and suppressing the readiness to learn that is part of their habit pool.

Rosenau (1986: 865–6) denies that the 'habit function' of decision-makers is unworkably 'nebulous', and is confident that the concept – and presumably other cognitive concepts – can be operationalized and made consistent with the canons of science. Here is where he and we part company and where the proponents of different types of 'dissidents' will need to argue among themselves. Although careful research may bare the perceptions of decision-makers in particular contexts, strict empiricism will probably not take us much further. 'Dissidents' will share our doubts about the likely fruits of empiricism, but they may differ as to whether generalizations can be made about decision-makers' perceptions in particular ideological contexts or whether perceptions are inevitably idiosyncratic because they are filtered through the personal 'glasses' of individuals.

Erase the 'International' and 'Domestic' Boundary

The presence of an impermeable wall between 'interstate' and 'intrastate' political arenas is enshrined in the 'classical tradition'. In reality, the two are not only 'linked', but actually constitute a single arena that encompasses countless individuals as well as numerous layered, overlapping, and interacting political authorities and other groups. These actors, in turn, are variously engaged in many, often interrelated issues. In this perspective, there is no 'international politics' or 'domestic politics' – there is only 'politics'. Politics is a seamless web, and we should be engaged in seeking a unified theory – or at least an approach to understanding – of politics *sui generis.*

A corollary of the practice of dichotomizing is thinking of the cast of global actors as a constant, with the territorial state the continual star of the show. The propensity to assume the state system as a *principal* and even *permanent* feature is inherited from eighteenth- and nineteenth-century Europe. Shedding our historically selective lenses reveals that the cast of actors in global politics has always been variable. Territorial entities are composed of many nonexclusive groups – organized horizontally and vertically – interacting at, between, and among various levels. Many relationships and institutions cross state boundaries, including formal and informal intergovernmental regimes and a great variety of private or 'mixed' intrastate and transnational entities (like firms, religions, charitable groups, and political party and labour organizations).

Political life is Janus-faced, and the fate of actors on both sides of the 'great divide' of state boundaries is knitted together. Issues germinate, spill over from, and have consequences for both sides of that divide. Competition for human loyalties is visible not least in the pulling and hauling that takes place between the 'domestic' and 'international' arenas over issues of foreign policy. That very language – evolved from the metaphor of the sovereign state – disguises what is actually taking place. In reality, competition for the loyalties of elites and publics is simultaneously underway among numerous groups and institutions situated within and without 'sovereign' boundaries. Both 'insiders' and 'outsiders' are actually involved in a single political process and seek allies among one another.

The concept of the 'national interest' serves to mask this pulling and hauling, but individual positions on specific issues usually reflect values that are the consequence of loyalties to something other than 'the state'. One supports higher or lower tariffs because one's labour union desires to protect jobs, one's corporation fears retaliation in European markets, or one's family likes Japanese cars and televisions.

Conduct Research Flexibly Among Levels

The conventional notion that scholars must choose among levels of analysis remains an unnecessary impediment to theory building. The interaction of a great variety of actors in a layered environment requires us to move freely among levels. In some cases, individuals or small groups are appropriate units of analysis, and insights drawn from individual or 'groupthink' psychology may be useful. In other instances, organizational or cybernetic theory may be relevant because of the centrality of bureaucracies and other large organizations. In still others, the emphasis may need to be upon regimes or other systemic attributes. Whatever the emphasis in a given case, additional insights can always be gained *by viewing the same issue from several different levels.* And, multi-level analysis becomes essential when generalizing across issues and actors. What is lost in parsimony is regained in the richness of analysis.

The issue-specificity of actors has important structural implications. When Waltz (1979: 102), for instance, declares that '[a]mong states, the state of nature is a state of war', he is also (wrongly) arguing that both the cast of actors and the structure in which they interact remain constant. Since the cast of actors is a key structural attribute, changing issues by definition means changing structure. Some issues resemble the 'state of nature' described by Waltz. Others, however, are characterized by norms and institutions that not only preclude violence, but also foster community or, in Bull's (1977: 4, 5) words, 'an arrangement [that] promotes certain goals or values' and 'sustains elementary, primary or universal goals of social life' (life, truth, and property).

Some of the recent literature on the 'agent–structure' problem, drawing both from scientific realism and structuration theory, is innovative in dealing with levels of analysis. Alexander E. Wendt (1987), for example, decries Keohane's emphasis on state 'agents' at the expense of regimes (structure) and Waltz's and Wallerstein's reverse emphasis upon structure at the expense of state agents. According to Wendt, scientific realism, by admitting the causal impact of 'unobservable generative structures', clears the way for appreciating that agent and structure are engaged in a continuous and dynamic interrelationship. It is agent–structure interaction that determines the nature of society (rules of the game, institutions, and so on).

This approach is to be applauded for its determination to move back and forth across levels of analysis, and it is consonant with a number of other, earlier views. Despite theorists' determination to focus on a single level of analysis, many (perhaps inconsistently) have long been comfortable with the assumption that an individual's choices are constrained by personal preferences and by environment, and also that choices of individual agents are reciprocally related to the environment. Some years ago, Harold and Margaret Sprout (1969) defined an 'ecological triad' encompassing actor, environment, and the actor–environment relationship. Bruce M. Russett (1972) adopted the provocative analogy of a 'menu', wherein an individual diner's choices are limited both by what the diner likes to eat and by what foods the restaurant serves. Presumably diners' choices affect future menus, or the restaurant is headed for bankruptcy.

Structuration theory itself 'does not tell us what particular kinds of agents or what particular kinds of structures to expect in any given concrete social system' (Wendt 1987: 355), which *should* be refreshingly open-ended. Unfortunately, the actor–structure discussion has so far proceeded with depressingly familiar overemphasis both on the state concept and on the international–domestic dichotomy. The contribution of structuration theory has, therefore, been limited principally because it has too uncritically accepted the 'generative structures' version of realist mythology to which we referred earlier.

However, weaving together observations about the distribution of attitudes and the agent–structure problem, it becomes clear that there is not a single agent, but many, and a consequent variety of structures that arise from their relationships and shape, in turn, the attitudes and behaviour of agents. We must consider phenomena both from a micro- and a macro-perspective, the latter conceived not as a single level, but as the panoply of interrelated actors and relationships in which the individual is enmeshed. Rosenau (1986: 866–7) gets it right:

[B]y their very nature, the macro processes and processes of any social system are rooted in and sustained by the habits that prevail at the micro level. ... To be sure, the more firmly macro structures are in place, the more they reinforce the habitual patterns of the micro actors who are embraced by them. This is why global structures and processes do not readily change. ... Notwithstanding this central tendency, however, micro-macro interactions cannot be taken for granted because the impetus to fundamental parametric change can originate at the micro level.

Toward a New Conceptualization of Global Politics

Revising our thinking in relation to the direction toward which we are trying to move will produce a significantly different approach to world politics than the approaches that have dominated the field in recent years. The new approach will:

- emphasize the subjective side of world politics and balance it with the 'objective' side that has long been the mainstay of positivist scholarship;
- be sceptical about the prospect for discerning permanent 'laws' of politics;
- avoid dichotomizing between 'internal' and 'external' politics;
- be sensitive to historical context;
- recognize the normative/ideological bases of theory and practice, the reciprocal relationship between them, and the difficulties this poses in seeking reliable 'evidence';
- seek to describe and explain the competition for human loyalties among a wide variety of (often) overlapping polities of many types.

Authority Patterns

Organizing concepts around which to rebuild theory include 'authorities' or 'polities' and the attendant human loyalties that uphold or undermine them. 'Authority', as we use the term, denotes nothing more nor less than *effective governance*.

We propose to take seriously David Easton's (1965) durable definition of politics as 'the authoritative allocation of values' by a 'political system' within its societal environment. We are, nevertheless, uncomfortable with Easton's concept of a 'political system', because it seems to imply a Platonic degree of discreteness, autonomy, power, and exclusivity that few, if any, real-world political entities have ever achieved. Moreover, Easton excludes from the realm of the 'political' nongovernmental social asymmetries, and this is unjustifiably restrictive. Lastly, we are not inclined to follow Easton in reserving 'authoritative' for the (supposedly) legally binding actions of governments. Value allocation, in our view, is authoritative if it is 'merely' effective; government action, whether legal or not, is not always binding in the sense of effective; law is only one possible source of the legitimacy that enhances the capacity of political actors to govern effectively (as an 'authority' or 'authoritatively'); and a wide range of governmental and nongovernmental entities may, in fact, govern effectively and thus each be an 'authority' or 'polity' within their particular domain(s).

The effectiveness of governance ultimately rests on the loyalties of those who are governed and on their willingness to provide resources to the collectivities of which they are part. Few, if any, authorities govern effectively on the basis of sheer coercion. Individuals obey authority not usually just to avoid punishment, but because they expect some benefit(s) in exchange, including both material benefits and the (often underrated) psychological satisfaction inherent in group identity and ideology. Authority, then, is an exchange phenomenon in which loyalties are provided to surrogates in return for value enhancement (or relief from value deprivation).

Today, as in the past, global politics reflects sometimes isolated, but often criss-crossing, webs of loyalties. Each is a social network, with a territorial scope of sorts, in which participants *perceive* one another as sharing some trait(s) that place them jointly in a situation of actual or potential advantage or disadvantage. Although individuals have many things in common – most of which remain unperceived – it is the perception of linked fates that produces a social network and lays the essential foundation for authority.

Our premises demand that we focus future research on questions of how authority patterns and attendant human loyalties evolve, overlap, and interact. Questions of this order can be addressed only through systematic analysis of a wide variety of historical and contemporary cases. The key intellectual issues are 'political', but only a few historical sociologists, neo-Marxist world-system analysts, political anthropologists, comparative politics specialists, and archaeologists have seriously concerned themselves with political evolution. The revisions in scope and method that we should like to encourage have implications far beyond any traditional conception of international relations as a field, let alone a discipline.

One assumption is that 'the authoritative allocation of values' has never been confined just to governments (unless defined so as to include all forms of political organization) or even to governments conceived as non-unified actors and supplemented by various overarching intergovernmental regimes. Territorial, legal, and organizational boundaries exist, but none encompass governmental/intergovernmental authorities with full control of the allocation-of-values process. Bureaucracies may enjoy extensive (albeit not exclusive) control over selected processes. In some cases, they presume to allocate values authoritatively only for those residing within the territory of a single state. In other instances, they allocate on a far greater scale, as did the British Admiralty and Foreign Office in the nineteenth century. By contrast, governments in the 'developing' world are often not effective allocators in any sense. Instead, such 'authorities' behave as special pleaders or lobbyists abroad and enjoy only very limited control over persons and things within and beyond their legal frontiers.

The allocation of values also takes place through a host of nongovernmental social networks that routinely cross state boundaries. Such networks have their own territorial conception of the world. Families and kinship groups have their homes, sedentary tribes their lands, nomadic tribes their home range, religions their faithful, political parties their party members and supporters, ethnic groups their ethnic 'nation', transnational corporations their production centres and markets, and so on. Various social elites and institutions engage in politics, sometimes in cooperation with, sometimes in conflict with, and sometimes without reference to governmental/intergovernmental elites and institutions. Each society is distinguishable, in part, by its specific division(s) or patterns of authority. Nevertheless, in a more profound sense, when it comes to explaining behaviour, it is inaccurate to conceive of a single political system or a single society. Individuals are enmeshed in a complex web of relationships, inextricably intertwined with other governmental and social entities.

When values cease being allocated in an acceptable fashion by one or another elite, loyalties fade, and the stage is set for their redistribution and a consequent shift in authority patterns. This process commonly occurs gradually (though not always, as in times of world war) because human loyalties are almost by definition slow to change.

Thus, there is often a discernible time-lag between events with a fundamental effect on the distribution of values and a significant shift in authority patterns.

Theory and the Competition for Human Loyalties

Loyalties can be shared among numerous authorities, and the manner in which they are divided and redivided is central to politics of all kinds. Competition for loyalties has been an engine of political change since the dawn of time. Elections, wars, and even advertising – though apparently disparate enterprises – may all be seen in substantial part as contests for loyalties. Onuf (1989: 243–4) remarks:

> World politics are still the terrain upon which belief systems are most intensely contested. No differently from priests, today's propagandists, ideologues, teachers, and publicists attempt to spell out the meaning and significance of the human situation in ways that inevitably affect the distribution of influence and rewards.

When a particular actor or type of polity (e.g. city-state, theocracy, chiefdom, empire) challenges dominant political affiliations or attains prominence in a given place and time, theory also emerges (or is revitalized) that reflects and helps to legitimize that polity. Such theory is essentially ideology. The emergence of absolutist monarchies in Western Europe during the 'early modern' era, for example, assured the growth of a 'statist' theory based on such concepts as divine-right monarchy, sovereignty, and the balance of power.

The symbiotic relationship of theory and practice appears to be universal. The rise of the polis in ancient Greece went hand in hand with the glorification of the city-state (Aristotle's 'man is a polis being') and the idea of citizenship. The triumph of an imperial institution in China coincided with the spread of Confucian doctrine, and the existence of administrators schooled in Confucian principles fostered imperial unity. Without a belief in the divinity of pharaoh, no Egyptian ruler could have even temporarily overcome the forces threatening the collapse or division of that civilization. The power of the Catholic Church in the medieval era rested not least upon its control and self-serving interpretation of the holy scriptures, and church doctrines – with their synthesis of political, legal, and theological themes – provided some stability for a turbulent age. Contemporary international regimes derive authority from widespread presumptions about the dictates of 'interdependence'. Ultimately, there are as many such examples as there are patterns of authority.

All societies are characterized by competition among authorities, each with its own symbols and resonant ideas. Returning to the example of the Middle Ages, there were Western and Byzantine variants of Christianity, several 'heresies' (e.g. Albigensian, Arian, Manichaean), at one stage popes in both Rome and Avignon, and ascetic orders decrying the worldliness of the hierarchy. The Holy Roman Empire waxed and waned, various kings argued about rights of investiture, and powerful towns and local nobles were loathe to recognize any higher authority. Debates over the interpretation of scripture had important implications for authority patterns generally.

If secular rationalism might inform the reader of holy scripture as well as the doctrine handed down by church hierarchy, what might be next? The answer, in part, was the Reformation, with its subversive implications both for the Church of Rome and secular authorities. Martin Luther's agonized pleas to his followers to obey their princes were not the sort of message that followers of Oliver Cromwell wanted to hear.

As these examples suggest, the *domain* of authority – that is, the number of persons, territory, and range of issues for which an authority effectively allocates values – is implicitly or explicitly limited. There are broad loyalties to entities like 'family', 'tribe', 'class', 'ethnicity', 'nation', or 'government' (the normative order of the state) that may help elicit obedience to authority over a wide range of issues. By contrast, specific authorities like the Greek amphictiony supervising the shrine of Delphi operate only in highly specialized areas of political life. Observers are likely to view different authorities as germane to particular issues and, therefore, as the ones to be obeyed regarding those issues. Perceptions of such interrelated matters as function, past success, aspirations for the future, and control over rewards and penalties influence which authority an individual will heed with regard to any issue.

From a micro-perspective, individuals in any time and place identify with selected groups, and their loyalties to groups are tested with regard to specific issues. Issue conflicts force them to make invidious choices among the positions proffered by competing authorities and, hence, to rank their own loyalties. A succession of such conflicts may force a major re-evaluation and reordering of loyalties. In the medieval period, for example, how did nobles (some of whom were also bishops) choose between and among pope and emperor, extended family, and local secular and/or religious authorities, and why did they make the choices they did? In early twentieth-century China, what bonds tied military officers to the Manchu, the Kuomintang, the communists, local warlords, and other would-be authorities, and how did such bonds influence political outcomes? These are the kind of questions that characterize a micro-perspective. Broadly speaking, they tap the changing cognitions, perceptions, and skills of individuals.

By contrast, a macro-perspective would adapt variants of the seven variables identified by Dina A. Zinnes (1980: 10–12) as ways of mapping and distinguishing among international systems. The maps of historical systems will include: (1) number of competing authorities, (2) distribution of resources among those authorities, (3) the issue-positions and issue-objectives of competing authorities, (4) the location of power within authority patterns, (5) the pattern of affect among authorities, (6) customary rules that govern interaction among competitors, and (7) the accorded status of competing authorities.

Unlike most conventional descriptions of international systems, however, this macro-perspective includes issues and examines the variables identified above for each key issue. In other words, we allow for the likelihood that the values of the variables and the rates and nature of changes in them will differ among issues. Issues appear like towns on an ordinary map, and authority patterns resemble roads that pass through and link the towns. Where several authorities converge at a single issue, we can anticipate competition, as inhabitants are required to select among them. If the same authorities are present in several issues, those issues are linked, so that outcomes in any of them will have an impact on others. In seventeenth-century Europe, for instance, religious disputes were enmeshed with issues concerning the political and economic relationships of local monarchs to the imperial centre, and localities to one another, as well as with issues affecting powerful personalities and various underclass ambitions.

Polities and Global Relationships

History reveals a world that has always been a crazy-quilt of polities – foci of authority with varying scope and influence; distinct in some respects and overlapping, layered, and linked in others; competing and cooperating in a quest for the allegiance of persons and control of stakes; and involved in a continuous process of allocating values that have almost always been in limited supply.

Even prehistoric hunter-gatherers and nomadic herders had a complex process for allocating values. Early entities that archaeologists classify as 'states' evinced characteristics customarily associated with 'modern' states, such as territory, executives, legislatures, judges, bureaucracy, taxes, military, interest groups, and social classes, as well as problems of succession, peer-polity and sometimes centre–periphery relations, alliances, wars, and trade.

The notion of the world as a 'living museum' points up the fact that institutional artifacts from every stage of human political evolution may still be found. Just as there are remaining pockets of Stone Age culture and predominantly agricultural societies, so too there continue to be tribes, city-states, surprisingly autonomous cities and other political or functional sub-divisions, myriad ethnicities, latent and more substantial 'nations', classes and masses, interest groups, political parties, monarchs, popes and patriarchs, transnational corporations, transgovernmental organizations, alliances, and putative neo-imperialisms.

Much of political significance over the millennia has derived from the interaction of entities that might individually be located at different points along a continuum of political evolution, yet the study of such interaction has been largely precluded owing to preoccupation with levels of analysis. Although we assume a continuum of political evolution, this does not imply that movement along it entails 'progress' in any value sense. Some political options close – even as others open – when population increases, environmental pressures grow, economies and social strata become more complex, communication and transportation improve, and relationships with other groups present threats or opportunities. Family-level groups tend to be subsumed into local polities, and these into regional polities, but the different strata neither completely disappear nor achieve full autonomy. For the most part, each assumes importance for members for different issues, but the most interesting cases are those in which they collide.

Historical analysis helps to explain the relative success and longevity of more encompassing polities. The effort of conquerors to eliminate competing authorities is often a recipe for continued conflict and instability. By contrast, in cases where new rulers seek to coexist with the old, are tolerant of 'foreign' mores, or utilize a strategy of co-optation, the resulting cross-cutting of authority patterns often functions well. Rome was prepared to tolerate and make use of local religions and nationalisms. Roman citizenship as well as other economic and political rewards were accessible to non-Roman subjects, provided they paid nominal allegiance to Rome and its gods. Conflict arose mainly when local authorities – the Jews and early Christians in particular – refused to reciprocate Roman tolerance, and when Roman subjects felt the balance between rewards and penalties had shifted against them. Centuries later, the British Empire adapted earlier models, especially the Roman, with remarkable success. Indigenous elites in India, Asia, and Africa were educated in British schools and were co-opted to manage imperial institutions.

Political evolution has never been unilinear. 'Empires' and 'states', for example, have at least temporarily in the past 'devolved' into 'chiefdoms', as happened in Italy under the Lombards and in post-Mycenaean Greece, respectively. More inclusive polities appear to simplify the political universe, yet may contain the seeds of their own destruction. They incorporate but do not completely overwhelm old loyalties; their very success in creating centralized power may set off a struggle for control; and centralization may result in an ideological revolution, economic take-off, or 'foreign' adventures that, in turn, have an impact upon social groups and loyalties. The fact that older entities have been absorbed into newer and larger ones does not mean that the former are irrelevant, but may merely mean a shift in the political venue and a new set of rules for waging conflict.

Throughout history/prehistory, divergent polities have coexisted in varying degrees of isolation from one another, and the collision of previously isolated authorities symbolizing entire cultures has been especially dramatic. Between the eleventh and the fourteenth centuries, for instance, global politics experienced successive shocks owing to the outward expansion of Latin Europe and the movements of nomadic tribes from central Asia. From Western Europe, crusaders set out to the south and east, intent on forcing the submission of Byzantium and Islam. And from central Asia, waves of Turkish and Mongol warriors overcame the Byzantine Empire and imposed their rule on large areas of Russia, China, and India.

In later years, the European voyages of 'discovery' 'encountered' the Indian empires of the New World and, although the Indians either died of disease or were 'conquered', their gold and crops had monumental consequences for Europe. Still later, imperial expansion imposed a thin veneer of European 'rule' and 'statist' bureaucracies over a tribal reality throughout much of Africa and Asia, which was to surface again to plague the 'new states' in those areas after 'independence'.

At the present stage of history, much of humanity is organized into discrete territorial units. The symbol of the state in some cases elicits a substantial measure of habitual obedience and considerable resources from citizens. However, by any standard – territory, ethnicity, GNP (gross national product), industrialization, military capability, governing capacity – contemporary 'states' have little in common. They are as different as persons, dogs, and whales are in the 'mammal' category. To aver that humanity is divided into 'states', though technically correct, is also trivial because it obscures the equally important fact that humanity is divided in many other ways as well. As in the past, key identities will continue to vary for individuals, binding and separating them, sometimes issue by issue.

There are few consensual rules of behaviour among the inhabitants of many contemporary countries, and there is little loyalty to an abstract state. In Lebanon, society breaks down along religious, ideological, and charismatic leadership lines; in Cyprus, Greeks and Turks refuse to coexist; in Burma, tribes like the Kachin confront Burmans; in Iraq as well as Iran and

Turkey, a large Kurdish minority continues to struggle for political autonomy. In Colombia and Peru, drug lords offer income to the underprivileged,
control large parts of their respective countries, terrorize government officials, and enjoy links with transnational drug cartels. The list is seemingly
endless.

Not only in strife-torn countries are there limits to the applicability of
rules of behaviour; everywhere they apply to some issues but not to others.
In many Moslem societies the state cannot intrude in matters of faith or
dictates of the Koran. In Israel, governments are hopelessly fragmented as
Jews in two major parties, who are themselves divided on secular and religious issues, negotiate alliances with a host of small religious and single-issue
parties. What we are describing may sound suspiciously like our old friend
'pluralism', and it does owe something to that concept. Pluralism, however,
carries the relatively limited connotation of 'multiple centers of power, none
of which is wholly sovereign', coexisting under the overarching authority of
the democratic state (Dahl 1967: 24). Where is the nation-state in this definition? Its presence is a vague, almost chimerical one; the state is absent as
an active participant or actor. Government agencies can, of course, participate in a pluralist arena, but there is no 'sovereign' player. Rather, the state
idea calls to mind the metaphor of God the Watchmaker,[4] in that it appears
to have set the rules of the game, started the game in motion, and then disappeared from the scene of the action. Pluralism reminds us that however
reassuring the state is from a metaphysical point of view, it gets in the way
when we analyze the processing of real political issues.

A New Research Agenda

We have identified the extent to which we share the scepticism of a growing
number of 'dissident' scholars in our field and where we part company with
them. Rather than rejecting empiricism and admitting wholesale relativism,
we are arguing for a new research agenda that will explore the evolution,
overlapping, and interaction of authority patterns and attendant human
loyalties from past to present. Such analysis will necessarily identify dominant and competing patterns, as well as continuities and changes over time,
and attempt to explain both the reasons for the patterns observed and the
important consequences that have flowed from them. Such analysis, for
example, might have alerted us to the intensive vertical pressures that were
building up against the governments of major states during the past 40
years and whose efforts are now visible as elements of an emerging world
order. We would have been able to 'see' that, even at the height of the Cold
War, polities as diverse as multinational corporations and banks, 'unconventional' guerrillas, terrorist, and peace movements, and ethnic separatists
were circumscribing the 'traditional' statist dominance of foreign affairs. In
sum, the dramatic change we are witnessing is nothing less than a contest
among authority patterns.

Historical/prehistorical periods vary dramatically in terms of authorities, loyalties, and issues. Some epochs are characterized by many polities, and some have relatively few. In some instances, authorities are highly linked, and in others they remain largely isolated from one another. They may be relatively homogeneous in some eras and very heterogeneous in others. They may be specialized and exist only in relation to a few limited issues, or they may be unspecialized and function across a wide range of superficially unconnected issues. Authority patterns may exhibit vertical organization, as in territorially-defined entities, or they may be predominantly horizontal, as in class-, religious-, or caste-based groups. Vertical and horizontal patterns may overlap, at least with regard to some issues, as is the case today, thereby creating unusual loyalty dilemmas.

A 'snapshot' approach will not capture the dynamic process through which authority patterns evolve. Change and the forces that produce it should be an important concern. Polities decay from within and are challenged from without. Of special interest are those epochs that are 'transitional', when the hegemony of previously dominant authorities is contested and loyalties are seduced to new authorities through the critical issues of the day.

Such periods involve major shifts in collective value hierarchies owing to contextual and situational factors that heighten perceptions of deprivation of some values and reduce anxieties about others. Shifts in values may result from evolutionary environmental changes (e.g. technological development or ecological change), or they may be sharp and sudden as a result of cataclysmic events (e.g. wars, plagues, and famines).

The relatively leisurely evolution in polities that accompanied the introduction of guns and gunpowder, the discovery of iron, and the great voyages of discovery illustrate one model, and the dramatic shifts in loyalties and institutions following the Thirty Years War and World War I illustrate the other.

It is essential to break away from 'statist' preconceptions derived from most theorists' exclusive focus on the modern West. To this end, theorists should give special attention to pre-modern times and non-European experiences. Only such a shift in focus will make it possible to discern what is constant from what is genuinely unique about contemporary political life.

While reviewing our craft, we must avoid becoming hopelessly bogged down in epistemological debates. Preoccupation with epistemology is an occupational hazard especially among self-conscious social scientists and devotees of formal theory. We share Thomas Biersteker's (1989: 267) conclusion:

> What ... we need most at this point is not a premature celebration of post-positivist optimism, but concrete, self-reflexive, nuanced, and theoretically-informed research. We need work that takes post-positivist criticism seriously and constructs plausible explanations of important subjects.

Ultimately, we have to stop critiquing (or defending) our own or others' theories, damn the epistemological torpedoes, and proceed full speed ahead on uncharted seas. The best way to start afresh is to abandon traditional conceptualizations and return to a study of politics in general, with a focus on authorities/polities, human loyalties, and value allocation.

Finally, students of international relations must stop trying to defend an imaginary 'disciplinary turf'. Acting upon the prescription we have advanced requires us not only to venture beyond our field's familiar boundaries, but also to tolerate the effrontery of others messing about in *our* intellectual territory. It is not constructive to trot out the epistemological problems that have too long paralyzed us to prove that interlopers are hopelessly naive.

Instead, we should acknowledge that all the social sciences and humanities are experiencing theoretical pluralism, but that each exists because it gives emphasis to an important facet of social reality that is less central to the others. Then we can recognize that many of us are interested in similar questions and do not need one another's epistemological baggage. What we do need is one another's expertise and the window on reality that each discipline's subject focus provides. Only then can we begin to integrate the apparently disparate insights of geography (e.g. location, climate, population, natural resources), biology (e.g. disease), technology (e.g. weaponry, communications), economics (e.g. production and markets), sociology (e.g. social strata), archaeology (e.g. non-historical evidence), anthropology (e.g. social mores), philosophy (e.g. religion, ideology), psychology (e.g. personality, group identity), language (e.g. concepts), and others into a broad understanding of politics. The task is a formidable one, but nothing less will suffice.

2 Values and Paradigm Change in Global Politics (1988, 2003)

One consequence of the behavioural revolution was to evoke unrealistic expectations of cumulative progress in understanding global politics. Yet, even in the absence of cumulation, acceptance of Thomas Kuhn's epistemology permitted optimism. If progress had previously been imperceptible, this was no longer the case because science itself constituted something of a revolution in the field, which would as a consequence shortly enter a stage of 'normal science'.

Our intention is not to reopen the stale and unrewarding science-versus-traditionalist controversy, nor do our views fall neatly on one or the other side of the positivist–post-positivist divide. We will argue that among the reasons for theoretical stagnation in the field are the materialist bias of Western science and the European tradition of global politics. This leads us to conclude that there are crucial differences between the evolution of theory in the social sciences (including global politics) and Kuhn's version of the natural sciences that render much of his analysis inapplicable to the former.

The Source and Role of Values

Kuhn (1970: 164) himself highlighted the most significant difference between the natural and social sciences when he wrote of 'the unparalleled insulation of mature scientific communities from the demands of the laity and of everyday life'.

In this respect, the contrast between natural scientists and many social scientists proves instructive. The latter often tend, as the former almost never do, to defend their choice of a research problem chiefly in terms of the social importance of achieving a solution.

In other words, the work of social scientists is generally infused by a commitment to serve the needs of the society of which they are members, and such a commitment is routinely reinforced or weakened by government and community norms and incentives. Patrick McGowan and Howard Shapiro (1973: 224) summarize well the impossibility of freeing research from its normative roots – although they shy away from the full consequences of this – and make the critical point that even the quest to separate facts from values reflects a normative claim:

> If normative preferences are not explicitly stated, then they are always implicit in the research – for even the desire to do a 'scientific' study is a normative decision. In addition, scholarship is a social process that in the end must justify its cost to society by the benefits it creates. Many social scientists feel today that social science is a tool in the struggle for a better world – for example, a world with a more equitable distribution of wealth and less violence. ... For many, then, their systematic orientation to the study of foreign policy derives from their normative interests in policy evaluation and prescription.

Indeed, one of the founders of modem realism, E. H. Carr (1962: 2), was fully aware of the normative underpinning of the scientific enterprise in global politics, including his own antipathy toward norm-made illusion. It was, after all, the dolorous consequences of a 'twenty years' crisis' as much as any rationalist disagreement that led him to write as he did:

> The science of global politics ... has been created to serve a purpose ... Our first business, it will be said, is to collect, classify, and analyse our facts and draw out inferences; and we shall then be ready to investigate the purpose to which our facts and our deductions can be put. The processes of the human mind do not, however, appear to develop in this logical order. ... Purpose, which should logically follow analysis, is required to give it both its initial impulse and its direction.

The facts that scholars amass and the phenomena that preoccupy them are selections derived initially from a set of specific value-based concerns. Those concerns lead them to focus attention on selected facts and phenomena at the expense of others. Thus, their version of reality necessarily spotlights some aspects of the world while keeping others in shadow. If the theorist chooses to take cognizance at a future date of what previously has been ignored, that choice reflects a shift in normative concerns rather than a paradigm change in the Kuhnian sense.[1] Carr (1962: 4) sees this to some extent as a condition of the physical sciences as well, but notes correctly how much more difficult it is to isolate facts from values in the social sciences:

> The purpose of research in global politics is not, as some claim of the physical sciences, irrelevant to the investigation and separable from it: it is itself one of the facts. In principle, a distinction may doubtless be drawn between the role of the investigator who establishes the facts and the role of the practitioner who considers the right course of action. In practice, one role shades imperceptibly into the other. Purpose and analysis become part and parcel of a single process.

For the most part, both natural and social scientists are aware of the intrusion of their values into the research process and make efforts to control their impact. But it is far more difficult for social scientists to do so successfully because of the pervasive influence of society upon them and their perceptions. The relative absence of objective concepts confounds the task even more, and policy preferences are routinely clothed in the garb of abstraction. Although natural scientists hope that their theoretical insights may *in the end* have an impact upon society, social scientists hope for such an impact, but as soon as possible.

The synthesis of purpose and analysis is evident in R. J. Rummel's (1976: 11) autobiographical reflection, which could probably be echoed by many in our profession. 'My lifelong superordinate goal', Rummel declares, 'has been to eliminate war and social violence; only by understanding this goal's genesis and enveloping cognitive structure can DON'S [Dimensionality of Nations project] research and my current re-orientation be grasped.' How different than this was the normative commitment of German historian Heinrich von Treitschke, who equated war with the 'grandeur of history'. And how well do these contrasting admissions reveal the starkly different normative climates of the societies in which they were written! It is not uncommon for pundits in impoverished or subjugated societies to devalue peace in the name of goals such as prosperity and independence and to promulgate theories that would achieve these ends through violence. These preferences can be debated, but no final proof can be offered as to the inherent superiority of one set of values over the other.

Jacob Bronowski's (1978: 127–9) arguments against the 'naturalistic fallacy' in the natural sciences are, if anything, even more germane to the social sciences. Bronowski suggests that normative consequences inhere in scientific discovery for at least three reasons. The first is that discovery reveals that certain forms of conduct are 'obviously ridiculous' and that one ought to tailor one's own actions so as not to be ridiculous. The second is that science informs us of our capabilities as human beings and 'that it is right that we should practice those gifts'. Finally, and most importantly for Bronowski, scientists must behave in certain ways in order to learn what is true, which is the object of their calling:

> What is the good of talking about what is, when in fact you are told how to behave in order to discover what is true. 'Ought' is dictated by 'is' in the actual inquiry for knowledge. Knowledge cannot be gained unless you behave in certain ways.

It is hardly surprising, then, that theoretical debates among political scientists reflect different normative commitments that are indirectly revealed in competing claims over which actors should be studied, which level of analysis is most appropriate, which variables are critical, and which issues are most pressing. Thus, assertion of structural primacy over agency is hardly acceptable to those dissatisfied with the status quo any more than advocating limiting the franchise to propertied classes in the name of stability is acceptable to 'diggers' or 'levellers'.

What is striking about these debates, and what distinguishes them from debates in the natural sciences, is that essentially the same arguments and emphases tend to recur through time despite superficial changes in concepts and language. And, as we shall suggest, such debates recur because they revolve around enduring normative themes. The key assertions and themes of realism and idealism, for example, have been present in intellectual discourse about global politics at least since Thucydides. In this sense, realism and idealism (or liberalism) are *Gestalten* with more or less clear ontologies rather than specified paradigms or theories as defined by scientists. As such, they are inevitably value laden, and their normative implications are often better refined and structured than their predictions or explanations.

Thucydides' *Melian Dialogue* and Thrasymachus's argument with Socrates in Plato's *Republic* are enduring reflections of the antinomy between power and justice. Centuries of European political theorists served the roles of realists and idealists. Machiavelli and those later known as Machiavellians consciously propounded their versions of realism in contrast to the so-called idealists of their time. The old realist–idealist debate is currently manifested in debates among structural realists and liberal institutionalists, on the one hand, and against unrepentant neofunctionalists, postmodernists, and constructivists on the other. (However liberal or reformist, no theorist wishes to be labelled 'utopian'.)

Such debates are no less value laden than their precursors. Leading schools of thought in global politics are as much a part of the *Zeitgeist* of their age as are dominant theories of art and literature; all are part of the *ductus* of a culture (see Ortega y Gasset 1948: 4). Indeed, the continuing devotion to science in global politics is a phenomenon that will always be associated with late-twentieth-century America and the numerous symbols of its 'modernity'-pragmatism, technology, non-representational art, functional architecture, and so forth. All reflect a similar ethos, fully as much as did *The Trojan Women* of Euripides and Thucydides' *History*.

Changing fashions in art and literature, changing social values, and the wrenching nature of such shifts are commonly reflected in fierce, though often arcane, conflicts over aesthetics and purpose. The triumph of baroque forms, for instance, gave testimony to a growing belief in human perfectibility and rationality, whereas the ascendance of non-representational art was but one of many clues that society had come to sense the growing impact of the unconscious and the non-rational on human behaviour. More obviously, we are repeatedly reminded of the unbreakable link between art and political ideology – both the reflections of more fundamental social values – in the legacies of great artists such as Pablo Picasso and Francisco Goya and of authors like Rudyard Kipling (imperialism), Maxim Gorky (socialist realism), and many others. The values reflected in their work reveal the social context in which they were formed and allow us to glimpse the collective values of their time and place. The intimate relationship between politics, and art and music has been appreciated and commented upon by successive generations of scholars; Plato, Hegel, Kant, and Marx are but a few of those who have been preoccupied by this relationship. Ultimately, art, like political theory, reflects choices among competing value systems. Thus, Pierre Bourdieu's (1984: 6) analysis of the consumers of culture might be applied equally well to consumers of political ideas: The science of taste and cultural consumption begins with a transgression that is in no way aesthetic: it has to abolish the sacred frontier which makes legitimate culture a separate universe, in order to discover the intelligible relations which unite apparently incommensurable 'choices,' such as preference in music and food, painting and sport, literature and hairstyle.

But what are the source and nature of the values to which we have been alluding?[2] Values are abstract aspirations for improving the human condition that may be pursued only indirectly through the acquisition of scarce objects that serve as stakes in political contests. In this way, stakes are the building blocks of what political scientists, especially realists and neo-realists, call 'interests'. When perceived in this way, interests are less ends in themselves (as realists and neo-realists claim) than they are reflections of the values that underlie them. In this sense, then, politics may be regarded as an unending quest for value satisfaction and as a process in which values are allocated and reallocated. Abstract values are sought as consummatory ends with intrinsic worth, while the stakes that represent them are merely instrumental in terms of value satisfaction. The former are universal or nearly so, while the latter are subject to significant sociocultural variation.[3]

The definition of individual or group interests, derived from values, is the core of self-identity, and bundles of different interests necessarily produce multiple identities. Context, of which the key element at issue is defined in terms of 'what is at stake', largely determines the individual identity that is triggered and actuated at any moment and, therefore, the direction and intensity of individual loyalty.

Although values are largely universal, value hierarchies periodically change in response to contextual and situational factors that heighten perceptions of deprivation of some values and reduce anxieties about others. In this way, interests, far from being static, continually evolve. Such shifts may be slow and imperceptible, resulting from evolutionary or secular environmental changes (e.g. technological development and ecological change), or they may be sharp and clear as a consequence of cataclysmic events (for example, wars, plagues, and famines).[4] Although individual value hierarchies vary, they can largely be deduced from socially specific collective norms. The collectivity determines the limits of what is culturally and socially acceptable and legitimizes certain values at the expense of others.

Value hierarchies represent *collective* perceptions of value deprivation (though there may be variation among individuals) and reflect *collective* experiences and neuroses. Their collective nature is institutionalized and reinforced by mechanisms of socialization, including family, education, and role. Political leaders must share and articulate key values and, in turn, seek to anchor them ever more firmly in order to foster cohesion and consensus. The scope and domain of such hierarchies are determined by additional factors such as the extent to which environmental changes or cataclysmic events are shared symmetrically and the degree to which peoples are interdependent or isolated. Thus, the Black Death, which afflicted all of Europe, had a profound impact on the value hierarchy of all who witnessed it.

Value and identity hierarchies find expression in the normative temper of a society and an era, which in turn conditions intellectual direction and philosophic predisposition. Theories of human nature, for instance, which are commonly the bases of elaborate theoretical edifices, are among the most obvious manifestations of changing value hierarchies and consequent normative predispositions. The 'timeless' commentaries on human nature by the early Christian scholars or by the likes of Rousseau, Locke, and Hobbes are not timeless at all; they are concrete articulations of the value hierarchies of particular eras and places. Thus, Hans Morgenthau's (1946) bleak realist view of human nature flowed from the atrocities of World War II:

> There is no escape from the evil of power, regardless of what one does. Whenever we act with reference to our fellow men, we must sin, and we must still sin when we refuse to act; for the refusal to be involved in the evil of action carries with it the breach of the obligation to do one's duty.

Whatever the prospects, then, for applying scientific methods to studying political phenomena, political science will continue to develop more like one of the arts than one of the sciences unless or until political scientists can isolate themselves from the milieu whose problems they seek to address. This, we believe, is an impossible task and therefore not one even worth attempting.

The Normative Basis of Theory

Although a feedback loop of sorts is involved, political dialogue is most accurately seen as a *reflection*, rather than a *cause*, of the normative temper of an era. And it is the shift in that temper, rather than the appearance of Kuhnian anomalies, that stimulates what are characterized as paradigm shifts in global-politics theory. Such shifts occur under conditions of rapid change and stressful events that generate an atmosphere of unpredictability and instability, a sense that somehow new and baleful forces are at work that will alter existing conditions in ways as yet not fully apprehended. In these circumstances, prior patterns of behaviour and standard procedures either no longer seem able to perform the tasks for which they were established or appear unsuited for new tasks that are identified. What James Rosenau (1986: 861) has felicitously termed the 'habit pool ... that is fed and sustained by the diverse wellsprings of human experience' is dramatically changed during such times.

Although the causal sequence remains unclear, such periods seem to be associated with the genesis of sharply different individual and collective identities and norms that constitute a very different subjective environment than in the time preceding them. This environment may be characterized by new or changed religious, scientific, social, or ideological concepts. The emergence of Christianity and Islam and the collective self-identity of groups of people as Christians and Muslims accompanied sharply etched normative climates that altered the political bases of the worlds in which they occurred. The scientific ideas of Hippocrates, Galileo, Darwin, and Einstein, among others, forced the reconsideration of humanity's place in the cosmos and fostered the emergence of powerful, normatively infused political doctrines and movements.

Changes in the subjective environment may be triggered by, and may in turn trigger, qualitative technological and economic shifts and major unanticipated events, especially wars and environmental disasters. Often the subjective and objective worlds change simultaneously, though this is not necessarily the case. Fifth-century Greece was one such period. This era witnessed the development of tragedy as a literary form by the Athenian poets, the philosophic relativism of the Sophists, the introduction of empirical diagnosis by Hippocrates of Cos, the development of mining at Mount Laurion (which provided precious metals for a monied economy), the earthquake and helot revolt in Sparta (464 BC), the plague in Athens (430 BC), and the Peloponnesian War. These events provided the framework for Thucydides' view of the world. The late-fifteenth through early-seventeenth centuries in Europe was another tumultuous period that witnessed a renewal of the plague, the rise of Protestantism, the ideas of Brahe, Galileo, and Kepler regarding the physical universe, the spread of movable type, the rifling of guns and the boring of cannon, and, finally, the Thirty Years' War – all of which combined to constitute a sharp break with the past and to usher in fundamental revisions of the normative order. In recent years, the revolution in microelectronics, with its implications for overcoming distance and devaluing territory, has had a similar effect. Changes of such magnitude point to new issues in need of resolution, new opportunities to be exploited, or both.

More recently, two types of changes have taken place in the subjective dimension of global politics. On the one hand, the decline of Marxism–Leninism was followed by the proliferation of free-market and modernist cultural self-conceptions, which have accompanied and reinforced globalisation while undermining territorially limited conceptions of state citizenship. On the other hand, there has been a veritable explosion of ethnic, religious, tribal, and even 'civilizational' self-identities – some historical and some new – that also compete with citizenship identities and threaten existing sovereign territorial arrangements. The consequences have been most dramatic in the developing world, where statist identities imposed by colonialists have yielded to prestatist identities, resulting in conflicts that threaten state survival. These events are examples of what Rosenau (1990: 128) calls 'the breakdown of traditional norms and the authority crises into which states have entered'.

Typically, major authority crises are accompanied by revisions in identity hierarchies and in the nature of political communities. Contemporary authority crises are also related to the declining importance of 'citizen' as an identity and the erosion of the territorial state as the dominant form of political organization. In earlier centuries, the authority crisis accompanying the European Reformation and religious wars was associated with the emergence and maturation of the territorial dynastic state, legitimated by 'the notion of personal sovereignty to buttress traditional divine right doctrine' (Hall 1999: 86). New norms produced new identities: 'Against king and particularistic privilege,' revolutionary leaders invoked 'the "rights of man and the citizen", "justice", "liberty, equality, fraternity", and citizenship for the "people" and "nation"' (Mann 1993: 193). 'Citizen' succeeded 'subject' as a core identity with the wedding of nation and state during the French Revolution and in the nineteenth century with the growing activism of the European bourgeoisie and the extension of the suffrage.

An authority crisis within Arabian tribal society was associated with the emergence of Islam in the seventh century. Islam and Islamic identities constituted a new and revolutionary normative order associated with a theocratic empire that at its peak stretched from Spain to the Oxus River of central Asia.

Authority crises reflect revisions in the normative order. Intervening between changing identities and political communities on the one hand, and revision of the normative order on the other, are perceptions of linkages among stakes at issue in the global arena and the hierarchy of issues on the global agenda. Fears of value deprivation, identification of new opportunities for value satisfaction, or both, occur as old stakes disappear and new ones emerge. Although these processes are continuous, they are especially intense during periods of potential or actual shifts in the global status hierarchy, when the enfeeblement of high-status actors encourages challenges to an existing distribution of stakes and the energizing of low-status actors spurs their ambition. For instance, the decline of traditional trade unions in the West and the growing obsolescence of traditional industries at a time of recession and high unemployment in the 1980s transformed into stakes many social and economic benefits and entitlements that until then had been regarded as sacrosanct.

As new stakes become available for contention and old ones are removed from contention, new issues emerge, old ones are redefined, and the salience of issues on the global agenda may be revised dramatically. Changes in issue salience redirect attention toward the values that underlie the newly important issues and away from values that are associated with declining issues. Accordingly, the value of prosperity, which in the United States had dominated the value hierarchy during the Great Depression, became a secondary concern with the outbreak of World War II and its aftermath, during which time physical security and freedom became principal preoccupations. As memories of the war receded in the 1960s and 1970s and the relative salience of key issues continued to change, values such as peace, health, and human dignity assumed greater importance.

Key Normative Dimensions

Changes in the global agenda of issues, and in the value hierarchy underlying that agenda, invariably produce new normative emphases, which are reflected in what we have called the normative temper of an era. Normative shifts occur along several dimensions, often at the same time. Among the most important of these are mutability/immutability, optimism/pessimism, competitiveness/ community, and elitism/non-elitism.

Mutability/immutability is the degree to which it is believed that human affairs and the conditions that shape them can or will be purposefully modified. In traditional cultures, the status quo in human affairs is accepted as inevitable and unchanging, and the conditions in which people find themselves are viewed as beyond control or manipulation. Arguments that attribute behaviour to the supernatural, to human nature, or, sometimes, to structural conditions commonly assume immutability. By contrast, modern Western science assumes almost unlimited mutability.

The normative implication of a belief in immutability is that efforts to change the human condition are at best a waste of time and at worst dangerous and illusory. In any event, such efforts ought not to be made. Political realism in its several versions tends to view political conditions as relatively immutable, whether owing to 'human nature' (Morgenthau), 'original sin' (Niebuhr), 'death instinct' (Freud), or 'system anarchy' (Waltz). Following Hegel, such theorists believe that the dilemmas of politics 'cannot be rejuvenated, but only known' (cited in Carr 1962: 11). Although realists and neo-realists accept that alterations in the distribution of power continuously occur, they see the struggle for power as a permanent feature of the international landscape. It is power theorists to whom Robert Gilpin (1981: 5) is referring when he writes of 'the Western bias in the study of international relations' as an obstacle to analysis of political change. Nowhere is this emphasis on immutability more succinctly expressed than in Hans Morgenthau's (1978: 4) observation:

> Human nature, in which the laws of politics have their roots, has not
> changed since the classical philosophies of China, India, and Greece

endeavoured to discover these laws. Hence novelty is not necessarily a virtue in political theory, nor is old age a defect.

For Waltz (1986: 341–3), global structure, rather than human nature, is the source of immutability. Although he admits the possibility that the global system could be transformed from anarchy to hierarchy, such transformation is highly improbable because states mimic one another's behaviour, most importantly in acting to balance one another's power. Thus, John Ruggie (1986: 152) concludes that 'Waltz's theory of "society" contains only a reproductive logic, but no transformational logic', and 'continuity ... is a product of premise even before it is hypothesized as an outcome'. Realists and neo-realists, argues Robert Cox (1986: 211), 'have tended to adopt the fixed ahistorical view of the framework for action characteristic of problem-solving theory, rather than standing back from this framework ... and treating it as historically conditioned and thus susceptible to change'.

This emphasis leads political realists to criticize those who seek to reform prevailing conditions, claiming that such individuals are 'divorced from the facts ... and informed by prejudice and wishful thinking', and that the laws of politics, rooted as they are in human nature, are 'impervious to our preferences' (Morgenthau 1978: 4). Since experimentation entailed an element of peril, prudence became the prescriptive hallmark of political realism. The prudent leader would understand the immutability of historical laws and eschew bold efforts to transform humankind or the global system.

In contrast to realists, those whom realists dismiss as idealists blame 'the failure of the social order to measure up to the rational standards on lack of knowledge and understanding, obsolescent social institutions or the depravity of certain isolated individuals or groups' (Morgenthau 1978: 3). For them, social engineering is both possible and morally compelling. Constructivists, for example, allow for changing meanings and identities that can entail fundamental transformations of global politics and for cultural changes that produce such altered meanings and identities. Over time, interaction can produce changed interests and identities. For their part, liberals allow for shifting state preferences – 'the fundamental social purposes underlying the strategic calculations of governments' (Moravcsik 1997: 513) – emerging from experience with international cooperation and shifting domestic interests, norms, and ideas.

Unlike the realist/neo-realist world in which human nature, structure, or both produce negative feedback that keeps on reproducing the same old world, liberal theory allows for non-linear change owing to 'a disproportion between the magnitude of the cause and the results, which will depend on the system as a whole' (Jervis 1997: 146). Moravcsik (1997: 535) continues:

> Liberal theory offers a plausible explanation for historical change in the international system. The static quality of both realist and institutionalist theory – their lack of an explanation for fundamental long-term change in

the nature of international politics – is a recognized weakness. In particular, global economic development over the past five hundred years has been closely related to greater per capita wealth, democratization, education systems that reinforce new collective identities, and greater incentives for transborder economic transactions.

Specifically, as more and more key actors share similar domestic values and institutions, their behaviour, according to liberals, will converge (Moravesik 1997: 540). In this way, domestic change can produce trust and cooperative relations that succeed conflict and vice versa. This, according to liberals, explains the end of the Cold War.

Optimism/pessimism constitutes a second critical normative dimension. Unlike mutability/immutability, which describes the degree to which it is believed that change can be engineered by human intervention, optimism/ pessimism refers to the direction in which change is headed and whether such change is the consequence of purposeful modification or not. More simply, it describes the answer given to the question: Are conditions likely to improve or not? Nevertheless, as the previous discussion of realism suggests, those who see conditions as relatively immutable are also likely to view change in a distinctly pessimistic light. After all, if the forces of change cannot be governed and directed, change itself is likely to be fickle, unpredictable and, ultimately, dangerous. There are, of course, significant exceptions to this intellectual propensity. Classical Marxists, for example, view history itself as an engine of progress governed by laws of economic development that will in time improve the human condition. And, as Waltz (1959: 18ff) points out, even those who start from an assumption that human nature is relatively immutable can be divided into optimists and pessimists. There are obviously degrees of immutability that allow for varying assessments of the potential for change.

Overall, however, optimism is at least partly a function of belief in mutability. Natural and behavioural scientists and social reformers share an acceptance of the possibility that the cumulation of knowledge and the application of that knowledge can improve conditions and behaviour. (This claim emerges from Bronowski.) The implication of such optimism is that it is the obligation of those with knowledge and insight to apply these for the benefit of humanity. In the context of political life, liberalism tends to be associated with optimism and conservatism with pessimism. Since degrees of optimism or pessimism would appear to be associated with discernible psychological profiles, it may be possible to predict the future political and scholarly orientations of individuals by suitable tests administered during their formative years.

Jeremy Bentham, who sought to deduce a universal ethic, typifies the synthesis of optimism and mutability through the application of reason. Buoyed by the apparently limitless prospects opened by the industrial revolution, Bentham decreed that, since humans sought pleasure, 'the greatest happiness of the greatest number' was the only possible guideline for collectivities. Such a guideline could be followed only by cooperation, and its content could be determined only by informed public opinion. Hence, Bentham and James Mill lauded the egalitarian effects that they saw as flowing from education, public knowledge, and by inference, political democracy. And it was this dedication to the cause of democracy that, perhaps more than any other factor, characterized nineteenth- and early-twentieth-century idealism. Since individuals sought their own happiness and since peace was instrumental to achieving this, only democracies could assure international peace, as only this form of government could accurately reflect popular interests and sentiments.

It is no coincidence that intellectual optimism and scientific advances are associated with eras and places where the norms of the culture were characterized by waves of optimism – Renaissance Italy, late-eighteenth-century France, Edwardian England, and pre-Depression America. Whereas pessimism encourages political conservatism and inertia, waves of optimism inspire great efforts to give history a nudge. Political revolutions, for example, generally occur in the context of growing optimism, or at least a belief that the improvement of conditions is probable once the weight of existing institutions is swept away. Not surprisingly, advances in natural science suggest to laymen that optimism is not misplaced.

In the context of global-politics theory, the post-war ascendance of political realism in part reflected a rejection of the prevailing optimism of the 1920s and early 1930s. Yet realism is not a doctrine of unrelieved gloom. Realists do see the possibility of ameliorating the effects of international conflict by the judicious management of power, especially its balancing. As a whole, advocates of a scientific approach to the discipline in the 1960s and 1970s, while retaining many critical assumptions of realism, reflected an increasing optimism about the prospects for overcoming the most dangerous problems of global politics insofar as the methods of the natural sciences were to be applied to an understanding of them.[5] However, growing fears about environmental, political, and economic trends in the early 1970s produced a renewal of pessimism.

And, the pessimism of the 1970s was a significant aspect of the revolt against realism, a new emphasis on 'spaceship Earth', and the re-emergence of doubts regarding the ultimate prospects for a science of global politics. Not surprisingly, this revolt accelerated after the end of the Cold War.

A third normative variable that is central to global-politics theory is that of *competitiveness/community*, that is, the degree to which welfare and deprivation are perceived in relative or absolute terms. '[P]ower', declares Waltz (1979: 192), 'has to be defined in terms of the distribution of capabilities'. Are evaluations of status and value satisfaction made in comparison to others, or are they made in terms of an absolute level that changes over time? The former emphasizes competition for scarce resources and the latter, linked fates and interdependence. When evaluation is made in relative terms, it implies that greater value satisfaction can be achieved only at the expense of others; changes in the absolute level of well-being matter less than the distribution of costs and benefits among competitors.[6] Outcomes are viewed in zero-sum, rather than positive- or negative-sum terms.

Emphasis on competition intensifies as perceptions of scarcity grow. One need not, however, necessarily assume such a convenient relationship between the two dimensions. Highly competitive doctrines such as Adam Smith's version of capitalism or late-nineteenth-century social Darwinism became popular in exuberantly expansionist eras. By contrast, theories of interdependence and 'limits to growth', which are at least in part based on perceptions of scarcity, emphasize the shared condition of humankind and the absolute nature of value enhancement and deprivation. Nor does there seem to be any necessary connection between competitiveness/community and optimism/pessimism, despite the common assertion that pessimism encourages competitive evaluations.

Political realism, with its emphasis on national interest, falls on the competitive end of the spectrum, and it is hardly surprising that this tradition took root in Europe after the Middle Ages, when numerous small states found themselves cheek to jowl. Morgenthau's (1978: 231) definition of global politics 'as a continuing effort to maintain and to increase the power of one's own nation and to keep in check or reduce the power of other nations' highlights the realist emphasis on the relative nature of status and security in the global system. Although there is no implication that a scarcity of political goods conditions the intensity of competition, it is the assumption of an absence of central power and trust that is fundamental to this analysis. In other words, scarce political space creates pressure toward zero-sum relationships. Efforts to equate the national interest with a global interest through international law and organization are dismissed as 'legalistic-moralistic' (Kennan 1951: 82), 'too wildly improbable' (Burnham 1943: 34), or, more generally, idealistic. Efforts to achieve justice must, in the realist vision, give way to the more basic search for security that can limit the prospect of relative loss with scant possibility for universal gain. The competitive world that political realists see is not anarchic, however, though it has the potential to become so. Classical realists from Thucydides on have seen their task as preventing such potential anarchy from becoming reality. The prevention of unrestrained violence in the international system and the management of the sources of such violence are key values that loom behind realist claims of the inevitability of interstate conflict.

For neo-realists, anarchy is the most important source of conflict in global politics. As a result of anarchy, competition is, for Waltz (1979: 74), 'pervasive', and competition, in turn, induces rational competitors to emulate the most successful among them. Anarchy in realist/neo-realist thinking permits only one interpretation because it is a condition in which betrayal is always possible and trust, therefore, never complete.

By contrast, those whom realists label idealists have argued that informed reason reveals a harmony of interests that can be sustained only by cooperation. Peace, for instance, constitutes a public good that cannot survive intense competition and parochial rivalries. 'I believe', declared John Stuart Mill (cited in Waltz 1959: 97), 'that the good of no country can be obtained by any means but such as tend to that of all countries, nor ought to be sought otherwise, even if obtainable.' Since democracies share the same values, there is no reason for conflict among them, and it is these values – nurtured and disseminated by education and a free press – that, to many so-called idealists, provide the real bases for a world community even in the presence of sovereign states.

In practice, emphasizing competitive elements in global politics necessitates undervaluing prospects for international, supranational, or transnational organization, whether formal or informal. Actors that are more powerful, wealthier, or more skilful should, it is implied, see to their own well-being and security before concerning themselves with some 'abstract' global good unless it can somehow be shown that the two are identical.[7] The global good may be secured but only in the manner of Smith's 'invisible hand' if actors follow the dictates of national interest.

By contrast, idealists perceive individual and collective good as identical and, in any event, believe that the former must give way to the latter if they are somehow incompatible. It is not the interests of states – fictitious corporations – that hold their attention but rather the shared interests of the individuals who constitute them. 'If it were not for extraneous interference, and a remediable measure of ignorance and misunderstanding', wrote Arnold Wolfers (1962: 86) of this perspective, 'there would be harmony, peace, and a complete absence of concern for national power.'

The devaluation of the norm of equality by those who emphasize competition tends as well to make them relatively elitist in their perceptions of global politics. This normative dimension entails perceptions of who ought to be involved in the making of decisions and the management of issues. Elitists emphasize that the possession of some attribute – for example, wealth, power, or skill – renders some individuals or groups legitimate leaders (and others, followers).

Among global-politics theorists, elitism takes the form of an assertion that certain actors in the global system are and ought to be responsible for significant outcomes that affect the system as a whole. An elitist emphasis can be manifested at different levels of analysis. At the system level, for instance, it may assume the form of claims that the discipline should limit its focus to 'sovereign' entities and exclude nongovernmental and transnational interactions. In a more extreme form, it may implicitly or explicitly entail the assertion that only the governments of 'great powers' or 'superpowers' matter and that the interests and aspirations of minor states can (and by implication, ought to) be ignored except in unusual circumstances. This realist bias is, in part, a reflection of a belief that order and stability are best assured in a system governed by a few who share common norms and are relatively satisfied with their status.

Realist admiration for the virtues of the eighteenth-century European state system, which was characterized by a shared value consensus within the narrow stratum of rulers and professional diplomats, is elitist in this sense. For realists in general, the avoidance of catastrophic war is the most important of values. In order to secure this, they are prepared to assume as irrational the value hierarchies of those for whom the risks of war might be preferable to the perpetuation of unbearable political, economic, and social conditions. They assume that the great powers are somehow more responsible than lesser powers, presumably because the former have so much more to lose than the latter. The poor or the weak might be tempted to behave rashly and promote instability in order to improve their status. Whether this argument takes the form of opposition to nuclear proliferation or praise for the ability of the balance of power to preserve the independence of major states, it is profoundly conservative and elitist. In effect, it is an international version of the argument that there should be a property or educational qualification as a prerequisite for enfranchisement.

The Wilsonian critique of balance-of-power politics was dismissed by realists as utopian because it did not take sufficient account of the role of power in global politics. Yet what probably incensed realists most was his (Wilson's) denunciation of the prevailing elitist ethic. It is not simply that Wilson denounced aristocratic rule within states, but also that he rejected a condominium of the great powers. His assertion of the rights of nationalities and ethnic minorities, along with his praise of democracy and the rights of small states, constituted a brief in favour of greater participation at all levels of global decision-making. There is an added irony in the fact that, although Wilson was accused of being naive for advocating such participation, he effectively predicted what has become an elemental process in the global politics of the late twentieth century.

At a different level of analysis, elitism may also take the form of assertions that foreign policy should be left in the hands of small coteries of professional diplomats. Such arguments are often made in the context of expressions of concern about the allegedly injurious impact of public opinion or shifting electoral majorities on the possibility for formulating consistent and farsighted foreign policy. Walter Lippmann (1955: 29), for instance, saw the 'devitalization of the governing power' as 'the malady of democratic states'. For their part, realists consistently lament the passing of the age of the professional diplomat and the onset of the era of mass politics. George Kennan (1951: 81) believed that 'a good deal of our trouble seems to have stemmed from the extent to which the executive has felt itself beholden to short-term trends of public opinion in the country and from ... the erratic and subjective nature of public reaction to foreign-policy questions', and Morgenthau (1978: 591) cited as one of his 'four fundamental rules' that '[t]he government is the leader of public opinion, not its slave.' In sum, the elitist bias of political realists is characteristic of their perception of all levels of analysis just as Wilson's anti-elitist bent was present in his views of both internal and external political life.

Conclusion

This brief analysis of the sources and nature of evolving theory in global politics is pessimistic about the prospects both for developing a cumulative science in the discipline and for paradigm advances of a Kuhnian sort. Notwithstanding significant advances in data collection and method, our analysis views the discipline as mired in an unceasing set of theoretical debates in which competing empirical assertions grow out of competing normative emphases that have their roots in a broader sociocultural milieu. Dominant norms tend to vary through time in concert with shifts in perceptions of the sources of value deprivation and satisfaction; and such norms, therefore, reflect the hierarchy of issues on the global political agenda. In effect, social norms mediate between circumstances and events and the perceptions of analysts and practitioners.

Our analysis suggests, furthermore, that dominant theories of an age are more the products of ideology and fashion than of science in the Kuhnian sense. Their sources are relentlessly subjective. If the natural sciences somehow evolve in linear fashion regardless of their social and cultural contexts, knowledge generation in the social sciences – including global politics – may more closely resemble that in the humanities, which is inevitably infused by the ethos of the era. Global politics will, therefore, continue to be characterized by a welter of competing theories that reflect significant political, subjective, and normative differences. Only when the global system enters a period of rapid and stressful change will a dominant theory *superficially* resembling a Kuhnian paradigm possibly emerge for some period of time. In all likelihood that 'new' theory will be old wine in a new bottle. It will reflect a changing normative environment and will yield pride of place once that environment again changes.

3 Reconstructing Theory in Global Politics

Beyond the postmodern challenge (2002)

Introduction

There is a well-justified tendency to associate an obsession with language and word games with extreme relativists or post-structuralists. Of course, playing with words is the very bread and butter of theorists of all stripes, not the least those of us who profess to be focusing upon 'international relations' (IR). So, as IR (somehow the acronym seems less controversial) theorists ourselves, we can perhaps be forgiven for raising the definitional question at the outset. If we are to move theory beyond the postmodern challenge, we have to be clear what 'postmodernism' actually is. Ah, we hear the Wittgensteinian chorus shout, wouldn't you like to 'know'?

Premodernity, Modernism, And Postmodernism

Postmodernism is not one but a cluster of approaches to the world around us that share a belief that 'knowledge' is less a consequence of impartial enquiry than an expression of power relations in particular social and cultural contexts Far from being a neutral seeker after 'truth', the scholar, in Steve Smith's (1996: 30) words, 'is always caught up in a language and mode of thinking which, far from interpreting a world, instead constructs it'. Thus, it shares with other 'post-positivist' endeavours a rejection of strict science and an emphasis on the subjective and normative dimensions of knowledge. Its prominence in IR during recent decades is a consequence of the rapidly changing nature of global 'reality', scepticism about the paradigmatic power tradition and grand theory more generally, the failure of 'scientists' to live up to their promises, and the ensuing anarchy that characterizes theory in the field today. Although postmodernism has deconstructed and helped to undermine traditional theories, a result that in some quarters has been judged beneficial, it has made other more positive contributions as well. But in none of its guises has postmodernism proved able to provide a secure foundation upon which to reconstruct a theory of global politics. Indeed, many postmodernists would insist that that is exactly the point: postmodernism is not a theory that aims to (re)construct intellectual entities so much as resist such ambitions.

It is in this light that postmodernism is better understood. Postmodernism could not exist absent 'modernism' and the desire to transcend modernity or at least supersede it. Krishan Kumar (1995: 66–67) phrases it well when he writes that 'postmodernism is essentially a "contrast concept"': 'It takes its meaning as much from what it excludes or claims to supersede as from what it includes or affirms in any positive sense.' Well, yes, except that there remains some debate about in what sense postmodernism is 'post'. Have we gone 'beyond' modernism? Kumar observes:

> The 'post' of post-modernity is ambiguous. It can mean what comes after, the movement to a new state of thing, however difficult it might be to characterize that state in these early days. Or it can be more like the post of *post-mortem*: obsequies performed over the dead body of modernity, a dissection of the corpse. The end of modernity is in this view the occasion for reflecting on the experience of modernity; post-modernity is that condition of reflectiveness. In this case there is no necessary sense of a new beginning, merely a somewhat melancholy state of an ending.

But what is or was 'modernism'? Once again, we run into considerable ambiguity. As Kumar points out, 'modernity' and 'modernism' are terms often used interchangeably, and he prefers to use 'modernity' to mean 'all of the changes – intellectual, social and political – that brought into being the modern world' and to reserve modernism for the late nineteenth-century cultural movement in the West that was actually partially a reaction against modernity. The first meaning is the one most postmodernists adopt, although the second is useful as a reminder that – as we note shortly – contemporary postmodernism has antecedents, so in some respects it is not so much 'post' as reprise.

Modernity, in the sense of 'the modern world', begins in the West with the medieval transition from 'the ancient world' and continues through the Renaissance and Westphalia well into the second half of the twentieth century. Although important regional and local variations existed with regard to both conditions and the timing of political changes, a gradual end to the feudal order, a reduction in the influence of the overarching polities of the papacy and the Holy Roman Empire, the growth of city polities, and consolidation of sovereign states and their territorial boundaries occurred.

Economically, the same time frame saw the widespread expansion of capitalism, steady industrialization, increasing trade in an era of mercantilism, and the eventual emergence of a world economy. Society meanwhile became more complex, with a growing middle class, proletariat, and always an underclass of the poor. The gap between rich and poor also found an echo at the global level between 'have' and 'have not' countries. Intellectually, beginning with the Renaissance there was growing emphasis on the individual and a belief in the inevitability of human progress. The Renaissance and later the Enlightenment ushered in an increasing secular faith in human reason and especially positivism or science as the key to knowledge and an engine of progress that often conflicted with religious faith and church doctrines.

Some contemporary postmodernists – especially 'critical' and non-state-centric constructivists – reject various aspects of modernity in the historical sense that we have described, but the Great Satan for nearly all post-modernists is strict empiricism or positivism. To be sure, in the 1960s the prophets of a scientific revolution in IR theory preached that particular brand of salvationism like the collective guru of a cult. Interestingly enough, although they virtually equated 'scientist' with superman, few such scholars actually described themselves as 'modernist' in orientation. The assumption, perhaps, was that the scientific method was a timeless path to truth.

Much of the problem of realism, of course, is its persistent state-centric view of world affairs, a problem that stems in part from its embrace of modernity as proscribed in our definition. Statism has also been character-istic of most of the work of the strict scientists. Reification of the state, and therefore the exclusion of other actors, appeals to positivists because it is parsimonious. That such explanations are often gross distortions of a complex world sometimes seems less important than their supposed elegance.

Thus, the 'great debate' between 'science' and 'traditionalism' was not terribly 'great'. At root, the 'scientists' ignored theory while focusing on method. Indeed, since parsimony and statistical comparability were among their major goals, they needed to retain a model of global politics based on functionally homologous and exclusive units (states) for which there were plentiful data. Each of these units had to occupy an exclusive space so as to prevent the sort of medieval overlap that so complicated comparability. In the end, the scientists were much the same as the theorists described by John Agnew and Stuart Corbridge (1995: 83):

> [Among the contextual factors that have interacted to reproduce the dominant view about state territoriality found in such apparently different works as those of Waltz and Keohane] is the preference for abstract and 'closed-system' thinking among advocates of a scientific (positivist) approach to international relations. ... From this perspective a 'state' is an ideal-type or logical object rather than any particular state and, thus, states can be written about without reference to the concrete conditions in which they exist. If the system of international relations is thought of as an 'open system," such abstract (ahistorical and aspatial) theorizing becomes impossible. Causal chains would form and dissolve historically and geographically. They could not be reduced to a set of primitive terms that would hold true across space and through time. Essential state sovereignty is such a primitive term.

Ah, sounds again the Wittgensteinian chorus, neither modernism nor post-modernism has any meaning in the absence of 'premodernism' – and what, then, is that? A world of primordial and overlapping identities, 'tribalism', and variable political forms from cities to leagues and federations to empires plainly antedates the modern era. So, too, do intellectual attitudes other than Aristotle's, some of which bear an intriguing resemblance to present-day postmodernism. Felipe Fernández-Armesto (1997: 204) observes that Protagoras's 'guiding maxim' was that man 'is the measure of all things that are and the non-existence of the things that are not'. Socrates found that idea profoundly disturbing. 'Is this not roughly what [Protagoras] means', he said, 'that things are for me such as they appear to me, and for you such as they appear to you?' Socrates was sure Protagoras 'was wrong but got baffled in the attempt to disprove him'. Reports Fernández-Armesto:

> He confessed to 'vexation and actual fear' for what else could you call it when a man drags his arguments up and down because he is so stupid that he cannot be convinced and is hardly to be induced to give up any one of them?

Kumar (1995: 93–8) brilliantly explains that revolts against various stages or aspects of modernity have been going on, in one form or another, for a very long time. Unlike later revolts, the earlier movements seemed to retain a sense that the world could still be redeemed, not altogether unlike (we might suggest) some versions of contemporary postmodernist thought of a 'critical' variety. Kierkegaard and Nietzsche were considerably more pessimistic about the prospects for 'civilization' as were French writers such as Baudelaire and Rimbaud. Although often regarded as the epitome of early twentieth-century modernists, authors like Eliot, Proust, Woolf, Joyce, Strindberg, Brecht, and Faulkner also broke dramatically with many traditional forms, playing with ideas, and subject matter, and language through such techniques as stream of consciousness and free verse. Meanwhile, Stravinsky, Berg, and Webern assaulted established tonal music. Artists like Picasso and Braque, philosophers like Sorel and William James, architects like Wright or Le Corbusier, and psychiatrists like Freud and Jung were equally outrageous in their periods. Dadaists, during and after the First World War, 'attacked all the official ideas and institutions that had conspired to produce the mess', even art itself, 'the sacred cow of the establishment'. Surrealists like 'Dali and Buñuel aimed to show that the fantastic was as real as the reality revealed by modern science.' And so on.

Given all the precedents, we have to accept not only what Kumar terms 'the ambivalence of modernity', but also that of premodernity and postmodernism. Some of the arguments and visions of apocalypse or cries for reform have been around a long time and – yes, chorus – were relative in their degree of shock to the times in which they appeared. Marx was an 'alien' and 'outlaw' thinker in his day and still inspires some postmodernists.

But the political system and industrial economy built by Stalin was modernity at its most monolithic and oppressive. Similarly, as David Ashley (1997: 9) reports:

> By the 1950s, the work of abstract expressionists such as Jackson Pollock was being funded by the Central Intelligence Agency as part of an official state effort to demonstrate the American artists were more 'advanced,' more imaginative, and more 'progressive' than their Soviet counterparts. This propaganda effort ... was additionally intended to win the hearts and minds of avant-garde intellectuals, many of whom stubbornly continued to insist that Marxism had more to offer the world than Dwight Eisenhower's America.

That said, by contrast, it is somewhat easier to identify some of the principal 'schools' of postmodernist thought in present-day IR theory.

At one pole (happy to be there, except that being situated anywhere is an attempt at categorization and co-optation, and always an illusion) are the extreme relativists or post-structuralists, including James Der Derian, Richard K. Ashley, Jim George, David Campbell, and Michael J. Shapiro. These are the intellectual legatees of Jacques Derrida, Michel Foucault, Ludwig Wittgenstein, and others who insist that language has no inherent meaning and can only be understood, at best, in particular contexts. For Derrida the context is individuals, for Foucault social power relations, and for Wittgenstein the rules of a particular 'game' in which language is engaged. Since language has no dependable meaning and we can describe the world about us only through language, our views of the world are, likewise, undependable and fundamentally incommunicable to others. Theories cannot help but be value-laden. Language and its visual counterpart transmitted through the media images of a technological age should nonetheless be continually 'deconstructed' and their 'genealogies' explored to reveal the different versions of reality ('discourses') reflected therein. There is no such thing as a better epistemology, only hermeneutics or the philosophical concern with understanding and interpretation. New language must be invented and used, both to shock readers out of their complacency and to describe new understandings, however ephemeral they may be. There is no hope for any genuine human progress, only the inevitable 'alienation' and 'exile' encountered in an essentially meaningless universe.

'Critical theory', too, at least as invoked in certain quarters, also offers a textbook example of extreme relativism, and one that is often grouped with postmodernism in much contemporary literature. As Kublaková, Onuf, and Kowert (1998: 7) remark:

> Philosophers have used the term in a specialized sense that goes back to Immanuel Kant. In the hands of Marxist theorists, it acquired a different, though still specialized, meaning. ... Thanks to the diffusion of a

specifically neo-Marxist dialect, scholars in several disciplines now use the term in ways that neither Kant nor any ordinary person would understand. ... Not being critical might mean that a scholar is positivist or interested only in proposing policies to solve narrowly defined problems.

To confuse matters still further, consider the state-centric brand of 'constructivism' advanced by Alexander Wendt, which together with post-modernism, feminism, and others he groups into a 'family of theories' loosely classified as 'critical IR theory'. As Wendt (1995: 71–75) writes:

> All observation is theory-*laden* in the sense that what we see is mediated by our existing theories, and to that extent knowledge is problematic. But this does not mean that observation, let alone reality, is theory-*determined*. The world is still out there constraining our beliefs, and may punish us for incorrect ones.

Yet, Wendt admits to sharing central realist assumptions, for example, that international politics is anarchic, that states wish to survive and are rational, and he maintains 'a commitment to states as units of analysis, and to the importance of systemic or "third image" theorizing'. Perhaps the fact that one can be almost a traditional realist and just a little bit postmodern too helps account for the wide appeal of Wendtian constructivism.

Fortunately, in our opinion, there is another broad stream of constructivism that is far less tied to realism, initially arriving at US shores principally through the work of the British sociologist Anthony Giddens (1984) and filtered through the early work of Wendt (1987), then Onuf (1989,1995,1998), Friedrich Kratochwil (1989), and John Ruggie (Kratochwill and Ruggie, 1986). The take-off point is the relations between agent and structure. As Onuf, Kratochwil, and others discuss it, rules shape the relationships of a wide range of actors in global politics. Constructivists of this school are particularly interested in formal and less-formal international regimes, which are necessary and natural, rather than directly traceable to calculated state interests as in the Keohanian institutionalist explanation or even the slightly more venturesome vision of international society propounded by Hedley Bull. As Onuf most recently expressed it, rules form institutions, institutions form societies, and rules yield rule (what others might describe as patterns of governance).

This broad stream of constructivist thought has been particularly insightful with regard to the traditional organizing concept of sovereignty. As Walker (1993: 179) observes:

> The patterns of inclusion and exclusion we now take for granted are historical innovations. The principle of state sovereignty is the classic expression of those patterns, an expression that encourages us to believe

that either those patterns are permanent or that they must be erased in favor of some kind of global cosmopolis.

Onuf (1989: 142) notes that sovereignty 'is not a condition', rather 'an ideal that is never reached, in a world where each step toward the ideal takes effort and costs resources, possibly in increasing increments, to prevent even smaller amounts of unwanted behavior'. Thomas J. Biersteker and Cynthia Weber (1996: 11) similarly treat state sovereignty as a 'social construct', whose 'meaning is negotiated out of interactions within intersubjectively identifiable communities'. In their view, 'practices construct, reproduce, reconstruct, and deconstruct both state and sovereignty'.

Another focus in postmodern theory is the subject of identities. Identities are increasingly a concern of more mainstream theorists as well. Walker (1993: 162) again offers helpful insights:

> The usual categories and valorizations – of cultures and nations, of passions and Balkanizations – remain with us. Even so, a sense of novelties and accelerations is also pervasive. ... A common identity is precisely what we do not have. ... Modern political identities are fractured and dispersed among a multiplicity of sites, a condition sometimes attributed to a specifically postmodern experience, but one that has been a familiar, though selectively forgotten, characteristic of modern political life for several centuries.

As Walker explains, the notion of sovereignty remains as a mental anchor partly because of the absence of an effective substitute:

> ... The Cartesian coordinates may be cracked, identities may be leaking, and the rituals of inclusion and exclusion sanctified by the dense textures of sovereign virtu(e) may have become more transparent. But if not state sovereignty ... what then?

What, indeed?

Feminist theorists suggest that an important missing dimension has been gender. As Tickner (1997: 619, 629) stresses: 'While many feminists do see structural regularities, such as gender and patriarchy, they define them as socially constructed and variable across time, place, and cultures, rather than as universal and natural.' As she points out, further, although not all feminist theorists are postmodern or even post-positivist, most are often properly classified as 'critical' theorists and tend to have 'a preference for hermeneutic, historically based, humanistic and philosophical traditions of knowledge cumulation, rather than those based on the natural sciences'. In her view:

> feminists cannot be anything but skeptical of universal truth claims and explanations associated with a body of knowledge from which women have frequently been excluded as knowers and subjects.

The broader condition of alienation is a part of the description advanced by yet another strain of critical theory, typified by the work of Jürgen Habermas and the so-called Frankfurt School. Habermas maintains that, whereas class divisions were the main source of conflict and change in Marx's day, these have lessened in modern society to a point where big business, government, and labour have reached a compromise on welfare capitalism. The reader may object that that compromise now appears increasingly threatened. If so, that could either aggravate what Habermas calls the 'crises of legitimation' or perhaps open up more opportunities for constructive dissonance. Such crises arise, he believes, from the technocratic character of the political order in which ordinary individuals seem to have little role or direct stake. Hope for the future, in his view, lies in contemporary social movements – ranging from environmental groups to religious revivals that attempt to reinject values into political life and debate.

In Habermas we have thus moved well beyond extreme relativism, returning to a nominal foundationalism and with it the project of epistemology as a means to knowledge. As Fernández-Armesto (1997: 222) writes:

> Repelled by nihilism, [Habermas] has tried to rebuild the fragments of the 'deconstructed' world. His greatest enemy is the self; so he directs [us toward] truth [as] a collective enterprise, in which we learn from each other.

Reconstructing Theory in Global Politics

One IR colleague, Mark Boyer, recently remarked in a graduate seminar that he thought an appropriate label for the Ferguson/Mansbach 'polities' approach to global politics might be 'where empiricism meets postmodernism'. We also often seem to find ourselves grouped with postmodernists on panels at professional conferences, perhaps for good reason. As we explain later, we do share a number of assumptions with postmodernists. But despite this, it would be wrong to put us into the postmodernist pigeonhole. At the end of the day, we remain resolute empiricists and even appreciate an occasional effort to marshal data or evidence whenever it is available. Indeed, we have no inherent objection to strict science, only an abiding scepticism (based on past non-performance) that it can produce much in the way of convincing results in the study of global politics. Of course, science can never be value-free, and scientists in all fields are now more inclined to agree with that assessment than some of them were in the past. Perhaps in the social sciences that is partly a response to the barrage of critiques that they have endured from the postmodernists, as well as from post-positivists closer to the mainstream like us. Better theory, we hasten to stress, could make the positivist enterprise at least somewhat more productive.

Yet, in truth (pun intended), both the positivists and extreme relativists fail to convince us, although the latter would insist that that is proof positive of the validity of their arguments. As a gesture of goodwill, we similarly suggest that one familiar criticism of postmodernists does more to affirm the position of the extreme relativists than to refute them, to wit: with no standards for evidence, why should an observer accept their perspective more than any other? Or as Roger Scruton (cited in Fernández-Arnesto 1997: 203) put it: 'The man who tells you truth doesn't exist is asking you not to believe him. So don't.' Ah yes, but why then should we believe Roger Scruton?

Martin Hollis (1994: 241) sums up: 'All interpretations become defensible but at the price that none is more justifiable than the rest. If this is indeed the upshot, the circle turns vicious and the hermeneutic imperative to understand from within leads to disaster.' It is precisely this disaster that is unacceptable, especially when there would appear to be more constructive alternatives. Can we not discuss and debate ideas as well as we can, given our personal biases, weasel language, and imperfect information? For instance, we hope the readers of this chapter would agree that, whether or not they accept the arguments we are making, they understand what we are saying well enough – and that there are only a limited number of counter-arguments worthy of admission to the dialogue. To be sure, we may all be wrong, but we are not all normally engaged in tales told by idiots or in nonsense games.

As Charles Hostovsky (n.d.) has observed, for postmodernists, 'plainly expressed language is out of the question' because it is 'too realist, modernist and obvious': 'Postmodern language requires that one use play, parody and indeterminacy as critical techniques to point this out. Often this is quite a difficult requirement, so obscurity is a well-acknowledged substitute.' Top it all off by inserting 'a few names [e.g. Continental European theorists] whose work everyone will agree is important and hardly anyone has had the time or inclination to read [as in de/gendered-Baudrillardian discourse]'. Then hope that someone will not actually ask what you talking about, in which case you can always reply with more postmodern speak. Hostovsky is wickedly close to the mark. For fairness, we should lock postmodernists of that ilk in the same room with perpetrators of positivist jargon and endless equations and see who isn't bored to death.

Although there may be no such thing as 'absolute truth', there is often a sufficient amount of intersubjective consensus to make for a useful conversation. That conversation may not lead to proofs that satisfy the philosophical nit-pickers, but it can be educational and illuminating. We gain a degree of apparently useful 'understanding' about the things we need (or prefer) to 'know'.

We have had to confront this issue directly in our work on historical cases. The task is daunting, as historian Fernández-Armesto (1997: 227) readily acknowledges: 'Historians like me know, at least as well as practitioners of any other discipline, how elusive objectivity is.' However, to stand paralyzed and utterly ignore history because of the magnitude of the challenge would be absurd. It is nonetheless important to admit that historical research is inevitably *to some extent* theory-dependent and subjective, to look at as many sources as possible to get a firm notion of the range of interpretations, and then to make one's own informed judgment as to which interpretation(s) appear(s) to be the most plausible. The result is few givens – only probabilities, likelihoods, and sometimes only possibilities. We have to live with that amount of ambiguity and proceed as best we can. If our investigations seem to provide a more convincing view of political reality than other constructions, then that may be the most we can hope for.

In conclusion, we do want to set forth some of the major assumptions upon which we believe future theory construction should rest and to offer a few suggestions as to what seem to us to be among the most promising lines for future inquiry.

First, as we have stressed, theory must remain empirical in nature. Theory need not be falsifiable or testable, at present, to the extent demanded by strict scientists, but it should have some plain link to intersubjective reality, and we should strive to make our statements as falsifiable as possible. We agree with postmodernists that empirical theorists should openly acknowledge the normative concerns that guide the questions they raise and their analyses, and concur that the normative implications of theories should be fully and frankly explored.

In our view, grand theory is desirable and possible if it is relieved of overly restrictive empirical requirements. Parsimony is helpful, but is not an end in itself. Induction and correlative thinking limit us to what can be tested by existing data and methods; data and method drive theory rather than, properly, the reverse.

We must accept the inherent ambiguity of language. Language nevertheless should be used intentionally to communicate rather than to obfuscate or obscure. Deconstruction can be helpful in revealing layers of meaning, yet the ultimate goals should always be clarification and an effort to achieve a common stable of key concepts.

Turning to promising future directions for theory, we should start with a basic recognition that 'the subject is politics' in which *people* are engaged both individually and collectively. We need to avoid an error of the past, when much that took place under the rubric of 'behaviouralism' rarely involved actual observation of behaviour. Broad global, as well as less-encompassing, trends, and institutions at many levels and of various types shape the perceptions and constrain the choices that human individuals have. However, we must never forget that it is people who are the wellsprings of the patterns we observe. Micro-level changes affect the macro-level process and phenomena, and vice versa.

A central question is, how do people both organize themselves – and find themselves organized – for political purposes, that is, for value satisfaction and/or relief from value deprivation? We define *polities* as those entities with a measure of identity, a degree of organization and hierarchy, and a capacity to mobilize persons and their resources for political purposes. Each polity is an 'authority' (with a greater or lesser degree of legitimacy) in its own 'domain', those persons who identify with it and their resources, the space those persons occupy, and the issues over which the polity exercises influence or control. Thus, if one's approach is to be one of genuine 'realism', we should ask what individuals or more often collectivities (polities or authorities) influence or control which persons and resources in which issue contexts – and why? Sometimes there is widespread coercion, and always there is coercion applied to a few who refuse to be incorporated in any other way. However, our answer is that polities succeed mainly because they deliver the things that (at least) significant sectors of their constituencies want: material rewards and the not-to-be-underestimated psychological rewards found in group identity, as well.

One of the most important lines of contemporary inquiry is one that we, indeed, share with many postmodernists: a focus on identity. Polities are continually engaged in convincing their followers that they are, in fact, delivering the goods. One requirement is an ideology aimed at legitimating the exercise of authority and an active campaign of political socialization generally. Loyalties attach only to those polities that 'satisfy' them in some fundamental sense. No polity would long endure if it rested solely on coercion. An interesting puzzle is why an identity comes to the fore at a particular time. Multiple identities typically coexist, but conflictual situations, often elite generated, can arise that force individuals to choose which identity they will truly serve. In such situations, the choice will be either the identity they are forced to serve or, more often we believe, the identity that has earned their loyalty.

Global politics, in our model, has always encompassed numerous layered, overlapping, and interacting polities of many types (from families to empires) that coexist, cooperate, and conflict. Polities, identities, and loyalties may be overwhelmed and incorporated by others, but they almost never disappear entirely; rather they remain within the bosom of their successors in the form of what we have termed a living museum. History, far from 'ending', is forever being revived and at least partially re-lived. Some exhibits are currently on special show, some are in secondary and tertiary exhibits, and some remain in storage waiting to be re-exhibited in whole or in part. Contemporary political patterns, then, reflect history's revenge.

They also reflect future shock. Present-day trends in the global economy have helped to accentuate a divergence between parts of the world (and social sectors even within those parts) that are engaged and relatively profiting from economic globalisation and those that are not. Fragmentation and 'neo-tribalism' are most apparent in the developing regions. Drawn by colonial authorities, sovereign boundaries often cut across older (often incompatible) identities that are now resurfacing and that provide the ideological context for widespread civil strife. The governments of many of these states represent the privileges of a tribal, family, religious, regional, or military faction rather than serve as impartial umpires able to adjudicate subnational quarrels.

In contrast to the developing world, the developed regions seem to have concluded that war is almost inconceivable. The states of these regions have become enmeshed in larger political and economic systems and find themselves, consequently, less able to behave autonomously or formulate effective policies that can protect even wealthier citizens from the vagaries of the global market. Citizenship as the principal identity is being challenged by regional, professional, and even civilizational identities. At the individual or micro-level, the effects of the telecommunications revolution are varied. Better educated and technically 'wired' persons are increasingly empowered to live their personal and professional lives in cyberspace, withdrawing from traditional social relationships. However, they may reject that sort of microchip alienation and instead develop a far greater sense of proximity to like-minded persons or professional associates despite enormous geographical distances than to fellow citizens who are physically nearby.

As theory-building proceeds, several interrelated processes seem to us to be the most important, including those we have termed fusion/fission and Rosenau (1994: 255–81), 'fragmegration' – and their implications for governance. Cross-border concerns seem to require transnational institutions to address and manage them. In turn, major alliances like the North Atlantic Treaty Organization (NATO), trading groups like the European Union (EU), and the existence of transnational firms and banks offer important alternatives to smaller polities that wish to sever old relationships. Especially in an era when security concerns are somewhat diminished, potential breakaway countries (the Baltics), provinces (Quebec), or ethnicities (the Basques), or even groups that merely seek greater autonomy (the Catalans) find that smallness not only appears gratifying from a psychological standpoint but also, perhaps, is a genuinely viable option. Rapid change, increased contacts with foreign cultures, and the threat of cultural homogenization also engender a localizing backlash. Persons take refuge in local government, religion, ethnicity, profession, and so on, in order to know 'who they are' and maintain a sense of personal efficacy in a wider world that keeps impinging upon them.

The foregoing suggests that future theory will need to expand traditional conceptions of space and time. The political geographers are already out in front of most political scientists with regard to the former – though Walker has also been a pioneer – arguing for the utility of thinking about 'political space' rather than territory in the familiar way. 'Boundaries' may describe culture and identities as well as the domains of a wide variety of polities, which in any case vary by issue (the type of activity involved). Time effectively is speeding up.

Finally, any future theory will have to address change and continuity. An obvious question here is whether some sort of unilinear evolution or even 'progress' by fits and starts is involved; and the answer is almost certainly no. However, there is an urgent need for much greater historical perspective on the contemporary world. Any decent analyst, we believe, will have to establish what remains the same, what is changing, and what is the approximate rate of change. Those issues, in turn, send us back to more bedrock questions of what we should be using as benchmarks, what in fact it is that we are comparing.

The challenge of many, although by no means all, postmodernists is that IR theorists will never be able to resolve questions like these. Perhaps we will not, but we can and regularly do investigate and debate them – and thereby confound those cynics who insist that no communication is possible. Enlightenment in some final sense, whatever that may mean, will certainly never result. We theorists would be deeply disappointed, yea unemployed, if it did. Yet a greater measure of understanding may quite possibly come in ways that the strict scientists and extreme relativists never contemplated, but the wise of all ages would surely approve.

4 Historical Perspectives on Contemporary Global Politics

Promise and pitfalls (2008)

Reflect often how all the life of today is a repetition of the past; and observe that it also presages what is to come. Review the many complete dramas and their settings, all so similar, which you have known in your own experience, or from bygone history: ... the performance is always the same; it is only the actors who change.

> Marcus Aurelius, Emperor of Rome, 161–80 AD
> (Marcus Aurelius 1993: 832)

The only thing new in the world is the history you don't know.

> (Harry Truman, cited in Bradley 2000: 3)

We have recognized ... that there are certain trends – particularly in relation to the possible emergence of a 'new mediaeval' form of universal order – which do make against the survival of the states system, and which, if they went a great deal further, might threaten its survival.

> (Hedley Bull 1977: 275)

[T]here are ... major dimensions of the present era that have led to differences in kind and not just in degree when compared with earlier times

> (James N. Rosenau 1997: 22)

I claim that some of the most important characteristics of our world today can be appreciated more clearly by historical comparison. It is not that history repeats itself. Precisely the opposite: World history develops. Through historical comparison we can see that the most significant problems of our own time are novel. That is why they are difficult to solve: They are interstitial to institutions that deal effectively with the more traditional problems for which they were first set up.

> (Michael Mann 1986: 32)

Because we have an inadequate basis for comparison, we are tempted to exaggerate either continuity with the past that we know badly or the radical originality of the present, depending upon whether we are more struck by the features we deem permanent, or with those we do not believe existed before. And yet a more rigorous examination of the past might reveal that what we sense as new really is not, and that some 'traditional' features are far more complex than we think.

(Stanley Hoffman, cited in Holsti 2002: 23)

Political analysts since the earliest times have contemplated the past, although there is no more consensus today than there has ever been about what to make of it or to what extent it really helps us either to understand the present or to predict the future. Our contemporary post-international world features any number of apparently new phenomena that are actually old or refurbished, and our world may in fact be much more like the world before the rise of the sovereign state in Europe than that state-centric era. But we cannot know for sure what is genuinely new or old unless we have the clearest possible view of the past. Any assessment of change requires a baseline. For those who wish to make sense of the dynamic side of global politics, temporal comparison is essential. Our own work has led us to a comparative study of 'polities' in six pre-Westphalian historical systems (Ferguson and Mansbach 1996) and now is continuing with a focus on the ancient Mediterranean world, from whence come most of the examples used in this chapter.[1]

There are some analysts, however, including many historians, who are sceptical and even contemptuous of the claim that history helps us make sense of the present. They are inclined to accuse political scientists and others of ransacking the historical record in an effort to make and support sweeping generalizations. A frequent contention of historians is that history can only inform the reader about the particular epoch in which it took place – if that! Finley (1986: 31), for example, asks:

[W]hat is the point to a linear account over long periods of time? One can really know only one's own time, and that is sufficient anyway. The past can yield nothing more than paradigmatic support for the conclusions one has drawn from the present; the past, in other words, may still be treated in the timeless fashion of myth.

Plumb (2004: 17) similarly remarks:

Each of us is a historical being, held in a pattern created by Time, and to be unconscious of our historical selves is to be fraught with dangers, History, however, is not the past. The past is always a created ideology with a purpose, designed to control individuals, or motivate societies, or inspire classes. Nothing has been so corruptly used as concepts of the past.

Freeman is hardly more sanguine about the historical enterprise: 'It is in fact worth asking', he suggests, 'whether it is possible to understand Greece or any other part of the ancient world in any meaningful sense. It may be that scholars and archaeologists are simply imposing their own ideological frameworks on the limited and unrepresentative evidence that survives.' He warns the reader about his own meticulous single-volume history of three ancient civilizations: 'Virtually every page that follows conceals some controversy over which academic blood has been shed.' Yet, he concludes, it is nonetheless 'worth the effort' to produce such a volume (Freeman 1996: 12–13).

Studying the History of Global Politics: Benefits as Well as Pitfalls

Despite the difficulties and pitfalls involved in studying the past, there are many reasons why it is attractive and even necessary to do so. One generic reason is the famous response from George Leigh Mall, who, when asked why he was trying Everest, answered simply 'because it is there.' Well, why not? We *should* be inherently curious about history and prehistory, for it is nothing less than the record – or at least the stories – of the travails, triumphs, and failures of our own human species on planet earth.

Beyond simple curiosity, there is a persistent sense that the past can inform us about the present, explain why we act as we do, and even warn us against us the folly of our ways. The last is the essence of the familiar caution that those who do not read history are doomed to repeat it. Common assumptions are that the past is there to be 'read', that human nature has not changed, and that there are also recurring patterns in human societies and affairs generally. As David Lowenthal (1985: 4) expresses it: '[W]e feel quite sure that the past really happened; its traces and memories reflect undeniable scenes and acts. The airy and insubstantial future may never arrive; man or nature may destroy humanity; time as we know it may end. By contrast, the past is tangible and secure; people think of it as fixed, unalterable, indelibly recorded.' In the same vein, Finley (1986: 32) quotes Sir Isaiah Berlin on Tolstoy:

> Tolstoy's interest in history ... seems to have arisen not from interest in the past as such, but from the desire to penetrate to first causes, to understand how and why things happen as they do and not otherwise. ... And with this went an incurable love of the concrete, the empirical, the verifiable. ... History, only history, only the sum of the concrete events in time and space ... this alone contained the truth, the material out of which genuine answers ... might be constructed.

The point is also made eloquently by Thucydides, who encourages us to study his account of the Peloponnesian War for clues of things to come:

It will be enough for me ... if these words of mine are judged useful by those who want to understand clearly the events which happened in the past and which (human nature being what it will) will, at some time or other and in much the same ways, be repeated in the future. My work is not a piece of writing designed to meet the taste of an immediate public, but was done to last forever.

(Thucydides 1972: 48)

Some modern historians, like the eminent Hellenist, Peter Green, find not so much omens of the future, as guides to the present through its presumed 'organic relationship' with the past. As his research proceeded, he reports:

I could not help being struck, again and again, by an overpowering sense of *déjà vu*, [and being fascinated by] the ornate, indeed rococo glass in which Alexandria, Antioch and Pergamon reflect contemporary fads, failings and aspirations, from the urban malaise to religious fundamentalism, from Veblenism to *haute cuisine,* from funded scholarship and mandarin literature to a flourishing drop-out counter- culture, from political impotence in the individual to authoritarianism in government, from science perverted for military ends to illusionism for the masses, from spiritual solipsism on a private income to systematic extortion in pursuit of the materialistic and hence plutocratic dream.

He concludes:

Quite apart from some jolting lessons to be learned here about the constant elements in human nature ... – *déjà vu* on a truly cosmic scale – it is this depressingly familiar scenario, rather than the currently more popular Periclean myth, which remains in essence, the legacy of the Graeco-Roman world.

(Green 1989: 27–28)

History and Truth

Yet there remain a variety of reasons why historical truth is ever elusive. Every generation reinterprets the past in light of its own experience; the struggle over who controls the archives has practical political and policy consequences; and each individual has his or her own personal biases. However, as we view it, the fundamental problem has little to do with extreme-relativist postmodern premises about our inability to access 'reality' in any form. We insist that there is an abundance of 'true' historical 'fact', and empirical research is decidedly possible. But even for the best-documented eras there are huge factual gaps and serious problems with sources, as well as the question of what our facts 'mean'. Interpretation is not made any easier by the fuzzy concepts (e.g. 'empire' 'tribe', or even 'state') we use to organize our information.

Consider the paucity of reliable information relevant to our current project on the politics of the ancient Mediterranean. Most of what we think we know comes from relatively few written materials and, increasingly, from recent advances in archaeology[2] and dating techniques. For ancient Mesopotamia we have many cuneiform inventory tablets (still more not yet read); a few literary texts (the most famous, of course, the Gilgamesh chronicle); and monuments recording military victories, other royal accomplishments, and principles of law. For Egypt before Rome there are tomb inscriptions, some papyri fragments, and the Amarna letters treasure trove of diplomatic correspondence from a short period. If only the Alexandria Library had survived! Most of the chronology of Egyptian pharonic dynasties comes from a single source, a history of Egypt by Manetho, an Egyptian priest who wrote in Greek in the third century B.C., possibly for King Ptolemy I Soter. Manetho's actual history is now mostly lost, but the king-list survived as well as various citations and summaries of the history by other ancient and early Christian authors. However, the king-list has some gaps and obvious inaccuracies, especially for the crucial period when Egypt's civilization was just beginning to form.

As for Greece, Finley (1981: 10) observes: '[T]he "events" in the whole of Aegean prehistory can be counted on one's fingers.' Myths and traditions are 'highly problematical at best', and archaeology only 'reveals cataclysms' without telling us anything about the circumstances or personalities. There is a 'remarkable absence of monumental portrayal' and 'not a single dated object ... which is not an import'. All dates derive from archaeology. One breakthrough was the deciphering of Linear B, the early form of Greek script found on clay tablets baked in fires that apparently accompanied the destruction of Mycenaean centres at Knossos (c. 1400 B.C.), Pylos and Mycenae (c. 1200 B.C.), Thebes (c. 1320 B.C.), and elsewhere. Unfortunately, these records are only fragmentary, inventorial in nature, and cover a period of no more than a single year in each centre. Homer (Ionia c. 750?) draws on an older oral tradition and seems to describe the Heroic (Mycenaean) era, though some scholars argue that much of Homer reflects life in the ninth century (Fine 1983: 26). How far to trust Homer remains a subject for heated debate (cf. Chadwick 1976: 186 and Hammond 1986: 60 ff). The Boeotian poet Hesiod (*c.* 700 B.C.) provides a rare glimpse of life from the viewpoint of the non-ruling class, although his concerns are myth and metaphysics rather than narrative history (Finley 1986: 16).

The situation does not get much better later. Finley (1986: 22) again:

> No one before the fifth century tried to organize, either for his own time or for earlier generations, the essential stuff of history. There were lists – of the kings of Sparta and the archons of Athens and the victors in the various games. They could provide a chronology if we

knew what happened in the archonship of X or the reign of Y; but we do not know.

Herodotus, arguably the first historian, wrote in the third quarter of the fifth century, but his accounts, though wonderfully fascinating and colourful, are an often indistinguishable mix of myth, probable fact, and good storytelling. Finley (1986: 18) does give him credit for producing a fairly accurate chronology from about the middle of the seventh century B.C. Thucydides only gives us a few events and approximate dates about early Greece because that was not his main concern and he, like Herodotus and all Greeks for that matter, lacked essential information. Thucydides' account of the Peloponnesian War is more reliable, since he was a participant observer, but his very participation makes his objectivity suspect, and in any event he could not participate in, observe, or remember everything of importance. He tells us, for instance, that he had to reconstruct key speeches of Greek leaders from what he recalls was said or was appropriate to the situation.

Moving on to the Hellenistic era and Roman times, documentation substantially improves, but rarely is it nearly as plentiful as one would wish. The astonishing career of Alexander the Great generated any number of accounts during his brief reign and in decades immediately after his premature death, but none of those 'primary' sources survives in anything like its entirety. Later writers presumably had access to more of the original material than we now have, but all of them are highly unreliable or incomplete in various ways (cf. Bosworth 2003). Livy relied on a collection of legends for his history of early Rome, while Polybius and others patched together their accounts from what few actual records (or virtually none) they might have had to hand. Freeman (1996: 7) notes that there are only 1,865 Roman manuscripts which date from before Charlemagne, partly because so many were copied and the originals allowed to disappear. Many, including for example Books 40–45 of Livy, survive in but a single copy. No one, of course, knows what errors or omissions may have been introduced in the copying process. Although many new texts are still surfacing from epigraphic inscriptions on stone, pottery, metal, and sometimes wood, Freeman (1996: 7) believes, the 'amount which has been lost is staggering, and it may be the best of what was written'.

Putting aside the dearth of effects, the sheer distance produced by the 'veil of time' intrudes. In Lowenthal's (1985: 4) words, 'the past is a foreign country'. '[W]e can no more slip back to the past than leap forward into the future. Save in imaginative reconstruction, yesterday is forever barred to us'. We cannot get into the mindset or worldview of, say, a Spartan hoplite, not only because we cannot know what he as an individual was actually thinking, but also because our interpretations are severely affected by our own myths, predispositions, preoccupations, and concepts.

The gaps produced by sheer time are nowhere more obvious than in the case of key concepts of *war* and *democracy*. Regarding war, moderns find it difficult to grasp the degree to which warfare was almost a routine experience for males in the ancient world and, indeed, a deeply ingrained part of community culture. The command structure of Greek and Roman armies was a monopoly of the upper classes, but the liability inherent in that 'privilege' for them was that 'military command was inescapable (until the first century B.C.) at least at the "brigade" level'. Needless to say, poorer citizens were also nearly all enlisted in one capacity or another. Finley reminds us that 'Socrates fought in battle twice as a hoplite, at least twice when he was already in his forties.' In Finley's view:

> There is nothing in modern experience quite like this. War was a normal part of life; not all periods compared in intensity with the Persian and Peloponnesian wars or with the Hannibalic War, but hardly a year went by without requiring a formal decision to fight, followed by a muster and the necessary preparations, and finally combat at some level.
>
> (Finley 1983: 66–67)

There was thus no separate military class, military glory was an important road to political leadership, and virtually all politicians were expected to have had military experience and to continue to demonstrate their prowess in battle.

As for the concept of 'democracy', Cartledge (1993: 7), writing about ancient Greece, captures the crux of the matter brilliantly:

> [W]hat ... does and should it mean to us that 'democracy' was a Greek invention ... when our democracy is so different from theirs, both institutionally and ideologically? Or to put that question more brutally ... how was it that it was 'okay' for the Greeks to find the idea and practice of democracy perfectly compatible not only with the disenfranchisement of women, which was of course true of all democracies until the [twentieth century], but also with the outright enslavement of many thousands of human beings (including their fellow Greeks), whereas for us today that combination is not at all 'okay' on principle.

Green urges us to remember that even that limited form of democracy was far from universal in Greece and 'certainly not (as is sometimes supposed) coterminus with the rule of the city-state (*polis*)'. If we wanted to increase the confusion at this point, we could (but will not) diverge to consider what is often alleged to have been Spartan 'totalitarianism'. In any event, says Green, 'it was the Hellenistic rather than the classical legacy, politically speaking, that was transmitted, via Rome, to the medieval and modern world' (Green 1989: 17–18).

The 'facts problem' for historians parallels the issue confronted by social scientists in regard to the concept of 'rationality'. Even if we believe in rationality, it is very difficult to fulfil the factual conditions to buttress the claim, especially if we define rationality as selection of the *best* of *all* alternatives. Limits on individual knowledge and on researchers' efforts to get 'in the heads', complicates dramatically the task confronting rational choice and expected utility scholars. The 'facts problem' alone produces serious pitfalls in any attempt to read and draw insights about the present or future from history – or, indeed, about the past itself. We sense that there are things we urgently need to know 'there', but we also often discover, in the immortal words of Gertrude Stein (in quite another context), that 'there's no there, there'. [3] Or at least whatever 'there' we seem to encounter is frustratingly hard to 'know' with any degree of certainty.

The Struggle Over Meaning

Even if we had 'all' of the facts, we would have an additional problem. Facts apart from context have little meaning. Like a telephone book, a listing of facts provides nothing of theoretical interest or value. Facts allow us to draw a crude picture at best, but meaning only is possible after an observer has imposed some sort of theoretical framework upon those facts. That framework explains how facts are related and affect one another, and it is only partly derived from the facts themselves in the constant to-ing and fro-ing between induction and deduction. The framework also emerges from personal, political, and ideological predispositions of the theorists. This is especially the case in giving meaning to history because of the factual lacunae; it is equally a problem in global politics because of the accelerated pace of change that precludes the sorts of truth claims in science that tend to assume that change is exceedingly slow.

Thucydides *History* illustrates how historical analysis can quickly become a struggle over meaning, and how historians and history can be held 'hostage' to contemporary manipulation. For example, although Thucydides returns on several occasions to the question of why war breaks out, some scholars go no further than his initial explanation of war, as a result of growing Athenian power, to generalize about the virtues of everything from hegemonic and power transition theory to good old realist amoral moralizing and balance-of-power theory. Realists in particular have repeatedly tried to hijack Thucydides for their own ends. For some, the Melian Dialogue serves to legitimate power politics and the norms of 'might makes right'. For others, the story was even used as a metaphor for the Cold War in which 'democratic Athens', a naval power (read United States) and its allies, clashed with 'authoritarian Sparta', a land power (read Soviet Union) and its allies. Other interpretations abound. Some regard Thucydides' *History* as an attempt to put medical science to work; in this interpretation, the historian emulated his friend Hippocrates of Cos and employed the newly-discovered diagnostic method to the study of the social world. In another version, Thucydides, presuming acquainted with the work of the tragedians of his time, produced his own tragic vision in which the vibrant and idealistic Athens of Pericles is transformed into a cynical arena for demagogues, culminating in the plague and the disastrous Sicilian expedition and the destruction of the walls of Athens.

Looking at the past through present-day lenses inevitably entails distortion. Green (1989: 87–88) comments that 'every generation gets the nonsense it needs and deserves', for example, the New Age crediting of the Egyptians 'with being the guardians, if not the inventors, of every sort of hermetic wisdom, arcane science, prophetic skill, and perennial philosophy'. Such an interpretation, he insists, detracts from the extraordinary accomplishments of Egyptian culture in other arenas and 'is also seriously misleading, since it implies a gift for conceptualization which was the one thing, notoriously, that the Egyptians lacked, and which constitutes their most fundamental distinction from natural generalizers like the Greeks, who couldn't rub two facts together without coming up with a hot universal theory'. In Green's view, the 'natural focus of Egyptian civilization ... was not intellectual but theological, indeed theocentric'.

Green highlighted the same problem of seeing the past from the vantage point of the present in interpreting Greek history. Although admitting that some reported pronouncements of the Delphic Oracle were probably forgeries, influenced by special pleading, or akin to folklore traditions, he also dismissed as 'misleading in the extreme' Fontenrose's downgrading of the mystical role of the Delphic Oracle. 'Professor Fontenrose is ... a rationalist of the most convinced sort, and ... "it is a property of your rationalist that he is unable to understand any type of mind but his own."' Although Fontenrose 'claims to have followed exclusively objective criteria', according to Green: he has, perhaps unconsciously, set up a working model in which the only responses recognized as historical are, almost by definition, those that avoid any taint of ambiguity, second sight, or supernatural knowledge ... so that the whole archaic history of this extraordinary institution prior to the mid-fifth century can be treated with the same sort of patronizing and dismissive contempt that Victorian missionaries reserved for, say, Haitian voodoo.' (Green 1989: 103, 105)

The religious beliefs and practices of the ancients are especially hard to fathom from our contemporary remove. From the perspective of a world in which monotheism is so prevalent, it is difficult to make sense of a culture like that of ancient Greece with its enormous number of deities and their anthropomorphic foibles. Some analysts also suggest that Greece nurtured a secular and rational Western tradition. They spotlight Plato, Thucydides, Aristotle, atomists, sceptics, and others who seem to represent that side of Greece. But what to make, then, of the Greeks' active religious life (Dodds, 1964). To be sure, some ceremonies and shrines were closely associated with particular cities, yet was Greek religion a mere expression of civic pride?

Historians wishing to emphasize the development of a superior Western culture sometimes tell a story of Greek religion that suggests that it was a precursor of monotheism in general and Christianity in particular. Plato has had his usefulness in this respect too. Louise Bruit Zaidman and Pauline Scmidt Pantel observe that the initial approaches to Greek religion were two, prefiguration or survival. The prefiguration approach scrutinized the beliefs and practices of Greeks 'with a view to discovering soil that was especially propitious for the growth of a monotheistic religion like Christianity', including 'exclusive sects and mystery cults'. The effect of that interpretation was 'to refract Greek religion artificially through the distorting prism of Christianity'. Zaidman and Pantel concede that their own view of Greek religion, as 'a symbolic system with its own peculiar logic and coherence' similarly reflects 'our own, relativistic era'. Although current explanations are not irreconcilable, they do stress that for most analysts today Greek religion is either a successful blend of the cults and beliefs of pre-Hellenic populations and those introduced by later Greek peoples, or can best be understood as part of the ideological framework of the emerging Greek polis. By contrast, the survival approach searched for 'supposed traces of magical practices and primitive mentality' that might have persisted in classical Greece. That approach brought with it 'an entourage of would-be explanations that ... invoke the discredited notion of totemism (the idea that originally religion was essentially a matter of groups of people identifying themselves with objects in the natural world)' (Zaidman and Pantel 1992: 4–6).

We see the same effort at twisting history to help tell a story – in this case Greece as the cradle of democracy – in the debate over Greek 'hoplite reform'. The argument was that, at an early stage in the emergence of the polis, hoplite phalanx warfare became the dominant form of warfare, rather than the earlier form of combat waged primarily by aristocratic cavalry. Virtually all male citizens had to take their place side-by-side in the phalanx as equals in the defence of the city, and that equality inevitably spilled over into politics. In sum, hoplite warfare was substantially responsible for pushing Greek politics in a more egalitarian and democratic direction. Only relatively recently did archaeologist Ian Morris (1987: 197–201), working from evidence gathered at burial sites near Athens, conclude that hoplite warfare had been in use long before the period in question. To his mind, there was 'not a shed of evidence' for any change in Greek warfare tactics and certainly no reason to associate a 'hoplite class' with any shifts in Greek politics. It should be noted that the notion of a hoplite reform is still widely accepted, but the comfortable consensus that once existed is no longer entirely intact.

Interpreting facts poses serious problems, and so does choosing which facts to consider. Although there is inevitable factual overlap (thank goodness), each historian tends to look at or ignore certain types of facts owing to the inevitable mixing of norms in fact selection. Marxists pay careful attention to the means of production; Hegelians and Kantians, to ideas; realists, to military power; and so forth. Macro-historians of a Braudelian

(French *annales*) disposition are concerned almost exclusively with social, economic, and cultural history – and the conditions of everyday life in vanished eras and civilizations. As a profession, most historians today are, in our opinion, overreacting to a longstanding concentration on chronicles of kings and statesmen and focusing their attention almost exclusively on cultural and economic history rather than political history. No doubt the pendulum will swing at least somewhat back again, and meanwhile there are rewards from the current orientation. Yet, there is no escaping the situation that the sources of information upon which we must draw remain over-whelmingly elitist and male. As Freeman (1996: 7–8) observes for ancient Mediterranean history, what texts we have come 'overwhelmingly from those élite males with the leisure to write them'. 'The vast mass of the Greek and Roman populations and their subjects have vanished unheard.' Keith Bradley, a prominent modern authority on Roman slavery, 'records only one free slave'. 'Women's voices have also been lost.'

Historians and Social Scientists

Are historians and social scientists interested in global politics adversaries who are embarked on fundamentally different missions? In reality, nothing could be further from the truth. Although some social scientists admittedly blindside history – certainly to their detriment – every statement that historians make is laden with theoretical assumptions. To those historians who decry 'theory', we rejoin that all analysts are theorists and it is infinitely better to be aware of and frank about one's theoretical stance than otherwise.

Realist-Liberal Contest

There is a realist–non-realist antinomy (see Ferguson and Mansbach 2003: 61–87). in historical as well as international relations scholarship. The struggle over the meaning of Thucydides illustrates this tension. A more personal example from our point of view is macro-historian William McNeill's extended review (McNeill 1997: 269–74) of our 1996 book, *Polities: Authority, Identities, and Change* (Ferguson and Mansbach 1996). McNeill's critique 'seems' to be a straightforward attack on the way political scientists (mis)use history. He declares that we present our theoretical argument in the first two chapters and then 'devote almost all the rest of the book to illustrating how "world politics has always involved a crazy quilt of polities – foci of authority of varying domain and influence; distinctive in some respects and overlapping, layered, nested, and linked in others".' He continues: 'Given that they knew exactly what they were looking for, it is not surprising to find that they do indeed discover a "crazy quilt" of competing and "overlapping, layered, nested and linked" polities in each case.' To the contrary, he accuses us of being 'profoundly ahistorical': 'The authors seek general truths about polities and politics, and, sure enough, they find what they expect – a plurality of identities and loyalties in competition with each other everywhere and always.' 'Theory', he says, 'allowed the authors to create a series of pigeon holes into which they have to fit an impressive variety of information gathered through energetic reading of the best available scholarly accounts dealing with each of the cases they analyze.' He claims that we 'radically discount chronology' and go so far as to compare different sorts of polities across cases and periods (empires with empires, for instance). McNeill concludes that: collecting data about horizontal and then about vertical relations among rival polities, is like studying anatomy by describing organs torn from the bodies of different animals – comparing legs with legs, eyes with eyes, and so on – without ever trying to put the parts together into a single, living whole.

However, McNeill's *real* disagreement with the book is plainly one that he never acknowledges; that is, that the analysis he decries abandons key realist premises. Historian though he is, like all historians McNeill is also himself a theorist – in this case, a realist – and he is offended to the point of outrage that the 'polities' approach puts a variety of politics and their need to generate multi-dimensional 'value satisfaction' at the centre of the analysis rather than the familiar realist categories of coercion, armed force, and states. He insists that 'Ferguson and Mansbach are wrong to suppose that competition among all the diverse kinds of polity that they discovered will not continue to give pride of place to whatever authorities are able to organize and maintain superior armed force.' The Westphalian State is not under threat in the present era, because '[s]o far, no promising alternative to the territorial organization of armed force has even begun to emerge.' Like realists in the study of international relations, world historian McNeill is oddly caught in a state-centric 'prison of experience' (Dijkink 2001: 9).

The role of power similarly forms one key realist–non-realist difference that repeatedly changes fashions in the study of world history.[4] Not long ago, historians generally assumed that civilization diffused from major centres as advanced cultures passed on some of their superior features to backward regions. McNeill, for example, entitled the second chapter of the late-1970s third edition of his survey text, 'Diffusion of Civilization: First Phase to 1700 B.C.' (McNeill 1963, 1979). It is not hard to see in such an approach an orientation generated by European imperialism and post-World War II American hegemony and triumphalism.[5] Archaeologists, anthropologists, and other historians have subsequently countered the diffusionist position by suggesting that societies at particular sizes of population, type and level of production, and so on, tend to follow some of the same trajectories; and in any case that local cultures have always adapted and thus put their own indigenous stamp upon foreign ideas and institutions of any kind.

Another key subtext of the realist–non-realist debate in history, as in international relations, is that of change versus continuity (or, mutability–immutability) (Ferguson and Mansbach 2003: 27–29). The change–continuity question also makes its appearance in the processual–post-processual debate in archaeology. One of the 1960s pioneers of the 'new archaeology' or 'processual' archaeology, Lewis R. Binford, observed that everything his excavations unearthed was static, whereas what he and his colleagues were trying to discern was how societies related to one another and to other external influences, and what produced cultural change. As he saw it, the only appropriate methodologies capable of answering such questions were those of the natural sciences, because the main concern of social science was contemporary relationships that were no longer observable in static bones and stones. He became convinced that he had to focus his attention on contemporary people and their societies, and then to project backwards into the past through the material evidence they created, that is, 'to understand the dynamics of living systems and study their static consequences' (Binford 1983: 21, 100–1). In the end, processual archaeologists settled on environment as the prime shaper of social and cultural outcomes. Perhaps predictably, they soon were challenged by 'post-processual' archaeologists, who argue that what is missing in environmental determinism is a critical ideological dimension. Different societies process influences from their respective environments through their own value systems – with widely different results (cf. Hodder, 1986 and Refrew and Bahn, 1991: Chapt. 12). Anyone who is familiar with our work will not be surprised that we side with the post-processual perspective.

More broadly, most realists view history and global politics as static, a 'struggle for power' that is timeless and universal. However, some historians are liberals, who see the world as going 'somewhere' and who, therefore, tend to emphasize the uniqueness of different times and places. Thus, differences over meaning are compounded by whether or not the historian's training and epistemological leanings lead him to look for continuity between past and present or, perhaps more often the case, to emphasize the differences between them.

The liberal preference for uniqueness is reflected in Finley's controversial assertion that the ancients lacked any concept of 'an economy'. Finley emphasizes what is different and unique in contrast to what is similar or at least analogous. He argues (1985: 21–24):

> Of course, they farmed, traded, manufactured, mined, taxed, coined, deposited and loaned money, made profits or failed in their enterprises. And they discussed these activities in their writing. What they did not do, however, was to combine these particular activities conceptually into a unit. ... Hence Aristotle, whose programme was to codify the branches of knowledge, wrote no *Economics*.

Finley continues: 'There were no business cycles in antiquity; no cities whose growth can be ascribed, even by us, to the establishment of a manufacture; no "Treasure by Foreign Trade".' Therefore, the 'economic language and concepts we are all familiar with, even the laymen among us, the "princi-ples", whether they are Alfred Marshall's or Paul Samuelson's, the models we employ, tend to draw us into a false account'. For instance, he maintains that since wage and interest rates in the Greek and Roman worlds remained reasonably stable over long periods of time, it is wrong to speak of a 'labour market' or a 'money market'. Moreover, there is no record of an actuarial concept applied to the likes of maritime loans, which suggests that the grave absence of statistics regarding matters of economics is not an accident. The ancients simply were not interested in compiling that sort of data for later comparison. Not surprisingly, Finley's interpretation stirred considerable debate and is still contested (cf. Scheidel and von Reden 2002).

Agent–Structure

Another issue that both political scientists and historians must contend with is often summarized as the 'agent–structure problem'. To what extent are actions determined by structural forces over which decision-makers have no control? Neo-realists, in contrast to traditional realists like Hans Mor-genthau, typically weigh in on the structural side of the continuum. Ken-neth Waltz's *Theory of International Politics* (1979) is the leading representative of this perspective.

Among historians and political scientists, surely those who wrote on geopo-litics were among the most consistent structural determinists. Alfred Thayer Mahan, for example, argued that control of the seas was the key to world domination and helped convince Theodore Roosevelt of the need for a two-ocean navy. Others were Halfred J. Mackinder, whose theory that control of the Eurasian heartland was more important influenced Nazi Germany's disastrous decision to invade the Soviet Union; and Nicholas Spykman, whose idea that control of the rimland of the Eurasian land mass was more essential than a heartland strategy, offered an intellectual basis for America's post-World War II containment policy. These analyses smacked of single-factor geographical determinism and not only lacked staying power, but also in their day created substantial mischief. In reality, over the millennia, actual physical geography has had far less impact on politics than the other way around. Contemporary political geographers like John Agnew and Stuart Corbridge (1995) are also keenly aware that global politics is very much about 'mastering space' and not about geography dictating many political strategies. This is not, of course, to suggest that – even in the current era when some aspects of global politics appear to be increasingly de-territorialized – geographical proximity or topo-graphy retain no significance at all. For instance, United States relations with Cuba would no doubt have been very different if Cuba were an island in the South Pacific rather than 90 miles from Florida.[6]

By far the majority of international relations theorists have focused their attention on the twentieth century and especially the Cold War era after World War II. However, a significant and, indeed, increasing number of historians, political scientists, and other social scientists have made an effort to generalize about patterns of politics over a much longer time span.[7]

Structural bias is also evident in the work of the economic determinists. Most of the work on historical cycles, civilizations, or warfare to which we will turn shortly stresses politics more than economics. Exceptions are some of Jones's reasons for 'the European miracle', Gilpin's list of factors that ended the traditional cycle of empires, and Thompson's inclusion of world-system theory as one of three somewhat complementary approaches to understanding global war. Two other important theorists with an even more pronounced economics orientation, however much they may otherwise differ, are Immanuel Wallerstein (1974, 1979, 1984) and Paul Kennedy (1987). As the dean of neo-Marxist world-system theory, Wallerstein, like earlier Marxists, is an economic determinist. In addition to a world-system or world-economy, the bedrock concepts of his approach are mode of production and division of labour. He argues that prior to about A.D. 1500, most of the world was dominated by military–bureaucratic empires that were effectively systems unto themselves, with a division of labour that rarely extended beyond their frontiers and a similar mode of production that depended on surpluses generated by mass agriculture. From his perspective, the development of a world market economy, in tandem with the territorial state in Europe, changed everything. The world economy extended the division of labour beyond regional bounds and involved a predominantly capitalist mode of production. Henceforth the world-system would be one of strong states at the centre – not in every case capitalist states, for Wallerstein regarded the former Soviet Union as one of the privileged exploiters – weaker states in a semi-periphery, and still weaker states on the periphery. A crucial point, however, is that Wallerstein never has managed to explain how division of labour and mode of production might remain essentially the same for centuries while there took place dramatic shifts in political order, ideology, and relationships among polity types.

Should History be Periodized?

We differentiate among pre-international, international, and post-international epochs in global politics. Realist historians periodize using very different criteria than we do – power and power centres, economic system, technology, and so forth. But the basic question is should history be 'periodized' or not? On the one hand, periodizing facilitates longitudinal comparison. It also allows us to highlight key factors in global politics, especially changing political identities and loyalties and changing forms of authority and political community. Finally, it makes it possible for observers to focus on patterns of change and historical directions (if any). Therein, however, also lies a risk of imputing patterns of change and historical directions where none exist. 'Periods' like 'systems' are constructed and imposed by observers, tend to reflect their existing predispositions and premises, and, therefore, may lead to a process in which investigators are destined to find what they are looking for. In addition, periodizing runs the additional risk of leaving the wrong impression that historical change is largely structural in nature. The labels we tack onto decades or centuries almost never existed for the players in the historical drama themselves. In short, we must not confuse our periods with reality.

Two international relations theorists who have championed the use of history, Barry Buzan and Richard Little (2000: 387), note that there is a continual tension between those who view of history as a 'seamless web' and others who regard it as falling into distinct periods. 'The orthodox historical periodization assumes that there is something that binds the ancient world together in a way that is different from the way that either the medieval world or the modern world is bound together.' As Buzan and Little (2000: Chapt 18) emphasize, there are a number of problems with that sort of periodization. First, it is Eurocentric. What they term 'pre-international systems' persisted through the next two periods and profoundly affected their evolution. Second, it neglects the fundamental fact that history 'does not move at the same speed all across the planet'. For example, writing is 5,000 years old in some places, 2,000 in others, and 200 in others. Third, even the usual 1648 Westphalian date for the emergence of the sovereign state is questionable at best.

So far so good. Alas, at this point in the analysis Buzan and Little derail from the very promising unorthodox tracks they have laid for themselves. They posit a series of discrete historical eras punctuated by different types of supposedly dominant units. So we have hunter-gatherers giving way to other kinds of units, in succession, until 1500 (rather than 1648) when states become the dominant unit and impose their own standards of territoriality and sovereignty on the entire international system (Buzan and Little 2000: 274–5 and Chapt 18).

As for ourselves, far from implying historical direction in our own designation of historical periods, we argue that every historical period features something 'new' and much that is 'old' and also much that is 'reconstructed'. Of course, there are always genuinely new phenomena, if only because advancing science and technology enable us to do things in the present that we could not do in the past. And new ideas and concepts do arise. Thus, the European State was 'invented' by Europeans. Although it incorporated features from earlier polities, it was also different in some ways from any that existed before. We commonly refer to the present of global politics as 'a living museum', by which we mean that in looking at the contemporary world we can find many polity types, variants of polity types, identities, and loyalties that have existed through much of history. At a deeper level, many essential problems of politics are as old as history itself, even though they often appear in new guises and forms. There is change and continuity, and it is ways important to try to specify how much of each we observe.

Conclusion: The Necessity of History

Despite the undeniable risks in using history, we have little option other than to do so. Social scientists neither need to reinvent the wheel nor retreat to join 'critical' relativism and deconstruction. We concede that the past can sometimes be almost impenetrably complex; that there often is not enough 'evidence' or too much information to sort out properly; that it is always difficult and more than occasionally impossible to establish 'causation'; that significant exceptions seem to contradict almost any generalization; that no person can be an expert in more than one period of history and then may be so immersed their subject that they cannot put it into a broader perspective; and that no one outside of a particular historical time can be fully confident of reconstructing the perceptions of those who lived in that time, and so on.

However, the aversion of some traditional historians to 'theory' is a red herring, because, as we have observed, all historians have their theoretical biases too, which should be openly acknowledged. Nonetheless, we need to be aware of 'the spectacles behind our eyes' and also take additional precautions to improve the quality of the final product. Two are perhaps most important. First, the analyst can make a determined effort to look at a variety of sources that tell apparently different stories and perhaps emphasize different facts. Second, we must be prepared to modify initial assumptions based on what the ever-unfolding historical 'record' continues to reveal.

When seeking to theorize, especially about several long historical periods, there is no alternative to relying heavily on secondary sources. Indeed, given our view of the difficulty in arriving at a single version of historical 'truth', it is essential to see how and why historical authorities sometimes advance different interpretations of what happened, when, and why. When exposed to competing interpretations, we cannot avoid making careful and informed judgments about which interpretation(s) are the most plausible (see Martin 1989 and Novick 1988). But plausibility is hardly the same as truth. History, as we observed earlier, consists of competing stories many of which are true in a factual sense, differing only as to the way in which the facts are linked to give meaning. At the end of the day, there are few givens – only probabilities, likelihoods, and sometimes only possibilities. We have to accept that amount of ambiguity as unavoidable and proceed as best we can. If our investigations seem to provide a more convincing view of political reality than other constructions, then they will have at least some pragmatic value (Puchala 2003: Chapt 3).

When grave doubts about the reliability of the entire enterprise set in, there are several more important sources of reassurance. First, when we examine a number of different cases over thousands of years, it really does not matter a great deal to the theoretical arguments produced if a few key facts or interpretations that we or our sources advance in particular cases turn out to be wrong.

Second, although the past is no doubt irretrievable in some respects, it is nonetheless 'real'. There *is* an objective reality 'back there', however inadequately we are able to reconstruct it. Furthermore, for all our limitations and incapacity from this long remove to perceive life exactly as an Egyptian peasant, Hellenic monarch, or Roman Senator might have done, our perspective is actually far broader. We have more sources, understand much more about the world of his/her day, and also know how the story ended. Like the specialist historian, the participant observer is almost always too close to the action to appreciate what is going on, not least the wider currents in which he/she is caught up. In the words of Tudor historian G. R. Elton:

> [T]hose things we discover, analyse, talk about, did actually once happen. They happened to real people. ... They may not have known exactly what was happening, and ... the historian is entitled to think about his discoveries and to find a significance in them which may well have been invisible at the time. But his doing so does not affect the independent reality of the event; the historian is not entitled to suppose that he alone, by choosing this fact and ignoring that, creates history. On the contrary, no investigator is more firmly bound by his material, less able to invent or construct the object of his study.
>
> (Elton 1967: 77–78).

Third, it is humbling, but perhaps in some respects comforting, to know that the problems of using history are no less daunting than making sense of contemporary global politics. There is little or no agreement among defenders of different schools of contemporary international relations theory as to how to interpret the present and recent past – much less predict where history is headed. Making such tasks all the more difficult today are information overload (the opposite of the problem faced by historians of the ancient world) and the apparent acceleration of global change.

Consider some present-day debates. How are 'globalisation' and 'localization' best defined? By this or that definition, how 'global' or 'local' is the world today? Are globalising trends making for the continued advance of a 'human web' (McNeill and McNeill 2003), a global 'network society' (Castells 2000), a 'flat' (Friedman 2005) or 'spiky' (Florida 2005) world, selective 'denationalization' (Sassen 2006), or 'fragmegration' (Rosenau 1997)? Is globalisation still advancing, stalling, or in selective retreat? Are sovereign states losing influence or merely adapting to change? Is 'sovereignty' absolute, or has it always been 'organized hypocrisy' (Krasner 1999)? Are we seeing 'the end of history' (Fukuyama 1992) reflecting a consensus on the values of free market capitalism and political democracy? Does the concept of 'democracy' extend to the likes of 'transitional' post-Soviet regimes? Is it a reliable generalization that democracies do not fight one another? Or are we seeing, rather, a 'clash of civilizations' (Huntington 1996)? Is the world still essentially a society of states, is it unipolar and in the grip of 'empire'? If it exists, is such an empire 'American' or something akin to globalisation (Hardt and Negri 2000) or 'Westernization'? Do earlier examples of 'imperial overstretch' (Kennedy 1987) have continuing relevance?

Fourth and finally, we return to the point made at the beginning of this chapter. We study the past not only because it is 'there', but also because we sense history has important things to teach us about the elusive present. We are sympathetic to Stanley Hoffmann's view that 'a more rigorous examination of the past might reveal that what we sense as new really is not, and that some "traditional" features are far more complex than we think' (cited in Holsti 2002: 23). Michael Mann (1986: 32) surely is correct in arguing 'that some of the most important characteristics of our world today can be appreciated more clearly by historical comparison', although the jury remains out as to whether 'historical comparison' will allow us to 'see that the most significant problems of our own time are novel' and 'are interstitial to institutions that deal effectively with the more traditional problems for which they were first set up'.

Until now, much of IR theory has been narrowly grounded on a relatively brief and recent period in world history, either the twentieth century or at most the European era of the Westphalian State. History is now speeding up, and the Westphalian era seems to be transitioning to something like what Bull labeled a 'new medievalism' or what we prefer to call a 'post-international' world. To make meaningful judgments about continuities or (like Rosenau) about changes *in kind* in the contemporary world and global politics requires the longest possible historical perspective.

What are the enduring features and dynamics of politics? Politics, rather than 'international relations', should be the bedrock subject of our inquiry. Has Harry Truman got it right, that history simply repeats, if only we knew all of history? Or is Marcus Aurelius correct, that the performance is always the same and only the actors are different? If politics is the performance, certainly some types of actors/polities remain the same, all continue to evolve along with the context (stage setting) in which they operate, and some like TNCs (transnational corporations) or NGOs (non-governmental organizations) are far different from earlier prototypes.

With all due respect to Lowenthal, his otherwise felicitous phrase 'the past is a foreign country' is regrettable in its reference to 'country', a decidedly modern concept. However, who can gainsay the wisdom with which Lowenthal (1985: 412) closes his book: 'The past remains integral to us all, individually and collectively. We must concede the ancients their place, … But their place is not simply back there, in a separate and foreign country; it is assimilated in ourselves, and resurrected into an ever-changing present.'

Part III

The Complex Universe of Actors in Global Politics

5 The Web of World Politics (1976)

The Growing Irrelevance of the State-Centric Model

As we have seen, the doctrine of sovereignty triumphed by the seventeenth century. The doctrine owed much to philosophers such as Bodin and Thomas Hobbes who sought to explain and justify the emergence of centralized statist bureaucracies in France and England. The doctrine was largely the product of a search for order and stability after an era of feudal dissolution and religious strife. Although it was essentially a legal 'fiction', the doctrine provided a means of identifying international actors that was generally accurate and adequate for the period, even though oversimplified.

Global politics in the eighteenth century, at least in Europe, resembled a game of billiards in which the states appeared as homogeneous actors constantly caroming off one another. In this image 'the stage is preempted by a set of states, each in full control of all territory, men, and resources within its boundaries' (Wolfers 1962: 19). The major nation-states of the eighteenth and nineteenth centuries were self-sufficient units of relatively equal power. They were hierarchically organized and capable of protecting themselves against internal and external sources of instability and change. Their frontiers were clearly demarcated by international treaties. The Peace of Westphalia, which endorsed the principle of state sovereignty, was signed at a time when 'clear-cut, hard-shell, "closed" units no longer brooking' foreign interference were emerging (Herz 1959: 51).

Under these conditions international law and political reality coincided to a considerable extent. The state-centric model with its assumption of 'sovereign equality' reflected the essential ability of national governments to control their internal and external environments. These states disposed of sufficient territory and resources to defend themselves against foreign enemies and centralized the means of coercion within their territory. They were indeed subject to no higher secular authority. 'Now that power ... had become centralized, with its "headquarters" in impermeable units, and measurable in relation to other external power,' observes Herz (1959: 58), 'it made sense to translate power relations into legal relationships, to distinguish "rights" and "duties" of different states in their mutual relations, to speak of treaties "binding" nations, and so forth.'

However, there was always a discernible normative element in the doctrine of sovereignty as propounded by both Bodin and Hobbes. Whether or not a state actually possessed absolute authority over its citizens and could in reality regulate the citizens' relations with foreigners, it remained that the state should possess such authority. 'Bodin was convinced', declared J. L. Brierly (1963: 8), 'that a confusion of uncoordinated independent authorities must be fatal to a state.' In time what originally had been regarded as an attribute of a monarch came to be perceived as a quality of the state itself. Rousseau and the German philosophers of the nineteenth century were in part responsible for this shift in emphasis.

> With Rousseau ... the cult of sovereignty is justified by the rightness of the general will. With Fichte and the German romantics generally ... the emotional content of frustrated nationalism finds expression in the glorification of the state .... With Hegel ... philosophical absolutism is reflected in ... the concept that the State as a harmony of the whole society is the absolute power on earth.
>
> (Larson 1965: 25)

But, the facts of political life and the fiction of sovereignty were congruent only during the brief era of monarchical absolutism and, even then, only in Europe. Yet, 'so strong had the hold of sovereignty upon the imagination of political scientists become', argues Brierly (1963: 13–14), 'that when it became obvious... that the personal monarch no longer fitted the role, they [political scientists] started a hunt for the "location" of sovereignty, almost as if sovereignty, instead of being a reflection in theory of the political facts of a particular age, were a substance which must surely be found somewhere in every state if only one looked for it carefully enough'.

The Relative Irrelevance of Sovereignty

In earlier centuries the doctrine of sovereignty had an empirical basis. Today this doctrine does not have such a basis. All nation-states are subject to diverse internal and external conditioning factors that induce and constrain their behavior. American elections are influenced by events in Saigon and Peking, and American and British petroleum prices are affected by decisions made in Baghdad, Tripoli, or the headquarters of international petroleum corporations. James Rosenau (1969:2) describes this situation well:

> Almost every day incidents are reported that defy the principles of sovereignty. Politics everywhere, it would seem, are related to politics everywhere else. Where the functioning of any political unit was once

sustained by structures within its boundaries, now the roots of its political life can be traced to remote corners of the globe.

The confusion between sovereignty as prescription and the practical issue of state power is the main reason why it is so difficult to employ the concept of sovereignty meaningfully. No nation-state disposes of sufficient resources to prevent foreign intrusions upon its freedom of action or to realize and select goals without competing or cooperating with other actors; no nation-state enjoys the unqalified loyalty of its citizens. Dual and multiple loyalties are common today as illustrated by many communists who are at the same time loyal nationalists and ardent believers in a world movement. Although all nation-states enjoy some of the legal privileges of sovereignty (for example, all member states in the United Nations General Assembly have equal voting rights), in practice some states are obviously more 'sovereign' than others.

Certain units that manifest the trappings of sovereignty or are recognized by others as being sovereign do not and cannot behave independently. States such as Nepal, Outer Mongolia, and Bulgaria arc, at best, marginally independent, and their behaviour in the global arena can usually be predicted by reference to some larger state. 'Micro-sovereignties' such as the Republic of Maldives and the Comoro Islands are scarcely relevant to global politics.

Students of global and comparative politics have begun to recognize that many of the more than 50 nation-states that have acquired formal political independence since World War II and have been admitted as 'sovereign equals' to the United Nations are vastly different than those states that constituted the global system of the eighteenth and nineteenth centuries. 'There is surely at least a *prima facie* case', argues David Vital (1969: 155–6), 'for asserting that one of the notable characteristics of the modem international scene is the growing disparity in human and material resources to be found where important categories of states are compared – with the result that the only genuine common denominator left is the purely legal equality of states that carries with it only such tenuous advantages as membership in the United Nations.' Oran Young (1972: 131) declares: 'If the basic attributes of statehood are taken to be such things as a clearly demarcated territorial base, a relatively stable population, more or less viable central institutions of government, and external sovereignty, the contemporary situation immediately begins to appear unclear and confusing.' He continues: 'Many of the "new states", for example, are of doubtful viability in political terms, poorly integrated as communities, geographically fluid, and sufficiently dependent upon other states and organizations (albeit often on an informal basis) to compromise seriously their external sovereignty.'

With few exceptions, poor nation-states remain economically and/or politically dependent upon other actors, often the former metropole. For instance, several of the countries of what was formerly French Equatorial

Africa continue to rely on France to provide minimal economic and social services, and one of them, the Republic of Chad, was involved in a civil war in which the government depended upon French troops and arms to retain power. Similarly, Israel relies on the United States, and Cuba on the Soviet Union, for a semblance of economic stability. Certain states, notably the former Belgian Congo (Zaire) after 1960, the Dominican Republic in 1965, and Bangladesh (formerly East Pakistan) since 1971, have required the assistance of international organizations, not only for economic and social services, but for administrative guidance as well.

After World War I it became fashionable to assume that most states that comprised the global system coincided or should coincide with ethnically- or linguistically-defined national groups; hence, actors were commonly referred to as 'nation-states'. The destruction of the Austro-Hungarian, Ottoman, and Russian empires during the war appeared, to many historians and political scientists, to have brought the evolution of the state system to its close. States whose frontiers did not reflect national boundaries were considered anomalous. What few scholars and statesmen grasped, however, was that the nation-state, like the empire, was the product of a particular historical train of events and was 'therefore bound to disappear in the course of history' (Morgenthau 1973:10).

Currently, throughout Africa and Asia there are self-proclaimed states in which any coincidence between legal and national frontiers is imaginary. 'If the entry of the third world onto the stage of modern socioscientific consciousness has had one immediate result (or should have had), it is the snapping of the link between state and nation' (Nettl 1968: 560). Thus Nigeria, held up for a time after its independence in 1960 as a model of political development in Africa, was the scene of one of that continent's bloodiest civil wars. As is the case in many other former colonies in Africa and Asia, Nigerian loyalties remained parochial or tribal. Members of the various Nigerian tribal groups had a greater affinity for fellow tribe members living outside the state than for members of other tribes within the state. Nigeria was further cleaved along linguistic, religious, and economic lines. The existence of such profound cleavages explains in large part the recurrence of civil strife in many of the less developed areas.

Their lack of national identity and cohesion, coupled with their weakness and poverty, have made many of the newer states vulnerable to governmental instability, military coups d'état, and civil war. Perhaps the most extreme example of a national group that lacks a state is that of the Palestinians who were driven from or left their homes in what is now Israel or who live in the Israeli-occupied territories on the west bank of the Jordan River. Many of them are settled in refugee camps scattered in Egypt, Lebanon, Syria, and Jordan.

Owing to their lack of political and social stability, their military and economic weakness, and the linkages between domestic groups and foreign interests within their states, many of the Third World states are 'externally ill-defined, internally fragile and chaotic (calling) to mind sponges' (Waltz 1967: 205). Often they cannot prevent foreign intervention or externally-supported subversion and insurrection as well as more subtle forms of 'penetration'. The frustration engendered by this situation has often been behind the claims of 'imperialism' and 'neo-colonialism' made by their leaders.

Nonstate Actors

The far-reaching changes that have taken place in the global system since 1945 challenge not only the concept of sovereignty but also the adequacy of regarding the nation-state as the sole actor in world politics. Activities not accounted for by the traditional interstate model repeatedly direct our attention to more encompassing sets of concerns, requiring us to locate, enumerate, and describe a more complex universe of actors than before. After all, the state has not always been the *primary* actor in global politics and has never been the *sole* actor. And, unless we believe that history is irrelevant, we cannot even assume *a priori* that the nation-state will always remain the *most important* autonomous actor.

Before the emergence of the modern nation-state, global structure lacked the territorial divisions among units that characterize a world of 'sovereign equals'. A variety of other actors were generally recognized as constituent parts of the global system and its several subsystems. Mercenaries without national loyalties, empires consisting of several nations, bankers, clans, trading companies, tribes, religious groups, and nomadic groups (to name just a few) were all recognized as participants in the system.

Even after the rise of the nation-state system in Europe, other actors continued to exist alongside the state. James Field (1971: 355) points out that, paradoxically, it was during the eighteenth- and nineteenth-century struggles for national self-determination that such 'transnational individuals as the Marquis de Lafayette, Tadeusz Kosciuszko, Tom Paine, and the "titled freebooter" Lord Cochrane and such groups as the Philhellenes, Garibaldians, Fenians, and Zionists' were active. In addition, regions like Africa, Asia, and the Americas were characterized by units other than nation-states, such as empires, colonies, and tribes.

While national governments remain the principal actors in the contemporary global system, the past decade has witnessed an explosive increase in popular participation in 'affairs of state'. The global political process involves individuals acting as spokesmen, surrogates, or executioners for social and political collectivities. Private individuals usually participate only indirectly as taxpayers, voters, or (conscript) soldiers. Nevertheless, 'private' citizens or groups have increasingly intruded in world politics without reference to governments or interstate organizations. On occasion, even a single individual may behave independently and with impact. James Donovan, a New York attorney, negotiated the exchange of prisoners held in Cuba and arranged for the exchange of U-2 pilot Francis

Gary Powers for a convicted Soviet spy; Che Guevara fought for revolution in Bolivia; and H. Ross Perot, a Texas millionaire, flew to Indo-China to attempt to arrange the repatriation of American prisoners of war held in North Vietnam. Hijackings, kidnappings, assassinations, and street demonstrations illustrate some of the ways in which private individuals and groups have sought to modify the behaviour of national governments. Such groups, often lacking identifiable national affiliations, are 'difficult to punish in normal ways even for international crimes' (Bell 1971: 514).[1] The extralegal activities of James Bond, particularly against 'Spectre', illustrate an imaginative solution to the problem.

In the contemporary global system, certain units that appear to behave independently and whose behaviour has a marked effect on outcomes are not recognized as sovereign. Actors such as Al Fatah, the Viet Cong, the European Common Market, and even the Mafia play a larger role in global transactions than is customarily recognized. The Roman Catholic Church, for instance, 'has fashioned a transnational organization that provides it with a visible center from which its moral principles can be communicated and through which it attempts to exercise influence and social control' (Vallier 1971: 483). Similarly, the Ford Foundation 'has promoted economic planning in much of the less developed world' and 'is the largest financial supporter of social science research in Latin America' (P. Bell 1971: 466). Organizations like the United Nations and its agencies, NATO, and even the International Red Cross, while possessing neither the legal nor territorial attributes of sovereignty, are significant actors on the world stage. In certain cases, these organizations have developed large bureaucracies, have disposed of substantial budgets, and have acquired modes of routinized behaviour. They have gained the loyalties of civil servants or other functional groups, and many of their activities are perceived as 'legitimate' by nation-states.

It is increasingly evident that in the contemporary global system, as in political systems that existed before 1648, nonstate actors, often 'transnationally' organized, possess their own military capabilities, economic assets, and sources of information. The Palestinian guerrilla groups, for instance, dispose of organized military forces, negotiate formal agreements with Arab states, and threaten to undermine diplomatic understandings that were painfully achieved by representatives of major powers. Similarly, economic cartels and industrial corporations with productive and marketing facilities in several countries dispose of large-scale economic assets that provide them with substantial direct and indirect political influence. In some respects, multinational corporations such as International Business Machines and Shell Oil are more independent than a government such as that of Jordan, although the latter represents a 'sovereign' state.

Sheer size alone, however, does not reflect the impact that multinational corporations have on small countries or the threat that they may represent to the political and economic independence of these nation-states. As such corporations penetrate these countries, major economic sectors and large numbers of people may become obligated and responsive to foreigners. 'If a similar chain of command existed in public organizations', writes one observer (Evans 1971: 676), 'the poor country would be deemed a colony.'

> Because multinational corporations are private economic organizations, chains of command leading outside the state may multiply without ostensible loss of political sovereignty. Yet, national autonomy, the ability of a nation-state as a collectivity to make decisions which shape its political and economic future, has been diminished.

Conservatism in the Study of Global Politics

Despite the accumulation of conflicting evidence, most present-day students of global politics have been reluctant to abandon the state-centric model to which they have become so accustomed. In this respect, although the 'real world' has marched on since the era of Bodin, contemporary students of world politics have lagged behind. Even attempts to pioneer new approaches and methods have remained rooted in traditional concepts like sovereignty. The state-centric model has imposed research blinders and has inhibited an accurate mapping of the increasingly complex global system. As J. David Singer (1969a: 22) observes, 'The national state is – in most theoretical formulations – assigned too prominent a role, and... competing entities must be more heavily emphasized than has been customary.' Although it is 'mandatory to first describe the population about which one is generalizing' (Singer 1969b: 69), precious little time or effort has gone into performing this task.

The continuing state-centric bias is no better illustrated than in a recent edition of essays about international relations theory in which the editors conclude that, despite disagreements among the contributors, they all conceive 'the subject to consist of the individuals and groups who initiate and sustain the actions and interactions of nation-states' (Knorr and Rosenau 1969: 4). In addition, under contemporary international law only states are sovereign.[2] States and some international organizations have traditionally been regarded as the sole subjects of international law, and William Tung's view is not an uncommon one even today. 'International persons', Tung (1968: 39) declares, 'are primarily states to which rights and duties are generally attributed .... [The] position of states in the international community corresponds to that of individuals under municipal law.'

There are several reasons for this apparently conservative bias in the study of global politics. In the first place, empirical data concerning nation-states, particularly aggregate data, are practically the only data readily available. While many of the details of specific governmental interactions are denied to scholars for many years, we are confident that they will ultimately be made part of the public record and be available to historians. Moreover, information concerning the leadership, population, economic status, and so forth of nation-states is usually a matter of public record. Similar information about nonstate units is often hard to come by. Furthermore, newspapers, journals, UN reports, and government publications all tend to reify nation-states and to present data in tidy national pigeonholes.

Second, there is a natural desire on the part of scholars and practitioners to work with data that are readily comparable. Previously it has been assumed that all nation-states are sufficiently similar so that we can consider them as members of the same class of units. Each is sovereign, has its own GNP (gross national product), population, territory, army, and so forth. The assumption that similar nation-states can be conveniently distinguished on the basis of geographic criteria facilitates the tasks of aggregation and comparison and eliminates 'sloppy' overlap.

Yet some of these simplifying, albeit comforting, assumptions are misleading. 'Although many social scientists still insist on "comparing states" as if they were equivalent units', Ivan Vallier (1971: 501) reminds us that 'this is unfruitful.' Even though comparable data are difficult to obtain and calculate if we include nonstate actors, such data do exist or can be created. Many nonstate actors like corporations have a 'population' or membership, a 'government', and goals, objectives, and resources. As actors, nation-states and nonstate actors are certainly analogous and perhaps are even homologous.

The traditional mark of sovereignty nevertheless remains as a supposedly defining attribute of 'international' actors. It seems paradoxical that scholars, especially those who declare their desire to break away from traditional methods, should resort to traditional legal and diplomatic concepts to justify their continued focus on the nation-state. Their eyes are riveted to an artificial construct – an 'incomplete global system' – the existence of which is inferred as much from prescriptive norms as from empirical observation.

A final reason for the intellectual procrastination of many international relations scholars is that the study of international politics did not originate as an autonomous discipline, but evolved as an offshoot of the study of the state, as 'the untidy fringe of domestic politics'. As Martin Wight (1966: 20) suggests: 'The principle that every individual requires the protection of a state which represents him in the international community, is a juristic expression of the belief in the sovereign state as the consummation of political experience and activity which has marked Western political thought since the Renaissance.' But it is precisely because no national government exercises complete control over the individuals and groups for which it is legally responsible that nonstate actors can enter independently into relations with other actors.

The time has come to cast aside what Wight (1966: 20) terms 'the intellectual prejudice imposed by the sovereign state'. The conservative bias of the past, as Oran Young (1972: 126) remarks, has too long precluded 'the analysis of a wide range of logically possible and empirically interesting models of world politics'. Since scholars are concerned with investigating global behaviour, it is reasonable to propose that actors be identified and classified according to behavioural rather than legal or normative criteria.

Towards a New Conceptualization of Global Politics

All human activity may be analyzed in terms of purposive systems, each of which involves men intensively interacting with one another around particular activities. Thus we can identify ethnic systems, economic systems, defence systems, and so forth. Individuals and groups who occupy roles in such systems are functionally linked.

The Emergence and Disappearance of Actors

Individuals and groups become functionally linked as they discover that they share common interests and common needs that transcend existing organizational frontiers. They may then develop common views and even cooperative approaches to the problems that they confront. The complexity of contemporary modes of industrial production, for example, may generate a linkage between business firms in different countries that depend upon each other for raw materials, parts, expertise, or marketing facilities. Industrialists in several countries may discover that they share problems with which they can cope more effectively by pooling their resources; they may seek, for instance, common tax and pricing policies from the governments of the states in which they reside. In the course of collaborating, their common or complementary interests may grow and deepen beyond mere economic expediency. 'There is', argues Werner Feld (1970: 210), 'an emotive side to such efforts which produces in the staff members concerned with collaboration a distinct feeling of being involved in a "united or cooperative" endeavor.'

When one begins to identify the many functional systems that link men, the world appears 'like millions of cobwebs superimposed one upon another, covering the whole globe' (Burton 1968: 8–9). Functional systems themselves tend to be interdependent and related to each other in complex ways. Each system requires the existence of others to perform effectively; in this respect systems, too, may be said to be linked. In J. W. Burton's (1968: 8) words:

> Linked systems create clusters that tend to be concentrated geographically ... Linked systems tend to consolidate into administrative units ... Once consolidated... linked systems and their administrative controls acquire an identity and a legitimized status within their environment.

From this perspective, governments of nation-states may be seen as functional (administrative) systems whose central function since the seventeenth century has been to regulate and manage clusters of other functional systems. More accurately perhaps, in their function as administrators for many functional systems, states have been essentially multifunctional actors organizing collective efforts toward objectives which could not be realized by individuals in their private capacity. The boundaries of nation-states have tended to coincide with the boundaries of other functional systems, and therefore political frontiers have seemed to represent 'marked discontinuities in the frequency of transactions and marked discontinuities in the frequency of responses' (Deutsch 1966b: 15). States were able to control and limit the transactions which crossed their frontiers as well as those that occurred within their borders. As long as states remained relatively impermeable, they were able, for example, to regulate the economic or cultural relations of their citizens with those living abroad and with foreign nationals.

In theory, however, it is *not necessary* that the governments of nation-states be the umbrella administrative systems through which all other systems are regulated. The boundaries of such systems coincide with nation-state frontiers only insofar as national governments can control them and can independently open or close their state borders to transnational influences. Consider the situation of many states whose political or historical frontiers do not coincide with the national boundaries of groups residing within them. Ties may develop across borders, and loyalties may shift away from governments. There are many historical cases of such phenomena; the Austro-Hungarian Empire, for example, consisted of a patchwork of different national groups, and Serbian, Italian, and Croatian nationals tended to reserve their highest loyalties for fellow-nationals living outside the Empire and for the idea of 'their nation'. In recent years violence in areas as diverse as Cyprus, the Congo..., Nigeria, Canada, and Ireland suggest the way in which the loyalties of national groups may transcend the borders of states and lead to conflict.

The question of human loyalties is not one that can be settled once and for all; loyalties constantly shift as men perceive that their interests and aspirations are more fully represented by new groups. As Arnold Wolfers (1962: 23) noted some years ago, 'attention must be focused on the individual human beings for whom identification is a psychological event'. To the degree that human loyalties are divided between states and other groups, the latter can become significant global actors.

This is, in fact, what has happened. As Burton (1968: 10) reminds us, 'there is in contemporary world society an increasing number of systems – some basically economic, scientific, cultural, ideological, or religious – that have little relationship to State boundaries', and 'whatever significance geographically drawn boundaries had, has been and is being greatly reduced by these developments.' Of the various transnational exchanges, some of the more important and well-known include teaching and research abroad, study abroad, overseas religious missions, military service abroad, tourism, work in multinational corporations, and participation in nongovernmental and international organizations.

Functional systems have spilled across nation-state boundaries and in some cases have defied the efforts of governments to regulate them. Citizens

of many states find themselves linked in horizontal fashion, working together regardless of the wishes of governments. Thus, Jews in the United
States, Israel, the Soviet Union, and Europe are linked by loyalties that
transcend the interests of the states in which they reside. Leftist revolutionaries, industrial managers, international civil servants and others are linked
in similar fashion though for different purposes. Individuals have become
increasingly aware of the interests that they share with others in different
states, have communicated these interests, and have developed new loyalties.
In some cases these transnational affiliations have been organized and have
acquired their own administrative hierarchies, thereby becoming nonstate
actors in a more formal sense.

Several major trends have contributed to these developments. The proliferation and increasing potential destructiveness of thermonuclear weapons
have made the prospect of war between the superpowers 'unthinkable' and have
contributed to the erosion of the great postwar ideological blocs. Conventional
military force and intervention have become less effective in coping with certain
problems, as evidenced by the French defeat in Algeria and the American
debacle in Vietnam. As nuclear and conventional warfare have become more
expensive to contemplate and less effective, new means of gaining influence,
including guerrilla warfare, political terrorism, economic boycott, and political
propaganda, have become more common, thereby permitting actors lacking
the traditional instruments of power to exercise considerable influence and
enjoy considerable autonomy. Even more frightening is the possibility that
such actors may gain access to modern technology.

In addition, the diminution of the central ideological cleavage, the resurgence of Europe, China, and Japan, and the independence of a multitude of
small and poor nation-states in Africa and Asia have led to the emergence of
other cleavages, some global and many of a regional and local scope, and have
therefore encouraged the 'regionalization' or 'localization' of international
conflict. 'The structure of the international system', Jorge Domínguez (1971:
208) declares, 'has been transformed through a process of fragmentation of
the linkages of the center of the system to its peripheries and of those between
the continental subsystems of the peripheries.' The new conflicts that have
surfaced revolve around questions such as national self-determination, local
border adjustment, economic inequality and exploitation, and racial or ethnic
discrimination. These are questions that encourage the shifting of people's
loyalties away from institutions that formerly held their affections.

At root, the twentieth-century emergence of new actors in the global
system reflects the inability of territorially-limited nation-states to respond
to, cope with, or suppress changing popular demands. Popular demands can
be suppressed (and often are) by existing authorities; they can be fulfilled by
them; or they can lead to the emergence of new political structures designed
to fulfil them. Thus, when a state can no longer guarantee the defence of its
subjects, it may be conquered and eliminated as happened to eighteenth-
century Poland. Conversely, the integration of existing units, like the merger

of two corporations, or the creation of new nation-state actors such as the United States in 1776, Biafra (temporarily) in 1968, and Bangladesh in 1971, are partly the consequence of demands for a more capable and responsive performance of certain tasks–demands that were neither suppressed nor fulfilled.

Today the global system is complexly interdependent owing in part to improved communications and transportation. People's lives are being touched and affected ever more profoundly by decisions made outside their own national states. Their demands for justice, equality, prosperity, and independence tend to increase and further tax the capacity of existing nation-states. We are in the midst of a revolution of 'rising expectations' in which the achievements of people in one corner of the system generate demands for similar achievements elsewhere. When these demands remain unanswered, they may lead to intense frustration. Thus, the frustration of large numbers of Arabs at continued Israeli occupation of Palestine and the failure of Arab governments to satisfy their claims have led to the creation of Palestinian terrorist and liberation groups, the organization and behaviour of which are in part patterned after successful movements in Algeria, Cuba, and Vietnam.

In the contemporary world, demands such as those for defence, full employment, or social reform place overwhelming burdens on the resources of poor states. Others, increasingly, are beyond the capacity of *any* single nation-state to fulfil.

One way in which national governments may seek to deal with transnational pressures is through the creation of specialized intergovernmental actors which acquire limited global roles. The emergence of regional agencies and organizations and those associated with the United Nations attests to the growth of large-scale functional systems with their own administrative overseers. Such organizations reinforce pre-existing linkages or create new ones. Intergovernmental organizations that have achieved some measure of autonomy, however, are often engaged in highly technical and relatively non-political tasks. In those areas where governments resist transnational pressures, other groups may emerge.

Global Tasks

There are at least four general types of tasks that can be performed by actors:

1. *Physical protection* or security which involves the protection of men and their values from coercive deprivation either by other members within the group or by individuals or groups outside it.
2. *Economic development and regulation* which comprise activities that are intended to overcome the constraints imposed on individual or collective capacity for self-development and growth by the scarcity or distribution of material resources.

3. *Residual public interest tasks* which involve activities that are designed to overcome constraints other than economic, such as disease or ignorance, that restrict individual or collective capacity for self-development and growth.
4. *Group status* which refers to the provision of referent identification through collective symbols that bind the individual to others, provide him with psychological and emotional security, and distinguish him in some manner from others who are not members of the group. Such symbols are often grounded in ethnicity, nationality, class, religion, and kinship.

The behaviour of actors in the global system involves the performance of one or more of the foregoing tasks in cooperation or competition with other actors responding to the actual or anticipated demands of their 'constituencies'. Although governments of nation-states customarily perform these tasks 'domestically', tasks become relevant at the 'international' level when a government acts to protect its citizens from externally imposed change or to adapt them to such change. For example, the regulation of the domestic economy to create and sustain full employment is not itself an internationally-relevant task. When, however, tariffs are imposed on imports or the currency is devalued, the behaviour acquires significance for the global system. Others outside the state are affected and made to bear the burdens of the 'domestic' economic adjustment.

The suggested categories of tasks are, of course, in the nature of analytic pigeonholes, and many activities involve more than a single category. Most actors tend to perform several tasks for their members, but an actor may be specialized and perform only one type. The World Health Organization (WHO), for example, is largely concerned with upgrading global health standards (a residual public interest task). Armed mercenaries, on the other hand, are generally involved only in offering physical protection to those who require it and can pay for it. In practice, different categories of tasks are often perceived as mutually supportive. Hence, national groups may believe that only by unifying their 'nation' can they protect themselves; yet at the same time unification depends on self-protection.

Actors may add and drop tasks or enlarge and restrict them over a period of time. For example, only recently many 'welfare state' policies have been initiated by nation-states or intergovernmental organizations, thereby enlarging the scope of activities involved in the residual public interest category. Previously, such services were offered, if at all, by groups such as the family, church, or political party. Technological change, the behaviour of others, and the solution of old problems encourage demands for the performance of new tasks. Thus, modern technology and medicine, while solving problems that have bedevilled people for centuries, are partly responsible for growing global pollution and population pressures. If nation-states continue to cope only sporadically with these burgeoning problems, demands for pollution and population control may lead to the creation of significant intergovernmental and non-governmental political structures.

The increasing inability of modern nation-states to satisfy the demands of their citizens or to cope with problems that transcend their boundaries is partly the result of the growing complexity and specialization of functional systems as well as of the increase in the number of collective goods and benefits desired by individuals. In contrast, states in the eighteenth century were concerned principally with providing physical protection for members and insulating subjects from externally-imposed change. Individuals were able to provide for their own economic and social needs either privately or through small groups such as the extended family. Only peripherally and sporadically was the larger collectivity called upon to undertake economic and social service tasks or even to provide group status. Political philosophers were largely preoccupied with identifying the areas in which collective action was called for, and they tended to agree that these areas were narrowly circumscribed.

The increasing size and complexity of systems and institutions threaten individuals with a sense of helplessness in a world dominated by large impersonal forces where rapid change and 'future shock' are common. Many small and new nation-states are only barely (if at all) able to provide physical security, economic satisfaction, or social welfare for their citizens. On the other hand, often they do provide their citizens with an emotionally-comforting sense of national identity and 'in-group' unity. In this respect these states (as well as some nonstate units) can be seen as rather specialized actors in an increasingly interdependent world.

The Panoply of Global Actors

We can identify at least six types of actors in the contemporary global system.

The first type is the *interstate governmental actor* (1GO) which is composed of governmental representatives from more than one state. Sometimes known as 'international' or 'supranational' organizations, depending upon their degree of autonomy, they include as members two or more national governments. Since the beginning of the nineteenth century, the number of such organizations has increased even more rapidly than has the number of nation-states (Singer and Wallace 1970: 277). Examples of this type of actor include military alliances such as NATO and the Warsaw Pact, universal organizations such as the League of Nations or the United Nations, and special purpose organizations such as the European Economic Community (EEC) and the Universal Postal Union (UPU).

A second type is the *interstate nongovernmental actor*. Sometimes referred to as 'transnational' or 'cross-national', this type of actor encompasses individuals who reside in several nation-states but who do not represent any of the governments of these states. These groups are functionally diverse and include religious groups such as the International Council of Jewish Women, the Salvation Army, and the World Muslim Congress; trade unions such as the

Caribbean Congress of Labour and the World Confederation of Labour; and social welfare organizations such as the International Red Cross or Kiwanis International. While many of these actors seek to avoid involvement in politically-sensitive questions, some behave autonomously and do become so embroiled. This is illustrated by the role of the International Red Cross in the Nigerian-Biafran civil war and the conflict culminating in 1968 between Standard of New Jersey's subsidiary, the International Petroleum Corporation, and the government of Peru. The multinational corporation in particular is becoming a major transnational actor, rendering more obsolete the state-centric model of international interaction.

A third type of actor is commonly known as the *nation-state*. It consists of personnel from the agencies of a single central government. Though often regarded as unified entities, national governments are often more usefully identified in terms of their parts such as ministries and legislatures. On occasion, the 'parts' may behave autonomously with little reference to other government bureaucracies. The ministries that make up large governments bargain with each other and regularly approach 'national' questions with parochial or particularist views; each may view the 'national interest' from a different standpoint. For instance, it has been alleged that the American Central Intelligence Agency has, on occasion, formulated and carried out policy independently and without the complete knowledge or approval of elected officials.

Fourth, there is the *governmental non-central* actor composed of personnel from regional, parochial, or municipal governments within a single state or of colonial officials representing the state. Such parochial bureaucracies and officials generally are only peripherally concerned with world politics or, at most, have an indirect impact on the global political system. Occasionally, however, they have a direct impact when they serve as the core of secessionist movements or when they establish and maintain direct contact with other actors. In this context, the provincial officials of Katanga, Biafra, and, in the 1860's, the American South come to mind.

A fifth type is the *intrastate nongovernmental* actor which consists of nongovernmental groups or individuals located primarily within a single state. Again, this type of actor is generally thought of as subject to the regulation of a central government, at least in matters of foreign policy. Yet, such groups, ranging from philanthropic organizations and political parties to ethnic communities, labour unions, and industrial corporations may, from time to time, conduct relations directly with autonomous actors other than their own government. In this category we find groups as disparate as the Ford Foundation, Oxfam, the Turkish- and Greek-Cypriot communities, the Communist Party of the Soviet Union, the Jewish Agency, and the Irish Republican Army.

Finally, *individuals* in their private capacity are, on occasion, able to behave autonomously in the global arena. Such 'international' individuals were more common before the emergence of the nation-state, particularly as diplomatic or military mercenaries. More recently, one might think of the

Table 1 Actors Defined by Membership and Principal Task

	Physical Protection	Economic	Public Interest	Group Status
Interstate Governmental	NATO	GATT	WHO	British Commonwealth
Interstate Nongovernmental	Al Fatah	Royal Dutch Petroleum	International Red Cross	Comintern
Nation-State	Turkish Cypriot Government Officials	US Dept. of Commerce	HEW (US Department of Health, Education, and Welfare)	Biafra
Governmental Non-central	Confederacy	Katanga	New York City	Quebec
Intrastate Nongovernmental	Jewish Defense League	CARE	Ford Foundation	Ibo tribe
Individual	Gustav von Rosen	Jean Monnet	Andrew Carnegie	Dalai Lama

American industrialist Andrew Carnegie who willed ten million dollars for 'the speedy abolition of war between the so-called civilized nations', the Swedish soldier Count Gustaf von Rosen who was responsible for creating a Biafran air force during the Nigerian civil war, or the Argentine revolutionary Ché Guevara.

Table 1 relates actors to the tasks mentioned above and suggests the range of actors that exist in the global system and the principal tasks they perform. The entries in the matrix are illustrative and indicate that these actors at some point in time have performed these functions in ways relevant for the global system. Some categories may have many representatives; others only a few.

The Complex Conglomerate System

Our analysis up to this point enables us to return to the question of the structure and processes of the global political system. The contemporary global system defies many conventional descriptions of its structure as bipolar, multipolar, or balance of power. These descriptions account only for the number of states and their distribution of power. 'In particular,' declares Oran Young (1972: 136), 'it seems desirable to think increasingly in terms of world systems that are heterogeneous with respect to types of actor (i.e. mixed actor systems) in the analysis of world politics.'

We propose an alternative model of the contemporary global system which we shall call the *complex conglomerate system*. The concept of 'conglomerate' refers to 'a mixture of various materials or elements clustered together without assimilation' (Compact Edition OED 1971: 516). In economics the term is used to describe the grouping of firms of different types under a single umbrella of corporate leadership.

The principal feature of the complex conglomerate system is the formation of situationally-specific alignments of different types of actors using a variety of means to achieve complementary objectives. It is significant that many of these alignment 'conglomerates' lack the formal structure of traditional alliances such as NATO and tend to be flexible and ideologically diffuse.

For example, until recently one could identify conglomerate alignments that are essentially adversarial on the issue of Angolan independence. On one side were the Angolan rebel groups, the UN General Assembly, Black African states like Tanzania, the Soviet bloc of states, and even the World Council of Churches; on the other side were Portugal, the United States, and several major international corporations.

Table 2 further suggests the range of alignments that characterize the complex conglomerate system.

In summary, we should stress that the complex conglomerate system exhibits several other characteristics in addition to the primary one relating to the existence of many autonomous actors of different types and their grouping into diffuse, flexible, and situationally-specific alignments:

Table 2 Alignments in a Complex Conglomerate System

	Interstate Governmental	Interstate Non-governmental	Nation-state	Governmental Noncentral	Intrastate Non-governmental	Individual
Interstate Governmental	UN–NATO(1950)	UN–International Red Cross (Palestine)	EEC–Francophone African states	OAU–Biafra	Arab League–Al Fatah	Grand Muftiof Jerusalem–Arab League
Interstatenon Governmental	UN–International Red Cross (Palestine)	Shell Oil – ESSO (1972)	USSR– Comintern (1920's)	IBM–Scotland	ITT (International Telephone and Telegraph)–Allende opposition (Chile)	Sun-Yat-sen–Comintern
Nation-state	EEC–Francophone African states	USSR–Comintern (1920s)	'traditional alliances' (NATO)	Belgium Katanga (1950)	North-Vietnam–Viet Cong	US–James Donovan
Governmental Noncentral	OAU–Biafra	IBM –Scotland	Belgium–Katanga (1960)	New York Mayor–Moscow Mayor (1973)	Algerian rebels–French Socialists (1954)	South African mercenaries–Katanga
Intrastate Nongovernmental	Arab League–Al Fatah	ITT–Allende Opposition (Chile)	North Vietnam–Viet Cong	Ulster–Protestant Vanguard (1970)	Communist Party, USSR–Communist Party, German Democratic Republic	George Grivas–Greek Cypriots
Individual	Grand Mufti of Jerusalem Arab League	Sun-Yat-sen–Comintern	US–James Donovan	South Africa mercenaries–Katanga (1960)	George Grivas–Greek Cypriots	Louis of Conde–Gaspard de Coligny (1562)

1. The global system in traditional terms is steadily moving in the direction of multipolarity, with the breakup of the great postwar ideological blocs and the assumption of new global roles by Europe, Japan, and China. Concurrently, many new states have joined the system and the gap between the living standards of 'haves' and 'have nots' continues to widen. In addition, the Third World has begun to divide into resource-rich and resource-deprived states (the 'Fourth World').

2. Weapons with the greatest destructive capacity are deemed unusable, and military intervention by nation-states is becoming increasingly expensive. Economic adjustment among the developed countries is rapidly joining security as a major preoccupation of developed-country policymakers. Additional conflicts involve questions like national self-determination, local border adjustment, economic inequality and exploitation, and racial or ethnic discrimination.

3. Many poor and small nation-states are unable to perform the tasks demanded of them by their populations.

4. Global problems, such as oceanic pollution, are emerging that transcend national boundaries and overwhelm the capacities of individual nation-states.

5. Many means are available and are used to exert influence including conventional military force (nation-states), control of marketing facilities, pricing, and technology (multinational corporations), clandestine military force (terrorist and revolutionary groups), moral suasion (Roman Catholic Church), money and expertise (Ford Foundation), voting strength (Jewish community in the United States), and so forth.

6. Functional linkages create transnational perceptions of mutual interest and lead to regularized communication among status groups across state frontiers.

7. A high level of interdependence links diffuse groups in different nation-states and is fostered by modern communication and transportation facilities and complex production processes.

8. Nation-states are becoming increasingly permeable, that is, subject to external penetration.

9. The loyalties of peoples are increasingly divided among many actors and tend to shift depending upon the nature of the issue.

10. Discontinuities exist which are directly related to the salience of local issues and the level of political development of various regional systems.

6 Italy After Rome

Complexity at the nexus of the ancient and modern worlds (1996)

Our rather lengthy period of Italian history includes the end of the Age of Antiquity in the West, the Medieval era, and the dawn of the Westphalian system in Europe. No case encompasses a period of more varied and significant transformations among polities. We are dealing here with the gradual demise of the western branch of the Roman Empire, the intrusion of barbarian tribes, and the evolution of several major, interrelated rivalries during the Middle Ages among Western Catholicism, Orthodox-Byzantine Catholicism, and Islam, as well as among rather different forms of empire and city polities. Contests among Pope, Holy Roman Emperor, and cities persisted through the Renaissance and Early Modern era, when politics became more secular, the Holy Roman Empire faded, and cities – themselves internally transformed – were overshadowed by emerging Westphalian polities to the north.

Political Complexity

Italy was host to a bewildering array of competing polities. Tribal entities like the Huns, dynasties like the Merovingians, the imperial polity that emerged in northern Europe, groups of freebooters, the Church, and numerous city polities competed vigorously in Italy. Waves of invaders ebbed and flowed up and down the peninsula as Italians repeatedly served as pawns in the conflicts among powerful rulers.

Types of Polities

Italy's experience after the decline of the Roman Empire involved a wide variety of polities, with considerable overlapping and nesting.

Tribes

Tribes presented a continuing threat to the late Roman empire, though what constituted a 'tribe' is unclear. Most were *foederati*, like the Huns, whom Koenigsberger characterizes as 'a federation of clans and tribes under one king'. The Lombards, for some years after their invasion, imposed tribal rule over a large part of Italy.

In time, however, the Lombards found their ways of life transformed by Rome's cultural legacy. In fact, in Italy, tribe ceased to be a significant identity, while identities based on kinship found more than adequate expression in family and clan. The situation was somewhat different to the north among the Germans, where tribal identities persisted even when life-styles became more civilized. When, in the tenth century, Otto the Great spoke of the German parts of his kingdom, he talked of *Francia*, but he referred to its four duchies (ruled by members of his family) – each of which claimed a tribal origin – as Saxons, Franks, Bavarians, and Swabians (Ale-manni). Tribe, family, kingdom, and Holy Roman Empire identities thus overlapped.

Family

The basic unit of Italian society and those of Italy's neighbours was family or clan. Whatever the tribal nature of the Frankish kingdom, the Mer-ovingian kings thought of the whole of Gaul as a family property and their 'palace' as a mobile family household.

Centuries later, in 1152, when Emperor Frederick I Barbarossa ascended the throne, Germany was still suffering from a dispute between those who had supported Henry IV (Ghibellines) and those who had rejected him (Guelphs). Rather than a principled quarrel between papalists and imperi-alists, the conflict was really between Guelph supporters of the dynasty of Welf who opposed Henry's descendants and Ghibelline supporters of the hereditary dynasty of Hohenstaufen. When the Guelphs eventually lost, their lands were forfeit and all of the medieval duchies of Germany were redrawn. Thus began a process of disintegration of what little unity Ger-many had, until in the seventeenth century the 'empire' consisted of more than three hundred separate jurisdictions ruled by princes from noble families. These were a closed corporation whose number could not be increased except by their consent, interposing themselves as the *Reich-fürstenstand* between the emperor and his subjects.

In northern and central Italy the effective rulers of Italian city polities were groups of families dubbed the patriciates. One such group was the Book of Gold families of the Venetian Republic, but less exclusive patri-ciates, including well-heeled families of commoner origin, were the norm in many Italian cities. Most of the great commercial and trading companies and banking houses were identified with particular families. Family and clan – *gente* in Florence, *albergo* in Genoa – were often, quite deliberately, blurred through extended family linkages resulting from marriage or artifi-cial kinship. Hyde (1973: 104–5) explains that such *consorterie* predated the communes and continued to spread and evolve in the twelfth century. Most *consorterie* were either interfamily alliances or an important family with its clients. In every instance, the purpose was 'the conservation of the persons, property and interests of the members'.

Sometimes conserving the interests of an extended family militated against external authority and even civil peace. Typically, the *consorterie* regulated marriages and the inheritance of property and arbitrated disputes. Some enacted statutes or ordinances that were enforced by their own officials. Hyde points out: 'Where the members [of the *consorterie*] were the leading landowners in a particular area, the *consorterie* could easily acquire something like territorial jurisdiction.' Many extended families symbolized their independent status by constructing family towers, which can still be seen clustered in a few places like San Gimignano.

Vendetta was the accepted social code for repaying 'insults' in city polities. Family rivalries complicated other divisions – Guelph/Ghibelline, other parties, *popolo grasso/popolo minuto*, and so on – and resulting conflicts threatened public order in any number of cities. That was the immediate origin of the single *podestas* and *signori* whose appearance signalled the end of the republican tradition of the communes. In effect, many cities eventually installed family dynasties – of which the later Medicis of Florence were an example – local kings in all but name. Nevertheless, families outside of the ruling circle still preserved some of their traditional autonomy.

Towns and Cities

Italian society in the Middle Ages and later was unique both in its degree of urbanization and in the character of its towns and cities. What distinguished other European cities from those of Italy was that their inhabitants were engaged in trade, industry, or other commercial activity setting them apart from the rest of society and that leading burghers managed to establish their independence from kings, the landed nobility, and the Church. In Italy, towns and cities managed, to a great extent, to incorporate the landed nobility from an early stage and faced less resistance from external authorities (except the Church) because feudal structures were weak from the outset. Cities regarded their right to rule the surrounding countryside as a given, and a number of cities came to be ruled by merchant aristocracies.

There was a growth of towns and cities in much of Italy between 900 and about 1150. Many towns were new walled *castelli* settlements, some built by local lords and others by groups of neighbours acting on their own. Most of the people involved came initially from nearby. The very construction and maintenance of the walls may have been a factor in creating the communal spirit that developed in the twelfth and thirteenth centuries. Local identity was also enhanced by the association of cathedrals or *pievi* (mother churches) and patron saints with specific towns and cities.

Towns and cities, along with local bishops and priests, helped fill the authority vacuum created by the absence of kings and the weakness of the Holy Roman Empire. In northern and central Italy, the Carolingian counties (*contadi*), though still largely intact in the tenth century, rapidly disintegrated thereafter. Then in the twelfth and thirteenth centuries, towns and cities established a new system of *contadi* by extending their control into the surrounding countryside, circumscribing the collective government of lesser towns and villages and drawing *castelli* lords and other notables 'into the community of the whole city' (Reynolds 1984: 242). The process in Venice was somewhat different, owing to its Byzantine roots and unique geography. There a central city polity was formed, *c*. 1200, by literally bridging some 60 neighbourhood parishes.

Conceptions of town and city polities began to change in the mid-twelfth century when the term 'commune' came into fashion. The word had no real legal significance and was used to refer to everything from government, to the people of a community, or both. Yet a new sense of community identity did evolve, rooted in the practical achievement of greater independence. For many towns and cities there was a transitional stage in which local church authorities played a key role.

In this manner, Italian towns and cities re-emerged both as living-museum remnants of Rome and in the interstices within the domains of Church and Holy Roman Empire. Towns and cities did not suddenly appear as a result of some communal 'revolution', though the increasing independence of some may have inspired others. Degrees of autonomy varied for a long time, and it was not even clear who were citizens of these new communities. From the outset the consolidation of towns and cities also implied some loss of autonomy, or at least switch of allegiances, for neighbouring settlements. This process of consolidating continued until, in the late fifteenth century, most urban centres were overshadowed by Milan, Florence, or Venice.

The consolidation of a polity, as we have repeatedly stressed, is never complete, because the process involves establishing dominance over other groups and loyalties that tend to persist and because a new polity generates new institutions and groups. Consolidation breeds complexity, and so it was with Italian cities.

Economic and Social Polities

Important fraternities, guilds, companies, and banks often overlapped with family groupings. By the late twelfth century, many Italian towns and cities were 'positively riddled' by fraternities and guilds. We are inclined to accept Reynolds' (1984: 73–74) interpretation that their primary function was social – providing a sense of belonging in an unfamiliar town setting – though they also advanced economic interests, upheld standards, and regulated membership in crafts or trades. Most of the fraternities and guilds were involved in town government, or were downright subversive. Secular lords might fine or license guilds, and church authorities might use them to promote piety, but both religious and secular officials were deeply suspicious of sworn associations, viewing them as potential sources of heresy and political faction.

By the later thirteenth century, trading companies and banks had become powerful actors. Single-venture enterprises or family businesses developed into permanent firms drawing capital from a variety of sources. Some Italian traders settled in foreign trading centres, where they formed local associations or 'nations' for mutual advancement and protection. Large banks established such a symbiotic relationship with local and foreign governments, as well as various popes, that it was often difficult to determine who was beholden to whom. Edward III of England so drained the houses of the Bardi and Peruzzi that they went bankrupt in 1346 and ruined other leading families, which in turn made it difficult for Florence to raise money for its defence. In some cities, governments fell into the habit of borrowing locally at interest rather than levying a new tax, thereby amassing a substantial public debt. The public debt grew larger and larger until there was no hope of repayment, a problem officials dealt with by borrowing at enforced bargain rates – an ingenious form of direct taxation of patricians who had previously paid no direct tax.

A wild card among Italian polities were independent 'companies' of mercenary soldiers (*condottieri*), who became the virtual arbiters of Italian politics from about 1340 to 1380. Conditions, both inside and outside Italy, help account for the rise of the *condottieri*. George Holmes (1975: 104) explains it as a side effect of the Hundred Years' War. Following the defeat of France at the Battle of Poitiers and the devastation caused by the Black Death, it was hard for soldiers to find employment elsewhere in Europe. In Italy, by contrast, the progress of commerce and industry undermined civic militias, as did the reluctance of popular communes to elevate aristocrats to military leadership positions. Greater wealth also made it possible to pay the prices foreigners demanded for their services.

By the fifteenth century, the *condottieri* had become largely Italian. During the many wars of this period, only Venice had sufficient wealth and foresight to maintain anything like a standing army. In general, the *condottieri* of this century plundered less than those of the previous century because rulers and cities were consolidating their own defences. Ever inventive, *condottieri* leaders like Francesco Sforza countered such adversity by striving to capture themselves a city or group of cities that would serve as their permanent base.

Polities with Universal Pretensions

The two polities that occupied centre stage in the drama of the Middle Ages were an empire centred in Germany and a church in Rome. Both sought to inherit the mantle of Rome and exercise temporal authority over Christianity. Both the Holy Roman Empire and the Papacy were territorial empires that sought to extend their territory, and their struggle waxed and waned for centuries. In the end, both had to cede primacy to the territorial princes whose allegiance they sought.

During the period under consideration, however, there were other empires than the original Roman Empire, its Byzantine counterpart, the Holy Roman Empire, and the Papacy. In fact, Italy in the Middle Ages offers several examples of empires that were almost exclusively commercial and largely seaborne – notably Venice, Genoa, and Pisa. Each city had some land possessions – and Venice, at one stage, quite a large land area – and exercised authority partly through the application of force and use of local administrators stationed abroad. The primary goal of such empires was to acquire as many trading enclaves in the Mediterranean area as possible, usually captured or won as concessions from the Byzantines or others in connection with a crusade.

Indistinct Boundaries

'The word "frontier",' argues Peter Sahlins (1989: 6), 'dates precisely from the moment when a new insistence on royal territory gave to the boundary a political, fiscal, and military significance different from its internal limits. The "frontier" was that which "stood face to" an enemy.' However, 'frontiers' in much the same sense were characteristic of many polities before and after early-modern kings. Every polity has a territory, although its frontiers may not be clearly demarcated, contiguous or exclusive.

The complexity of Italian political organization in the period under discussion resists any statist interpretation. This complexity was made to appear even greater by the presence in the Middle Ages of what Benedict Anderson (1983) calls 'imagined communities' that reflected the aspirations of rulers and philosophers.

Competing Visions of Unity and Authority in Medieval Italy

Only once in its tumultuous history did Europe enjoy the sort of unity and central rule that characterized China for many centuries. This was the great achievement of Rome at its height. Italy avoided much of the feudalism that characterized other areas of medieval Europe. Instead, a multitude of independent city and regional polities emerged in Italy that began to compete intensively with one another. Under these circumstances, overlapping and divided political loyalties and identities became common, and the nesting of local polities within more extensive polities was widespread.

From Roman Church to Christian Commonwealth

The tumultuous two centuries between A.D. 400 and 600 saw the steady decline of Roman civilization in the West. In previous centuries there had been a steady growth in major cities at the expense of lesser towns, but now urban life either collapsed entirely or suffered major reversals. When 'older traditions of civil authority and secular administration became weakened, clerical power naturally assumed growing dominance, and in doing so, contributed the eclipse of secular traditions' (Markus 1990:226–7).

As time passed, the Church faced growing competition from several quarters and a gradual trend toward resecularization began, culminating in the Renaissance. The Holy Roman Emperor demanded his role in the governance of Christendom, and the notion of Christendom itself began to wane.

Empire Versus Papacy

The Papacy and the Holy Roman Empire were major polities during the entire period. From the outset, their domains and fortunes so overlapped that it is necessary to consider them together.

From Empire to Empire

With Rome's declining capacity to defend its western possessions, the pope inherited some of the glamour and burdens of Rome in the West. Also contributing to the preservation and spiritual renewal of the Church during the disastrous time of Justinian's attempted re-conquest – while beginning a tradition of separate institutions that would later be a source of tension as well as renewed inspiration – was the development of Benedictine monasticism. In the eighth century, missionaries from the English Church brought the concept of papal authority to the Continent, and eventually convinced the Frankish Church to accept it.

The pope's link with the Franks was a fateful one and came about primarily because of the continued threat from the Lombards. The pope waived return of church property previously seized by Charles Martel and agreed to consecrate Pepin III as king. In exchange, the Franks agreed to protect the pope from the Lombards. More important in the long run was that Pepin confirmed the Donation of Constantine, which recognized the pope as Christ's vicar on earth, made all bishops subject to him, and granted the pope full government powers over Rome and all Italy. The Frankish Church, as well, agreed to recognize papal authority and reform itself in accordance with his instructions.

The relationship between the Franks and the pope intensified, not without frictions, during Charlemagne's reign (768–814). Bishops actively participated in the government of Charlemagne's kingdom, symbolized by their gathering with counts in an annual *conventus generalis*. Charlemagne conquered the Lombards and became their king in 774, thus eliminating any possibility of the pope's playing the Lombards off against the Franks. In a revised Donation, king and pope divided Italy between them. On Christmas Day 800, the pope crowned Charlemagne in Rome, where he was proclaimed Caesar Augustus, the Christian Emperor of all Christendom. It was a portent of future disputes that Charlemagne later resented the pope's insistence that the coronation had ratified the Papacy's superior authority.

The Holy Roman Empire Ascendant

Saxon rulers revived the empire after a series of civil wars, and the ceremony elevating Otto I suggests the compromises required by the complexities of political theory in those times, complexities that owed much to a system based on 'a nonexclusive form of territoriality, in which authority was both personalized and parcelized within and across territorial formations and for which inclusive bases of legitimation prevailed' (Ruggie 1993: 150). The ceremony in Charlemagne's palace-chapel at Aachen was a double one, a secular 'election' involving the nobility, followed by a religious investiture conducted by the local archbishop. When the kingdom of Italy fell heir to Adelaide, Otto invaded Italy and married her. Having won his empire, Otto then sought to devise a means of governing it. Otto invented an ingenious new system: he would govern his kingdom through clergy (who, being celibate, could not found rival dynasties) and appoint them himself.

One snag in Otto's plan to rely on bishop-barons was that the system depended on the continued cooperation of the pope. An opportunity seemed to present itself when Pope John XII appealed for military assistance against a rival. Otto sent help, and John dutifully crowned him emperor. Otto then formally recognized the independence of the Papal State, which he immediately regretted. An ensuing quarrel led to Pope John's deposition, the installation of the more compliant Leo VIII, and the new pope's acceptance of the proposition that no future pope could be consecrated until he had taken an oath of allegiance to the emperor. During the first half of the eleventh century, the Papacy was at a low ebb. The emperor was far away, and Roman noble families appointed popes of their choice. So it continued until they disagreed to such an extent that, in the mid-eleventh century, there were no fewer than three popes.

When Henry III died and was succeeded by a woman, subsequent popes tried again to establish their independence. Then, under popes Hildebrand and Gregory VII, the so-called Investiture Controversy reached crisis proportions. Popes forbade clerics to accept secular commissions; Henry IV demanded his rights as emperor; the popes excommunicated Henry; Henry made war on Gregory VII; the pope escaped with the aid of the Normans (who paused to loot Rome); Gregory died in exile; the emperor tried to impose a compliant successor; and reforming cardinals instead succeeded in electing Urban II. Urban II boosted the authority of the Papacy by urging support for the First Crusade. Pope Calixtus II also came to an agreement of sorts with Henry IV and his son Henry V, by the terms of which elections to bishoprics and abbeys within the German kingdom would be a joint responsibility. The conflict between pope and emperor thus remained fundamentally unresolved, with implications for the continued disunity of Italy.

The contest between Holy Roman Empire and Papacy erupted again during the reign of the Emperor Frederick I Barbarossa (1152–90). To his mind, Roman law was sufficient ground for his authority, requiring no sacerdotal blessing. Not surprisingly, the pope was alarmed by Frederick, as were the Normans and the prospering cities of northern and central Italy.

Frederick might still have succeeded with his design, except that he over-estimated his capacity to subdue the communes. He and the cities could not have been further apart ideologically. As Frederick saw it, not only was everyone subject to him as Holy Roman Emperor, but also any proper town belonged to a feudal lord whose wealth rested on land. In his view, it was irregular for cities to have republican governments, not monarchies, and for upper-class citizens to draw their livelihood from trade and mix with ple-beians in business and politics. No wonder most cities were at war with their neighbours, and charges of corruption among magistrates regularly made. Frederick believed he was obliged to reorder matters. For their part, cities were guilty of all the ideas and actions that Frederick attributed to them – and, worse, a parallel hubris about their own putative ancient Roman birthright.

Frederick's armies swept south over many of Italy's cities, even capturing Rome. He obliterated Milan physically and legally, and tried to raise a compliant antipope. No sooner had the emperor returned to Germany than his success provoked an unprecedented reaction. The antipope failed to gain widespread recognition, and 16 Italian cities buried the hatchet long enough to form the Lombard League. The League rebuilt Milan, and its forces succeeded in defeating those of the empire. In a dramatic encounter, on 24 July 1177, Frederick submitted himself to Pope Alexander III.

The empire defeated, Pope Innocent III extended his discipline to rebel-lious kings and tried to reform a Church that seemed to be losing ground among believers generally. When Alfonso IX of León married a close rela-tive and Philip Augustus of France divorced, the pope brought them to heel by interdicting their entire kingdoms so that no services except infant bap-tisms and deathbed penances could take place.

The final round in the two-hundred-year contest between empire and church began with the crowning of Frederick II in 1215. Frederick recog-nized that, after over two decades of civil war in Germany, the empire needed a new base of power. He found that base in the *Regno* or rich Norman kingdom of Sicily. Pope Gregory IX, fearing that Frederick plan-ned to conquer all of Italy eventually and, resenting the emperor's initial reluctance to obey his instructions to embark on crusade, excommunicated Frederick in 1227. Although Frederick did set out and capture much of the Holy Land through skillful diplomacy, Gregory not only refused to lift the excommunication but also invaded the *Regno* and released Frederick's sub-jects from their oaths of allegiance.

War between emperor and pope was inevitable. Religious fervor in Italy reached a peak in 1233, the year of the great Allelulia, when many cities gave popular preachers authority to remake the laws. Church authorities sought to direct such fervour against the 'anti-Christ' Frederick, and Gregory did his best to revive the Lombard League. The next few years were chaotic as papal and imperial forces clashed all over Italy; Guelph/Ghibelline quarrels added still more fault lines within, between, and among city polities; and the cities failed to forge a united front against the threats to their independence. Pope Gregory died, and the emperor obtained a Ghibelline successor, Innocent IV – only to have Innocent turn against him. A General Council of the Church summoned by Innocent formally deposed Frederick, and papal forces defeated those of the emperor in 1248.

Thus ended for the near future any serious threat from the empire and the possibility of European unity under its aegis. German electors went on electing kings, usually from weak families chosen for the honour for that reason. Some kings marched briefly into Italy and crowned themselves emperor, but without lasting success.

The Imperial Papacy

The Papacy's authority, rejuvenated at great cost, almost proved its undoing. The pope claimed the right to make all appointments to bishoprics and other high church offices, entertain appeals from local ecclesiastical courts, tax the clergy, and maintain control of the important Dominican and Franciscan orders – as well as use the weapons of interdiction and excommunication against secular rulers whenever circumstances seemed to warrant. In 1296, when England and France were at war and their kings sought to tax their respective churches in that connection, Boniface VIII commanded the clergy to resist. The dispute escalated until Philip IV of France captured and held Boniface until he died, and then installed a French pope, Clement V, at Avignon.

In some respects, the Avignon 'Babylonian captivity' was the high point of the medieval Papacy. The Avignon popes established themselves in the midst of a powerful kingdom and a cultural centre for Europe as a whole, and achieved for the Church the administrative status of a genuine international organization.

Despite the successes of the Avignon popes, the essential bases for papal authority were eroding. Kings were starting to demand a cut from clerical taxes and were trying to influence papal appointments. The Papacy was also losing control of the education of both clergy and laity. Moreover, in 1376, Gregory XI's decision to return to Rome precipitated the Great Schism and further undermined papal authority. Educated clergy and laity looked less and less to Rome, and kings insisted on taking control over clerical appointments.

For all its strength and coherence in some periods, the Catholic Church was never a genuinely unified polity, and its identity tended to overlap with others. At the very pinnacle of Church authority, the pope and his ecclesiastical entourage resembled a secular feudal king who, with his court, ruled over the Papal State, collected vassals and tribute, and made war. Even popes who were reformist in spirit were far removed from what was happening in local communities. Bishops were literally rulers at a formative stage in some cities, and a 'cathedral, towering over its city, was a potent focus of civic loyalty, and its symbolic function was shared not only by its campanile, which summoned the citizens to prayer, counsel, or defence, but also by its baptistry, where all continued to be baptized in the same font' (Reynolds 1984: 83). Outside of the major cities, the 'untidy overlaps of secular and ecclesiastical units, combined with the apparent indifference of medieval people about the particular unit in which to act at any moment, often make it difficult to separate parish activity from the activity of villages or units of lordship' (Reynolds 1984: 83). In the countryside, mother churches had dependent churches (*tituli*, *capelle*), sometimes built by lesser lords, and there was a gradual decentralization of parish rights. Also, monasteries of various orders grew rich and independent, and managed village churches that they received as gifts.

Overlapping and Divided Loyalties in Medieval Europe

Pope and emperor occupied centre stage after about the year 1000, and it may be going too far to dismiss their contest, with Jacques Le Goff (1988: 96), as 'a mere shadow play behind which the serious events took place'. Nonetheless, much of what was vital in terms of political authority and identity lay elsewhere. During the Middle Ages, 'the reality for the west ... was not only the fact that government was split up into small particles but also the fact that vertical and horizontal powers were entangled. People ... did not always know to which of the many lords, the Church and individual churches, the towns, princes, and kings, they were subordinate'. As Hale suggests: 'Meaning lay in the familiar and near.' Any sense of loyalty to or involvement with larger polities 'was all the weaker because of the vigor of local associations and their ability to cater satisfactorily to the desire for mutual aid, spiritual fraternity, recreation and simple gregariousness' (Hale 1971:124–5). The family, not least because it was often the centre of production, continued to be *the* most important focus of identity and loyalty for the individual.

Communal Polities and Politics

The communes in Italy emerged with the waning of the Carolingian system, at a time when Christian ideology had triumphed and Church institutions were well established but the Papacy had not yet established practical control beyond part of central Italy. In time, the communes became powerful symbols of identity, though they set in motion institutional, economic, and social changes that simultaneously made government less manageable and society at large more difficult to govern. Like other successful polities, they ultimately helped create their own nemesis.

The feudal offices of marchio, count, and viscount came to mean little more than entitlement to lands and property enjoyed by certain families. During this confusing era, Hyde explains, 'it was the bishops with their stronger sense of office, their deep roots in the history of the city and their access to the virtues of its saints and martyrs, who were often able to rally the frightened and impoverished citizens' (Hyde 1973: 44–45). Emperors in a sense only made matters worse for the imperial cause when they tried to discourage the foundation of local aristocratic dynasties by giving celibate bishops secular authority. The bishops, then, were those who at least temporarily prevailed in the nascent-commune *civitates*.

Town rule became *somewhat* more secular when the concept of a 'commune' developed. A 'consulate' of citizens typically drawn from prominent families assumed control of local affairs from the bishop or other local church officials. The consulate was responsible – in principle more than practice – to a broader citizen council (*parlementum, concio*, or *aregna*) with membership of a hundred or more.

There were only three precedents for communal rule – and these were only tangentially relevant – in the old regime. One was the 'world of less formal associations which had at best been little more than tolerated at the lower levels'. A second was the feudal oath, which evolved into a consular oath enshrining 'the principle that authority was granted by the community' (Hyde 1973: 54–55). A third precedent was the ancient Greeks and Romans, who were 'rediscovered'. From the fourteenth to mid-fifteenth centuries, in early Renaissance Florence, there was a flowering of writings on 'civic humanism' inspired, in part, by that city's lengthy struggle to preserve its republic against assaults from the Visconti of Milan.

The 'idea of "community" as an ethical value' merged with 'the full might of the Christian value of love' (Black 1992: 120). No better symbol could be found of the living-museum effect and overlapping polities – blending ancient and medieval, sacred and secular – than the magnificent Romanesque cathedrals built, with a hefty contribution of city funds, to the combined glory of God and the commune. In church and civil processions alike marched many of the same grand families, heirs to feudal titles and oft-subdivided properties that once had been granted by the Holy Roman Empire.

Christian love and civic virtue were tested to the full as the communal experiment evolved. Even at the outset, intercity rivalries and aristocratic tower societies and their vendettas threatened the peace. Between 1150 and 1250, more serious problems accompanied rapid economic growth, increased migration to the cities, the rise of the guilds, and the conquest of the *contado*. As Hyde (1973: 106–7) explains, leading communes struck 'individual bargains with the families or consorterie, minor communes or religious communities' in the surrounding countryside. Cities expanded their territory and number of citizens. The communes 'did not build up a citizen body with uniform rights' but 'divided into numerous legal and social categories'. They simply nested, along with old and new polities, in communal niches. 'Each section with its resources of men and money and its own particular interests constituted a potential pressure group or faction.' No wonder communal history was tumultuous, 'for the communes were trying to practise government on conciliar principles in a society which remained intensely hierarchical.' Tower societies proliferated, while a wealthy *popolo* class of guild masters and other successful newcomers arose between the nobles or magnates on one hand, and ordinary labourers and the urban poor on the other.

The result of these developments was almost continual faction and party strife. At this juncture, Emperor Frederick I advanced into Italy, established his rule over many of the communes, and sent an imperial vicar or *podesta* to each of the captured cities to oversee its affairs. When the Lombard League finally defeated Frederick, the office of *podesta* lingered on in modified form. Many cities chose to elevate a single executive from outside their city to the post of *podesta* for a limited term, usually one year, to increase administrative efficiency and mediate among factions. There was a link here with intercity relations, which were at a delicate stage with the dissolution of the Lombard League. Cities exchanged *podestas* almost like royal marriages to pledge fidelity to a new alliance.

By the mid-thirteenth century, most cities had accomplished nothing less than a 'democratic revolution' in which the *popolo* gradually supplanted the older elite. This revolution typically took place in three stages: the *popolo*'s appearance as a powerful faction, the creation of a separate public body identified with the *popolo* that shared authority with the old council, and the *popolo*'s final success in dominating elected offices and administrative positions. However, the new arrangement hardly ameliorated civil conflict because some of the nobility refused to accept defeat and because of the divisiveness introduced by another contest among Frederick II, the papacy, and the communes. Rivals exploited long-standing animosities between and within cities, and even managed to construct fleeting political alignments that cut across city loyalties. One *popolo* might call on their counterparts in a neighbouring city for assistance against aristocrats, and aristocrats from one city might even appeal to the *popolo* in another. Once again, an emperor's strategy appeared to have a lasting impact, though civil conflict may have reached a level where the future was inevitable. Frederick II appointed despotic rulers over the communes he managed to subdue, and when he was finally defeated, the stage was set for a new age of the *signoria*.

The transfer of power to a single individual or family in most communes was the most important political development in Italy in the century from 1250 to 1350. Although the new *signoria* model spread most rapidly after Frederick II when the empire was in eclipse and popes were preoccupied with problems other than northern Italy politics, the complicated Guelph/

Ghibelline alignments of the thirteenth century increased the complexity and bitterness of factional strife in the cities. Meanwhile, the larger cities were extending their territory beyond the bounds of their previous *contado*, and warfare with bigger armies was becoming more expensive. In these conditions, there was a temptation to abandon republican squabbles for a single authoritarian leader.

The Florentine Experience

The example of Florence illustrates the perils of late medieval/Renaissance republicanism. One problem was the complicated and cumbersome government institutions necessary to give factions the representation they demanded and provide for sufficient rotation in office to make it difficult for any one to consolidate power. At the top were six *priori* and an additional standard-bearer of justice who served for only two months and could not soon be re-elected. These officials initiated legislation and conducted diplomatic relations. Below them were a *podesta* (executive) and *capitano* (judicial), who were always foreigners serving short terms, and various councils involving hundreds of citizens who did the actual legislating. However, this elaborate system was not enough to preserve republicanism during three periods of external threat, when even Florence felt obliged to submit to rule by a *signore*.

After the Duke of Athens, Florence remained republican, with one serious interruption, for about a century – until the Medicis gradually transformed it into a virtual monarchy. The system suffered a rude shock in 1378, when artisans and labourers (*popolo minuto*) who were not organized in recognized guilds rose in rebellion and terrorized the commune for several weeks. Its long-term effect was to strengthen the seven major guilds in the overall republican-oligarchical regime.

Although there had been a gradual trend towards single executives in Italy, the 'Age of the Princes' began with the invasion of the French Charles VIII in 1494 and continued through – and decades beyond – Charles V's decision in the early 1520s to challenge French control of Milan. It was an era of endemic warfare and political instability that further undermined what remained of republican rule. The Florentine Medicis and Machiavelli's *The Prince* are the symbols of the Age.

The Venetian Experience

The political evolution of Venice offers contrasts to, as well as parallels with, tumultuous Florence. What made Venice different were two factors present from the outset – its secure lagoon location distant from mainland conflicts and its ties with Byzantium. In fact, 'paradoxically, it was through her very submission to the Empire of the East that her independence was achieved and her future greatness assured' (Norwich 1982: 25).

Venice (under a *dux* or doge) started as a Byzantine dukedom, that is, with the sort of one-person secular autocratic rule that other Italian cities were to arrive at only later. The Venetians were also unique because they alone claimed to possess the body of the Apostle St Mark. Other cities might have patron saints, but St Mark was an Evangelist, a fact that 'would endow Venice with Apostolic patronage and place her on a spiritual level second only to Rome itself, with a claim to ecclesiastical autonomy' (Norwich 1982: 29).

Venice thus forged much of its special identity as a polity early on, but that identity continued to evolve and was never exclusive. The first five or six centuries of Venetian history were very violent, not unlike civil strife elsewhere in Italy, reflecting primarily the feuds and ambitions of powerful families.

By the mid-twelfth century, however, Venice like other Italian cities was calling itself a commune. Each new doge had to speak an oath, which grew more elaborate over time, detailing the restrictions he accepted on assuming power. The Ducal Councillors, the doge, and the three heads of the Forty constituted the *Signoria*, which acted as the government on a day-to-day basis. A genuine bureaucracy was almost nonexistent, since elected committees of the various councils ran almost everything except the church of San Marco. State Attorneys watched over the actions both of the several councils and individual officials. Venice at the local level consisted of some 60 to 70 parishes, each of which had a priest elected by the parish and installed by the bishop, and a parish chief named from one of the great families and supervised by the doge and Council.

A hundred or more families were involved in communal rule one way or another. The doge served for life, but other terms were short and nonrenewable, so persons tended to rotate through important posts. Moreover, in Venice as elsewhere, the rise both of new monied interests, including major guilds *(popolo grasso)* and artisans and craftsmen *(popolo minuto)* forced changes.

Venice maintained its republican constitution, but the Venetian system became more oligarchical and corrupt as the years passed. In 1310, a Council of Ten was created to act swiftly in the event of security threats. In the mid-fifteenth century, the General Assembly was abolished and the Great Council abandoned all pretense of seeking broader approval for changes in legislation. The Senate named several chief ministers to sit together with the *Signoria,* framing agendas and overseeing the execution of resolutions. Meanwhile, after 1381, the Book of Gold nobility who were eligible for service on the Great Council closed ranks, admitting no new families. Elections were often rigged; public service in elected or appointed office was increasingly sought for private gain, or avoided; and more disputes between individuals and factions resulted in violence and bloodshed.

Conclusion

Some analysts argue that the authoritarianism of Medici family rule in Florence – like the Venetian, Milanese, and papal polities – foreshadowed the bureaucratized European governments of later eras. To be sure, there was a gradual increase in the number of bureaucrats, and some effort was made to encourage appointments by merit. However, as Burke (1986: 215–18) emphasizes, there are several reasons one cannot carry the 'Renaissance state' idea too far. First, apart from later Venice, 'public administration was not separated from the private household of the ruler; loyalty was focused on a man, not an institution; and the ruler by-passed the system whenever he wished to grant a favour to a suitor.' 'A second consideration is the *sottogoverno*, the fact that some offices were sold outright, not to mention the continued importance of family connections and what was known euphemistically as "friendship" *(amicizia)* ... the links between powerful patrons and their dependents or "clients".'

Third, 'impersonal administration was impossible in what was still essentially a face-to-face society ... citizens might know officials in their private roles' (Burke 1986: 217–18). Hale (1971: 106) observes that 'even Machiavelli, writing as an ex-career civil servant, frequently used the word "state" in the sense of "those individuals in power for the time being".' It only took twenty minutes on foot to cross all of Florence. Most citizens were not directly involved in councils, but 'the sense of involvement in public affairs, through gossip, through sheer physical proximity, penetrated into all sectors of society' (Hale 1977: 15).

Finally, although a nascent bureaucracy's primary loyalty might, of necessity, be to the prince, he continued to face many competing identities and loyalties within the city at large. Distinct from, but often overlapping, the loyalties attached to the polities we have discussed were still others. Such identities and loyalties came to the fore when issues were perceived to affect them directly, and just as frequently subsided, fragmented, or blended into other identities and loyalties when other issues arose.

So it was at other levels. Cities fought cities with patriotic passion, yet:

> local patriotisms could merge into regional loyalties, and both at times could become aware of a larger shared identity ... a shared space ... which nature had appointed as a home; a sense that somehow 'they' had contributed something to the world that set them apart. It was this that, on occasion, led armies comprising mutually competitive peninsular units to battle against crude northerners with the cry of 'Italy'!
>
> (Hale 1985: 43)

At times Italy did come close to achieving a significant measure of unity, although the moment always passed. The Lombard League of 1167 against Frederick I included many cities. Later, in 1347, the megalomaniac Cola di Rienzi (the subject of Wagner's early opera) proposed a grand Italian Federation centred on Rome.

Italy finally joined the Westphalian club late in the nineteenth century, but a century later regional and city identities persist; there is still a pope in

Vatican City with a global diplomatic network, whose bankers are occasionally in the news. Factionalism and ideological extremes remain the norm in politics, despite the existence of major parties; fascist Mussolini, like Rienzi, sought to recreate the glories of Rome; post-World War II Italy has relied mainly on NATO for its defence and was an early enthusiastic advocate of the European Union; much of Italy's 'private' economy is autonomous, untaxed, and unaccounted for in 'national' statistics like GDP; and weak and divided politicians have had to wage 'war' against, first, the Red Brigades, and then the Mafia. And, with the disintegration of postwar political parties like the Socialists and church-affiliated Christian Democrats amidst charges of corruption, regionalism and fascism have again raised their heads with the Northern (Lombard) League and National Alliance respectively.

We are told that Machiavelli, for all his passionate desire for Italian unity, once responded to a friend's enquiry about the prospects for an Italian alliance with the comment, 'Don't make me laugh' (Hale 1971: 111–12). Let us reclaim the estimable Niccolò from contemporary realists and neo-realists and turn our attention from a static world consisting exclusively of Westphalian state polities to a richer universe of varied and constantly evolving polities.

7 Islam

The evolution of a messianic movement (1996)

The following examines the evolution of political forms in the Islamic world from its inception in AD 622 to the early thirteenth century, emphasizing the changing relationships among and within key polities that produced clashes among and revisions in allegiances and loyalties. During the period we are considering, the Islamic world was born, and an Islamic and Arab political and cultural universe spread in all directions and flowered from Spain to the frontiers of India. Muslims throughout the world today recall the epoch with pride, and many brandish it as a model to be emulated and as an alternative to the secular West.

Political forms and issues that appeared early on continue to vex the Islamic world. Of special interest was, and remains, the key role of competing ideologies in the form of religious doctrines and the difficulty they posed for the creation and legitimation of Westphalian states in the Middle East.

Then, as now, Arabs and non-Arabs had different perspectives on the conflicts among Islamic polities and provided alternative traditions for governing disparate peoples. At its inception, Islam was an Arab phenomenon, and then, as now, Arabic political identity was amorphous.

Introduction

The Muhammadan movement began as a rebellion against traditional Arab tribal practices, but the death of Muhammad triggered a struggle – the consequences of which remain with us – over modes of political organization and sources of political legitimacy. The elements of the conflict were exceeding complex, involving clashes between tribal and statist practices, struggles among kinship groups, differing class-based perceptions, and strongly-held religious positions.

System Discreteness and Structure

The Arab World Before Islam

The Arab world which was thrown into turmoil by the Prophet and his followers was one of tribal traditions, loyalties, and organization. The

Arabs were at the periphery of existing political and economic power in the Mediterranean arena which, in the early seventh century, was concentrated in two great rival empires to the north. The first, with its centre in Constantinople, was the Christian Byzantine empire, since the fourth century the heir to the eastern half of the Roman Empire.

The second great territorial empire, that of the Sasanians, lay to the east of Byzantium, encompassing Iraq and Iran.

Conquest

The Islamic polity never stabilized within secure boundaries and remained highly permeable throughout its existence. Islamic philosophy, science, and culture were enriched by Hellenistic, Jewish, Christian, and Persian traditions that survived the conquest and even flourished under the caliphate. Islam itself made universalist claims and recognized no territorial limits or frontiers, and the absence of a sense of territoriality also reflected the nomadic roots of the Arab conquerors.

By the time of his death, Muhammad already enjoyed personal authority over a considerable hinterland beyond Medina and Mecca, and he was determined to spread the Word of Allah to the four corners of the known world. His death, however, triggered desertions among tribal allies and efforts to return to traditional forms of government.

By the middle of the seventh century, all of Arabia, the Byzantine provinces of Egypt and Syria, and additional territory to the north and east had fallen to the young Islamic polity. By 643, imperial Islam had advanced into the Oxus valley and the frontier lands of India. Thereafter, the Umayyads swept across North Africa. By the end of the seventh century, the empire had incorporated Morocco and shortly thereafter in AD 710 crossed the Mediterranean into Spain.

The causes of this rapid success (and later decline) are complex. The charismatic qualities of the Prophet were a key asset, especially at the outset, but do not alone provide a sufficient explanation. The Mediterranean world appears to have been seriously weakened by barbarian invasions, plagues, failure to maintain agricultural projects, and the almost continuous wars between Byzantines and Sasanians, mainly for control of Iraq and Syria.

Many of the Arab soldiers had prior military experience and camels provided them with unprecedented mobility. Islam sanctioned the search for converts and religious conviction assured Arab unity and fervor, but there were actually relatively few conversions during the years of greatest expansion. Hitti argues that 'Islam owes its unparalleled expansion as a worldly power' to the idea of jihad (holy war) (1956: 55). The sense of destiny provided by religion was reinforced by early triumphs and rapid forward movement that at once excited the spirit of nomadic warriors and seemed to promise the ultimate victory of Islam. Hourani speculates that, as a faith, Islam spread fairly easily for a variety of instrumental reasons – among Arabs already living in the Byzantine and Sasanian dominions, officials of the former empire who wished continued employment, and immigrants to the new cities who wished to avoid taxes paid by non-Muslims (1991: 28–29). More importantly, the simplicity of Islam and its rituals, the absence of structure and hierarchy, its egalitarianism, and its tolerance for ethnic diversity facilitated its spread. Hitti claims that, while of each these may have had an impact, the key reason for conquest was economic (1956: 59–60).

Islam's expansion was also facilitated by the passivity of those who were conquered and their indifference about who ruled them as long as there was peace and reasonable prosperity. Finally, Islam's tolerance of other religions and liberal treatment of conquered peoples reduced incentives to resist and rebel. Supervision of the expanding polyglot empire was exercised by Arab soldiers in military settlements, which became centres of Islamic culture.

Polity Types

Three major types of polities coexisted uneasily within the medieval Islamic system. Tribes and tribal/clan loyalties dominated Arabia prior to the revolution begun by Muhammad, and tribal customs and loyalties were never far below the surface. The Prophet sought to replace tribal attachments with loyalty to a Muslim community of believers (*umma*). However, Muhammad's authority was putatively derived directly from Allah and not from the community he established in Allah's name, and all of his actions were believed to have divine sanction, which was unavailable to others after his death. Instead of legitimizing authority on the basis of past practice and tradition, Muhammad declared that his authority came from Allah alone, and he sought to establish an all-encompassing socio-political structure. Paradoxically, the identification of religious and secular symbols in Islam proved an insurmountable obstacle to institutionalizing imperial forms and practices after the death of the Prophet. The subsequent absence of stable territoriality in turn reinforced earlier tribal mores and affinities.

All later Islamic polities – the caliphate, the Ottomans, and twentieth-century Muslim Westphalian polities – have had to contend with nested memories of, identities with, and loyalties to the Islamic community. These remain latent for long periods and then threaten to erupt, especially during eras of rapid social and political change. Islamic politicians have to appear to be faithful to the forms dictated by Islamic law and the interpretations of that law by Islamic judges, and failure to do so invites political instability and personal disaster.

Tribe

Any understanding of Arabic politics, medieval or contemporary, must begin with an appreciation of its durable tribal and clan basis.

Within Arab tribal society, the extended family living together produced powerful loyalties. Since such a unit was not self-sufficient, it would be affiliated with a kinship group that could afford protection and, if necessary, seek vengeance on the family's behalf. Kinship groups identified with one another by claiming a common ancestor (who might be no more than symbolic) and thereby constituted a tribe. Such groups might be dominated by a single family that enjoyed prestige because of religious position, wealth, and/or military experience.

The coming of Islam posed a threat to tribal mores and challenged tribal loyalties. Dabashi argues that, far from being a reaction to the feebleness or corruption of traditional tribal society, as argued by others, Muhammad's 'charismatic movement' 'should be seen as a total expression of a new cultural order that challenged the Arab traditional system" and as an effort to "set up a radical discontinuity with the Arab past"' (1989: 17, 22).

That revolution notwithstanding, tribal forms nested within more inclusive Islamic polities, as these retained many of the tribal characteristics of their traditional precursor; and tribal solidarity, though eroded, was not eliminated. The society into which Islam exploded was, as expressed by Dabashi, one in which 'tribal solidarity constituted the single most cohesive element', and in which political authority was associated with factors like 'age, tribal genealogy, blood relationship, and religious functionaries' (1989: 20, 21). All of these factors express the traditional nature of Arab tribalism – especially, the centrality of the past for the present. Age was a prerequisite for tribal leadership in a patriarchal context, and 'pride of descent' (Saunders 1965: 4) was a key source of tribal unity. Kinship – blood relationship – was the basis of family, clan, and tribal loyalties, loyalties that remained powerful factors in the Islamic polity. Retention of tribal customs was virtually synonymous with maintaining the Arabic character of the movement. Tribalism and Arabism were inextricably woven together, and tribal influences continued to play a role in the advocacy of aspirational polities such as the 'Arabic nation'.

From the birth of Islam until the division and collapse of the Islamic polity, tribal habits and attachments remained strong. Muhammad himself used the same military strategy in seizing oases and raiding caravans against his Meccan adversaries as the Meccans had used against their rivals several decades earlier; and he acquired political support by adroitly adopting and manipulating the traditional role of arbitrator among tribes and clans. Muhammad was a member of a secondary branch of the Quraysh tribe, which was, through its control of trade routes and religious sites, the dominant political and economic force in Mecca and, therefore, in Arabia. As his preaching gained converts, Muhammad earned the animosity of leading figures in his tribe, ostensibly because he threatened traditional tribal authority; however, that opposition also reflected a long-term rivalry between two branches of the Quraysh. The same intra-Quraysh rivalry that led to Muhammad's flight from Mecca resurfaced years later in the struggle between 'Ali and Mu'awiya for the title of caliph and was an important element in the split between Shi'ites and Sunnis.

Tribal practices resurfaced almost immediately after Muhammad's death when a tribal council was held to select his successor, as well as in later debates over the selection of caliphs and the sources of their political legitimacy. The requirement that claimants to the caliphate demonstrate a familial relationship to Muhammad, for example, reflected the importance of genealogy as did the related role of primogeniture in succession to authority. Similarly, the central role afforded the chamber of deputies (*Dar al-Nadwah*) in Mecca, and the mixing of religious and secular functions in the chamber, reappeared in the form and function of mosques. The centrality of the *Dar al-Nadwah* in traditional Arab society was also reflected in the importance accorded by Islamic jurists to the legitimizing function of community opinion.

The organization of the imperial army was along tribal lines; units were tribally based, and conquered lands were divided among tribal groups. Clan and tribe members tended to associate with one another in the towns and cities of the empire and found themselves cheek to jowl with members of other clans and tribes. Indeed, the emergence of a single Islamic polity may have actually exacerbated tribal cleavages by facilitating contacts among geographically disparate members of tribal units.

Tribal and clan favoritism was widespread in the caliphate. Indeed, nepotism during the reign of the third caliph roused great discontent and was involved in his assassination.

'Uthman's successor, 'Ali, was also of Quraysh but of a different clan, and he was resisted by his predecessor's kinsmen – most important, the governor of Syria, Mu'awiya. The importance of tribal mores was again reflected in the resistance to 'Ali based on his responsibility for the death of the fathers of some of his opponents in a battle during which they fought against Muhammad. Mu'awiya, who like 'Uthman, was of the clan Banu Umayya, sought to avenge his kinsman, and the triumph of the Umayyads involved a reassertion of tribal prerogatives. The assassination of 'Ali and the caliphate of Mu'awiya (661–80) marked a shift in imperial power from Arabia to Damascus and the beginning of the Umayyad Dynasty.

The status and class differences that characterized imperial Islam also had their roots in pre-Islamic tribal society and politics. The practice of slavery, for example, was taken from pre-Islamic Arabia into the Islamic empire, as was the commercial hierarchy with merchant capitalists (*sayyids*) on top and tribal clients (*mawali*) at the bottom.

The Islamic Community (umma)

As the idea of the *umma* evolved, it came to refer to what Barbara Allen Roberson describes as 'a communal, though not a territorial society within which and through which people are to develop and enhance their moral behaviour' (1988: 89). The original community consisted only of Muhammad's wife Khadija, his cousin 'Ali; and Abu Bakr, though it shortly came to include his immediate companions. Three years later (622), he was invited to migrate (the *hijra*) to the settlement of Yathrib (later Medina or the city of the Prophet) by members of two tribes who were seeking an arbiter. Simultaneously, the community of Islam was formally established by the Constitution of Medina that was written by Muhammad on behalf of the believers who had followed him from Mecca and those in Medina. In other words, communal unity was not to be based on tribal or social affiliation, but on common religious belief, and tribal norms such as the blood feud were to be abandoned. Muhammad's idea of a community had little in common with the Westphalian polity. It was, as Dabashi observes, 'the most significant expression of Islamic solidarity against the traditional tribal structure' (1989: 76); and, in contrast to pre-Islamic tribal tradition, the community viewed all individuals, whether or not blood kin, as equals.

Between 624 and 632, Muhammad expanded the Islamic community and its power by force of arms until Meccan resistance had been crushed. In 630, Muhammad returned to Mecca in triumph, and the community of Islam found itself supreme across much of the Arabian peninsula. Two years later, the community's political, religious, and military leader was dead, and there was no one who could succeed him in combining these roles. The fact that three of the first four caliphs died violent deaths suggests how unsettled were the years following the passing of the Prophet. On the one hand, Muhammad's death triggered efforts by successors to elaborate bureaucratic institutions and forms necessary to govern the growing empire; on the other, it brought to the surface old tribal loyalties and identities that Muhammad had sought to suppress. Muhammad's effort to make 'religion, rather than blood' (Hitti 1956: 39) the basis of social organization proved only partly successful.

Religion and language enjoyed a symbiotic relationship in which acceptance of one necessitated the other, and both provided the means by which Muslims could identify one another. Together, religion and language marked, for Muslims, the critical demarcation between themselves and others and provided cement for a community united in theory. The Qu'ran and the traditional stories were almost only accessible in Arabic, and the common language of Islam provided an important sense of community among believers, just as Arabic poetry had been a source of solidarity to Arabs before Muhammad.

In addition to religious belief and ritual and language, architecture and art spoke of the unity of the Islamic community. Mosques were built in the centre of cities and towns to serve as sites for communal prayer. The fact that mosques were also used to conduct public business reflected the merger of governmental and religious functions. Common rituals – the 'pillars of Islam' – intensified the self-conscious similarity and unity of the faithful. It is a matter of dispute whether going to war to extend Islam was another obligation.

The idea of a community of believers retains much of its potency even in contemporary world politics. The powerful sense of 'we' versus 'they' that it propagated was and continues to be reflected in the Islamic contrast between 'the sphere of Islam' (regions governed by Muslims according to Muslim law) and 'the sphere of war' (regions not ruled by Muslims).

The Islamic Empire

Michael W. Doyle argues that, unlike most empires, the medieval Islamic polity did not begin 'with a centralized state directing a differentiated society' (1986: 105). Many of the attributes of a bureaucratized territorial polity were added *after* imperial conquest. An empire constructed on a tribal foundation, in Doyle's view, will not be durable, and the anomalous and transitory nature of the Islamic polity is perhaps best captured in Bozeman's metaphor of an 'empire-in-motion' (1960: 366).

The rapid spread of Islam and the movement of the centre from Medina to Damascus were accompanied by the proliferation of 'government attributes'. Tribal customs alone were inadequate to govern a polity of such enormous size and cultural diversity. And as power shifted from the Arabian periphery to the Syrian and, later, Iraqi heartland, the ruling elite grew urbanized and hostile to tribal mores; for their part, the 'Abbasid rulers found themselves increasingly dependent on Iranian and Persianized Turkish administrators. Nevertheless, the establishment of an Islamic polity continued to feature many tribal attributes.

The style of government administration was adapted from Islam's imperial predecessors. Although Arabic became the common language of administration, many of the same groups that had provided personnel to the Byzantines and Sasanians continued to do so for their new rulers.

Over time, recognizable interests emerged within the caliphate. Two of the most powerful were a military class surrounding the caliph and the merchants upon which the prosperity of the caliphate depended. Between the two there grew up an uneasy interdependence; the military required the wealth of the merchants, and the merchants needed the protection of trade routes, the maintenance of urban order, and the collection of taxes.

If the European concept of the Westphalian polity implies control from the centre, then the caliphate would not meet that criterion. The caliph's control was greatest in 'his' city and the immediate countryside. A permanent military presence was limited to key cities and a few highly fertile and productive agricultural centres.

Conclusion

The evolution of the medieval Islamic polity cannot be understood except by reference to a variety of polity forms that accompanied its birth, growth, and fragmentation. During the 500 years or so that imperial Islam prospered, three major types of polities competed for the loyalties and identities of Muslims – tribe, *umma*, and empire. Competition also went on among entities within each type of polity (among tribes and clans, branches of Islam, claimants to the caliphate, and rival caliphates).

Tribal identities that had dominated pre-Islamic Arabia remained important factors within the empire. Tribal perspectives, practices, and mores persist even in contemporary Arab societies, lending Arabic states a peculiarly tribal and clan coloration. The Muslim community only took root outside the Arabian peninsula years after the expansion of the empire itself. However, the community survived the empire, ultimately spread far beyond empire's limits, and remains a potent aspiration for Muslims in contemporary global politics. The caliphate, though it grew rapidly, proved an ephemeral political form, and the Islamic state never assumed the form of a Westphalian polity.

The Caliphate: The Limits of Dynastic Power

Unity based on Arabism and Islam proved elusive, and schisms based on tribe, clan, and even ethnicity were replicated and legitimized by religious divisions that made it difficult for the Islamic polity to survive. Some of those divisions remain potent in the contemporary Arab world. Indeed, the Arabs' common heritage – their religion – actually reduces their sense of national identity. As Anthony Smith declares:

> There is no reason why a common religious culture might not in principle act as the social cement of an Arab nation, were it not for the fact that the Islamic community of the faithful, the *umma*, by virtue of its very different inspiration and geographic extent, constitutes a rival. It creates a unity and a destiny that is, from a purely Arab standpoint, ambiguous. (1991: 63)

Introduction

The case of Islam is of interest precisely because of its failure to create a stable political structure like that enjoyed by Westphalian polities. Assuming the trappings of a despotic multinational empire, the centre of Islamic power shifted from the Arabian periphery, first to Damascus under the Umayyad caliphs (AD 661–750) and then to Baghdad under the 'Abbasids (AD 750–1258). However, the collision of polity types – secular empire, religious community, and Arab tribalism – impeded and remains a challenge to the stability of any secular political form in the Islamic world.

The Erosion of the Centre

The death of Muhammad threw the burgeoning community of Islam into turmoil. All Muslims agreed about the supremacy of God and His word as conveyed in the Qu'ran. Less clear, however, was how to govern the community of believers in the absence of the Prophet, and it was over this question that the community became irremediably divided. A successor to Muhammad had to be selected from the Islamic elite consisting of his early followers, the influential citizens of Medina with whom he had allied, and the leading families of Mecca. Among factors that were considered in identifying this successor were kinship to the Prophet, membership in his tribe, date of conversion to Islam, and acceptability to other tribal groups.

The Theory of the Caliphate

One of Muhammad's early followers, Abu Bakr, was selected as his successor or caliph (*khalifa*: the Prophet's successor), and political authority came to be centred around that position. The caliph, however, did not enjoy the authority of a prophet; he received no revelations and he could not easily claim the legitimacy provided one who was a messenger of Allah. Although the caliph became de facto leader of the Islamic community, he could claim no authentic religious sanction. God was the source of Muhammad's authority, and, for Muslims, secular authority without religious sanction was inconceivable. One consequence is that Islamic beliefs could never be fully co-opted by a government; this still remains the case.

Critical issues remained unresolved: Did a caliph possess religious authority, and, if so, what was its source? If a caliph lacked religious authority, what could be the source of his temporal authority? Were the tribal customs according to which caliphs were selected sufficient? Were caliphs infallible, and if not, could they be overthrown? Did law issue from the caliphs or the jurists, or was the Qu'ran its only legitimate source? Neither the Qur'an nor the stories of Muhammad's actions and prescriptions (*hadiths*) provided clear answers to these vexatious questions.

Muslim jurists sought to legitimize the caliphate by arguing that the caliph had been sent by Allah in order to maintain Islamic law and custom, a theory that became a source of continuing controversy. One of the most influential of the jurists, al-Mawardi, proclaimed in the eleventh century that the caliph enjoyed divine sanction through Muhammad to protect Islam and its community of believers, and must come from Muhammad's tribe. Al-Mawardi also argued that, although a caliph could delegate his authority to others, there could be only one legitimate caliphate at any time. This theory incorporated the traditional secular power enjoyed by Arab tribal chiefs and reflected, as well, Byzantine and Sasanian political influences. In fact, theory and practice regarding the caliphate diverged from the outset.

Competing Dynasties

Even more important to the fate of the Islamic polity than conflicts with external competitors like Byzantium or the later Christian crusaders were conflicts *within* the realm. The first imperial dynasty, the Umayyads, assumed power after a period of civil war and moved the imperial centre to Damascus. With the Umayyads, the caliphate came to be regarded as a hereditary or dynastic position, and caliphs increasingly relied on Sasanian and Byzantine bureaucratic procedures to augment the more informal modes of rule associated with their Arabic tribal origins.

Ummayad preeminence lasted for only eight decades and collapsed in civil war. The Ummayad caliphs had sought to institutionalize traditional Arab tribal practices and, in so doing, had alienated those who wanted the precepts of Islam to govern political life. In representing Arab superiority over non-Arab inhabitants of the empire, the Umayyads produced discontent on the part of 'the large numbers of non-Arabs who had become Muslims, especially in Iraq and the eastern provinces' (Watt 1974: 27).

Unlike the Ummayads, whose influence had been greatest in Syria and Arabia, the source of 'Abbasid power lay to the east, in Iran and southern Iraq. Like their predecessors, the 'Abbasids assumed power as part of an uneasy alliance and quickly turned upon their former allies. It was under the successors to Abu'l-'Abbas, especially al-Mansur (754–775) and Harun al-Rashid (786–809), that the medieval Islamic polity reached its political and cultural zenith. The shift in power away from Damascus was reflected in the construction of the city of Baghdad at a site which enjoyed a rich agricultural hinterland and controlled both the main north-south and east-west routes that linked the disparate provinces of the empire.

There are several events from which one might date the beginning of the collapse of the Islamic empire. One candidate is the establishment of a powerful rival caliphate in Egypt. The Fatimid caliphs sought to combine the roles of imam and caliph in themselves and emulated 'Abbasid pomp and ceremony.

Rival caliphates to both the 'Abbasids and Fatimids were established in Morocco (the Idrisids) and, more important, in Spain. Both areas were geographically remote from Cairo and Baghdad, and local officials acquired local interests and autonomy.

Thus, by the tenth century there was no longer a single centralized imperial entity or even a secular centre to which all Muslims could look. One caliph (Baghdad) governed Iran, much of Iraq, and regions to the east. A second (Córdoba) governed North Africa and Spain, and a third (Cairo) ruled Syria, Egypt, and much of the Arabian peninsula. Actual collapse may be dated from 1055 when the Seljuks, representing Turkish military mercenaries, seized power in Baghdad and governed through the figurehead 'Abbasid caliphs. An alternative date would be 1258 when the 'Abbasids were formally deposed by non-Muslim Mongols.

Hourani argues that a successful dynasty:

> needed to strike roots in the city: it needed the wealth to be derived from trade and formation of dynasties consisted in the conquest of cities. A conqueror would move up a chain of cities lying on a trade-route.

The creation and growth of cities in their turn depended upon the power of dynasties. (1991: 130)

Once in control of a core city, dynasties would try to appoint as provincial governors individuals who were beholden to them. Even if they were successful in placing their supporters, time usually eroded the ability of dynastic rulers to exercise authority at a distance, and provincial governors would increasingly come to exercise autonomy.

Imperial Decline

The employment of Turks in the imperial army and the failure to assure their loyalty were key factors in the decline of the empire. In the early ninth century, the manpower needs of the caliphate were met increasingly by the recruitment of soldiers from Turkish-speaking tribes in central Asia and the purchase of slaves. These 'slaves on horses' (Crone 1980) were aliens with no stake in the polity they pacified, and they were dependent on the caliphs whom they served. They neither enjoyed the political and social status of a formal elite nor did they acquire the stake in society of a landed elite.

Like the French kings at Versailles, the caliphs sought to distance themselves from popular urban forces and the pressures such forces might exert; they sought also to keep the army isolated from those popular forces. To this end, the caliph al-Mu'tasim (833–842) moved his capital north from Baghdad to the new city of Samarra. There, the political life of the empire was increasingly shaped by the leaders of the Turkish forces who also created virtual anarchy in Baghdad; simultaneously, the caliphate was threatened by the independence of strong provincial governors and by slave rebellions in southern Iraq.

On the surface, geographic impediments to unity and the shock of the Mongol invasions are sufficient to explain the imperial collapse. However, the former was not a determining factor, and the latter took place long after the empire had already been parcelled into hostile parts. In reality, the Islamic polity, having grown so quickly, never managed to stabilize itself or get beyond its tribal and clan-based origins.

Heavy taxation of conquered lands precluded deep loyalties, especially among non-Arabs and non-believers, and stimulated class differences. Islam provided a veneer of unity among Arabs, Berbers, Turks, and Persians, but it was not sufficient to wipe away deep cultural and ethnic self-consciousness that was reinforced by geographic distance and differences in wealth. Sectarian differences in Islam weakened the bonds afforded by religion. Finally, in AD 945, one Turkish military clan, the Buyids, seized power in Baghdad. The 'Abbasids remained nominal and shadowy caliphs until the middle of the thirteenth century. In 1258, Hulagu, the grandson of Genghis Khan, occupied and pillaged Baghdad and the remaining 'Abbasids were annihilated.

Islamic Continuity and Imperial Collapse

The collapse of the unitary imperial structure did not mean the disappearance of Islam. Instead, the weakening of loyalties to dynasties and
territorial frontiers intensified identification with religious symbols and
thereby reinforced the bonds uniting individuals in the community of Islam.

Many of the ideas and practices that evolved during the spread of Islam
retain relevance for contemporary Muslims. Key elements of this world view
are: (1) the world is unchanging; (2) the Islamic religion is a final answer to
all moral and religious questions; (3) Islam is intellectually self-sufficient
and neither rests upon nor requires insights from Judaism or Christianity;
(4) Islam is destined to become universal; and (5) all guidelines for society
can be found in the Qur'an and in the 'perfect' life followed by Muhammad.

The Contentious Religious Community: Schisms and Schismatics

If common religious beliefs initially fostered unity, differences in doctrine
served to legitimize competitors for power. Factionalism characterized the
ruling elite from the outset. In the years immediately following the death of
Muhammad, early converts and personal friends of the Prophet found
themselves at odds with 'careerists' from Medina and Mecca. Tribal loyalties also clashed repeatedly, and the elites in Medina and Mecca resisted the
efforts of governors of the wealthy provinces of Syria and Iraq to carve out
greater autonomy.

On the one hand, the bureaucracy that grew up around the caliphate was
necessary for day-to-day administration of newly urbanized centres and a
far-flung empire. On the other hand, it also produced alternate centres of
power that the caliph sought to control and with which he had to contend.
Increasingly the secular power of caliphs and later Islamic leaders was circumscribed by the 'holy law developed by jurists from the Qur'an and the
traditions of the Prophet' (Lewis 1993: 45). Since caliphs had no authority
to interpret Islamic law, the role of religious judge (*qadi*) became important,
especially since *qadis* enjoyed an exclusive right to interpret Muslim law
(*shari'a*). In this way, caliphs were deprived of authority to legislate or, at
best, had to share that prerogative with those who represented the Islamic
community. Like the caliphs, subsequent secular Islamic leaders have had
compete with one another to make it appear that their policies and actions
were compatible with the *shari'a*, described by Lewis as 'not only a normative code of law but also, an ideal towards which people and society must
strive', regulating 'every aspect of life, not only belief and cult, but also
public law, constitutional and international, and private law, criminal and
civil' (1993: 145).

Judges were trained in special schools (*madrasas*) that instructed them in
how to interpret and apply the *shari'a* or make inferences from it to matters
to which it did not explicitly refer. All in all, interpreting the law remained a

source of considerable authority in Islamic lands, especially when applied to phenomena unknown during the Prophet's lifetime.

Islamic society was violently divided by disputes over the bases of political and religious authority. Although clothed as doctrinal questions, the real issues involved power and rulership and were rooted in tribal and class rivalries.

The sometimes ferocious schism among the three branches of Islam – Shi'a, Sunni, and Kharijite – was never bridged, and it was partly responsible for the failure of Islam to produce a stable territorial polity. Although Sunnism triumphed, it would be wrong to regard it as religious orthodoxy because, in Watt's words, 'Islam has no machinery comparable to the Ecumenical Councils of the Christian Church which could say authoritatively what constitutes "right doctrine"' (Watt 1973: 6).

As noted earlier, Muhammad's successors could not claim a direct link to Allah; their authority could only be legitimized indirectly. Nevertheless, an empire existed; it had to be ruled, and disputes had to be settled. The cracks in Islam only became visible with the fifth caliph, Mu'awiya ibn Abi Sufyan (661–680), who assumed power after a civil war, which climaxed with the murder of 'Ali. 'Ali was a cousin of Muhammad, a close personal friend, the husband of Muhammad's daughter Fatima, and father of Muhammad's favourite grandchildren; he could, therefore, claim kinship, even a blood tie, to the Prophet. Mu'awiya, the governor of Syria, could assert no such claim. 'Ali's authority could neither be surrendered to others nor legitimately seized by them. As a result, with 'Ali's death, authority had to pass to his sons.

Shi'a

The *shi'at Ali* ('followers of 'Ali') refused to accept as legitimate rulers anyone except the male heirs of Muhammad, insisting that the caliphate required a family, not merely a tribal, link to the Prophet. Only if the line of succession went through the sons of 'Ali would a portion of Muhammad's charismatic authority be preserved. From the moment of the Prophet's passing, some of his companions were unhappy with the succession and would have preferred 'Ali. Their view reflected resistance to the resurgence of tribal traditions that followed the death of the Prophet.

According to one branch of Shi'a (the Imamis), there were twelve descendents of 'Ali – known collectively as the Twelve *imams* (spiritual leaders). Most of the twelve were believed to have murdered, but the twelfth and last *imam*, also called *mahdi* (leader guided directly by God), was believed to have disappeared in AD 878 and not to have died at all. Imami belief held that the *mahdi* would remain invisible until the day he chooses to return and rule all Islam. In other words, *imams*, unlike caliphs, were believed to be infallible and to enjoy a divine right to leadership of the Islamic community.

Initially, the Shi'a were only a loose group of opponents of Mu'awiya, but, in time, they became bitter foes first of the Umayyads and later the Abbasids. Spiritual and temporal power were, in their view, distinct; but, since the latter depended on the former, which could be held only by the male descendents of 'Ali, Sh'ites regarded all caliphs after 'Ali as usurpers. Since Muhammad was believed to have designated 'Ali as his successor, Sunni caliphs must be usurpers with no moral, legal, or religious legitimacy. Shi'ite beliefs were fundamentally incompatible with secular rule and bureaucratic institutions.

Sunni

Those who supported the Umayyads and accepted the legitimacy of the caliphs after 'Ali were known as Sunni (taken from *sunna*, which means 'standard practice' or 'normal and normative custom'). Caliphs, they insisted, should be selected from Muhammad's tribe according to the consensus of the community or its surrogates. The Sunni tradition was ostensibly based on the general principles of the Qur'an or on Muhammad's practice. In reality, Sunnism entailed a rejection of charisma and an acceptance of much of pre-Islamic Arab tribal tradition as the source of political authority and practice. Muhammad was viewed by Sunnis as a tribal, as well as religious, leader, and early caliphs had to be Quraysh.

More important (and anathema to their adversaries), when issues arose for which neither the Qur'an nor 'standard practice' offered a clear answer, Sunnis permitted leaders to decide or render an opinion based upon their interpretation of original religious sources. The Sunni tradition, then, was a pragmatic concession to necessity and changing circumstances. And even though all practices had to conform to the principles of the Qur'an, Sunni rulers permitted significant regional variation in customs and behaviour. The absence of any mechanism for making official doctrinal changes led to divergent practices and the proliferation of various Sunni schools of belief, but also encouraged tolerance of such divergences.

In time, the Sunni tradition became the ideology of the ruling elite, especially the 'Abbasids. 'Abbasid caliphs freely adopted religious symbols and used Islam to legitimize their rule. They claimed divine sanction by kinship with the Prophet and made decisions that putatively were based on the Qur'an and the Prophet's behaviour. The triumph of Sunnism probably permitted an imperial Islamic polity to survive as long as it did.

Kharijite

In the midst of the battle of Siffin (AD 657) between the supporters of 'Ali and Mu'awiya, 'Ali was persuaded to permit arbitration between him and his enemies in accordance with tribal tradition. The third and least known of the branches of Islam, the Kharijis ('those who seceded'), originated among those of 'Ali's supporters who turned against him when he agreed to this concession. The Kharijis argued that the struggle (which 'Ali was winning) should be decided by Allah alone, not by human arbitration.

Violence then ensued between 'Ali and the Kharajites, and in 661 'Ali was assassinated by a Kharijite.

Centred around Basra, Kharijites had much in common with the Shi'a. Like the Shi'a, they were unwilling to accept the idea of inherited rule or the possibility that secular politics could be severed from the religion. Authority, in their view, came solely from the community and was not reinforced by any external source of legitimacy; tribal sources of authority were explicitly rejected. Kharijites believed that Sunni Muslims were sinners who were no longer Muslims, and that violence should be used against them. By this logic, waging holy war (*jihad*) was a religious duty of all Muslims.

Classes

Doctrinal cleavages were linked to the emergence of socio-economic classes and hostility among them. To some extent, class and economic differences reinforced ethnic divisions. Not surprisingly the Arab conquerors became a privileged elite. For the most part, they lived apart from those whom they conquered and retained a sense of distinctiveness and superiority.

Non-Arabs who converted to Islam enjoyed theoretical, but not practical, equality with the Arab elite. Among converts to Islam – and in particular among Iranians who enjoyed an ancient culture – there was resentment against privileges given to those of Arab origin.

Christians, Jews, and others who were non-believers, but were tolerated, constituted the class of *dhimmis*. They and their property were under Muslim protection and they were allowed to practice their religion provided they paid tribute or tax (*jizya*). Although *dhimmis* could not participate in judicial proceedings involving Muslims or bear arms, were forbidden to wear certain colours associated with Islam, and could build houses of worship only with permission, the tolerated communities enjoyed considerable autonomy.

At the bottom of the social hierarchy were the large number of slaves who were captured in war or were purchased by Arab merchants. One special category of slaves – those purchased for military service – was destined to play a key role in the decline of the caliphate.

As a 'doctrine of opposition' to statist institutions and to the elites who managed those institutions, Shi'ism had a natural appeal to the poor and non-Arabic elements in Islamic society, especially in southern Iran. While the merchants of Mecca became Sunnis, many *mawalis*, especially those who chafed under the Arab Umayyads, took refuge in Shi'ism.

Islamic Law and the Jurists

There can be no stable and independent political structure in the absence of a legal framework to legitimize it and provide the guidelines for it to adapt to changing conditions. Since Islam regarded law and religion as identical, the purpose of which was to assure right conduct in this world in preparation for the next, it was almost impossible to establish a durable foundation for a secular Islamic polity. Government was regarded as an epiphenomenon, subordinate to religious dogma. The principles and practices of politics and government could evolve only with difficulty and had to find justification within the narrow confines of religious doctrine.

The Qur'an united Islam by providing a clear and simple code of ethics, fundamental values, and behaviour for individuals, enabling Muslims to differentiate themselves from non-believers, but providing little that might serve the practical day-to-day needs of government. Although it may be argued that the limitations inherent in religiously derived law contributed to the demise of the Islamic empire, it should also be noted that such law was vitally important in maintaining Islamic unity – the Islamic community – after the empire collapsed.

In time, the gap between theory and practice and between Islamic values like equality and the reality of despotism widened. Especially after the 'Abbasids had assumed power, the caliphs, their governors, administrators, and judges effectively legislated and adjudicated and, in doing so, took account of tribal customs and regional differences. Necessarily, they also sought justification for their acts and decisions in the beliefs of Islam. As the caliphs came to resemble oriental despots, Islamic law and society were transformed.

Islamic specialists in jurisprudence *(fiqh)*, really a body of religious scholars *('ulama)* – who combined the attributes of theologians, constitutional scholars, and political philosophers – tried to overcome the gap between theory and practice. The leading members of *'ulama*, which included leading *qadis*, teachers, and religious preachers, constituted a political and social elite. Religious scholars of all stripes agreed that law and government had to reflect the Qur'an, Muhammad's habitual behaviour *(sunna)* as recorded in traditional biographies and stories *(hadiths)*, and the wisdom of the Islamic community *(sunna* of the community) about what was just. However, caliphs and jurists differed about the meaning and relative importance of these sources of law and about how they related to one another. They argued especially about the role of contemporary community consensus *(ijma')*, which reflected local traditions (including those handed down in a tribal context), preferences, and interests. They also differed over the accuracy of the traditional stories about Muhammad and his companions.

Some scholars sought to apply reasoning to reach interpretations of the law. Others emphasized the customs of Muhammad and his companions in Medina, and still others gave greater weight to community consensus and interests. The jurist who had perhaps the greatest impact was al-Shafi'i (AD 767–820), who argued that the Qur'an had to be viewed as the literal Word of God on all matters referred to in it, whether large or small. Of equal importance, especially in matters to which the Qur'an did not refer, were the customs of Muhammad as traditionally handed down. *Ijma'*, he argued, was of lesser importance. But what was to be done in the event that the Qur'an or other traditional sources did not refer to an issue or was obscure about it, or in the event that conditions had changed? The dominant response was that they themselves, as the most competent religious scholars, should reach decisions by analogous reasoning from traditional sources; that is, that the *'ulama* could determine the community consensus.

The decisions and interpretations that jurists provided collectively constituted the sacred law or *shari'a*. The sacred law not only concerned public conduct, but also private issues of ethics, indeed, all aspects of life. Although such law was supposed to arise solely from Islamic sources, it actually mirrored local custom and tradition as well. On the one hand, the *'ulama* and its legal interpretations (*fatwas*) provided the caliphate with a critical source of legitimacy. Even though the jurists were divided, they were all within the Sunni tradition. On the other hand, jurists were a source of power independent of the caliphate; caliphs might be deterred from certain actions by fear of disagreement with jurists, or jurists might actually denounce a particular decision or policy. Indeed, within a century, the 'Abbasid caliphs had no input into determining the law. Thus, the imperial Islamic polity lacked the principal attribute of sovereignty as it evolved in Europe – the power to legislate and interpret the law. Consequently, as Roberson argues, Islam 'was not the captive of any government, nor dependent for survival upon the state, nor could it be predictably manipulated by centralized authority' (1988: 94).

Conclusion

The issues raised by medieval Islam remain relevant for the contemporary Muslim world. The effort of secular governments to harness the *umma* and deepen secular loyalties – or, as Roberson puts it, 'nationalize' Islam (that is, encourage those elements in Islam which support or rationalize the needs of a modernizing society) – have failed or are likely to fail. Arab national loyalties and frontiers have proved tenuous, and the barrier between internal and external politics almost non-existent.

The Islamic community and the religion of Islam continue to exert a stronger attraction for many Arabs than do Arab 'states' or the 'Arab nation' (a phrase that has roots in the original caliphate). Some of the region's sharpest and most dangerous conflicts, like those in Lebanon and Syria, can be traced to sectarian conflicts within the original Islamic community. The territorial polities of the Middle East were created by European rulers, and post-colonial nationalists and their political parties tried, but largely failed, to instil enduring national loyalties among citizens.

Instead, these polities reflect the nested consequences of their tribal origins. Modern Saudi Arabia traces its origins to the Wahhabi movement of the eighteenth century which, like modern Islamic fundamentalism, preached a return to strict obedience to the Qur'an and the teachings of Muhammad, and the rule of the Sa'udis began in 1921 at the expense of their tribal foes, the followers of sharif Hussein. In a word, contemporary Arab polities are weak in the sense that they are not the principal targets of loyalties of many of their own inhabitants. Whether one looks at Shi'ites, Alawites, Druzes, Hashemites, Maronites, or others that determine cleavages in the region, the potency of religious and tribal symbols inherited from the early years of Islam and even before are evident.

Efforts to make loyalties to the medieval Islamic empire identical or even compatible with loyalties to the Islamic community (or sects within it) succeeded only temporarily, if at all. The awkward relationship between *umma* and government that arose in the seventh century persisted and produced 'a religious outlook ... that was and is suspicious of the state' (Roberson 1988: 99). The triumph of the idea of an Islamic community separated from and superior to the non-Islamic world became frozen in time. As a result, 'Islamic reform is always governed by and drawn inexorably to the past: ... nothing in the present and future could possibly ever be as good as that exquisite society erected by Muhammad and transfixed forever by his death' (Naff 1981: 28). Islamic societies thus have found it difficult to accept change and adapt to modernity. In the words of Watt: 'One of the important points at which this ... unhistorical self-image of Islam affects contemporary events is in the idealization of early Islam, when it is regarded as a perfect society to which a return is possible and desirable; no such return can solve our contemporary problems' (1988: 142).

8 The Past as Prelude to the Future?

Identities and loyalties in global politics (1996)

Theory purports to tell us what to look at and, by inference, what can be safely ignored. By simplifying reality, theory helps us organize our beliefs about an ever-changing world and offers an intellectual foundation for policies. Bad theory almost inevitably means bad policies. Unfortunately, the failure to predict (or adequately to explain, even in retrospect) the end of the Cold War, adds powerfully to evidence from many other quarters that something is seriously wrong with our theories of global politics. International relations theorists have difficulty accounting for change, particularly when it arises from massive shifts in loyalties from one set of authorities to another. The demise of the Soviet empire surprised state-centric theorists, in part because their theories could not accommodate a revival of old identities. Such theories are equally useless when it comes to addressing mini-nationalisms, tribal violence in Africa, the globalisation of business and finance, or criminal cartels.

Surely we must discard and replace theory that fails to shed light on issues that any reader of today's headlines knows are most important. But replace it with what? In our view, we should conceive of global politics as involving a world of 'polities' rather than states and focus on the relationships among authority, identities, and ideology. Central questions are: In particular times and places, who or what controls which persons with regard to which issues, and why? How and why do old political affiliations evolve or die and new ones emerge?

Since political evolution and devolution presumably involve bedrock processes that are as old as political association itself, it is critical to escape our Eurocentric blinders and adopt the widest possible historical perspective. Our own response to this challenge has been to analyze six historical cases selected for temporal, cultural, and geographic diversity. The six cases are: (1) the world's first great civilization in Mesopotamia, which arose in the mid-third millennium BC and lasted until the Persian conquest in the sixth century BC; (2) the Greek world, from the Archaic period of eighth century BC until its conquest by Macedonia in 338 BC; (3) Mesoamerica, from the emergence of Olmec culture about 1250–1150 BC until after the Spanish conquest; (4) China, from the early Chou era of about 1100 BC until the end of the Han era in AD 220; (5) the Islamic world, from AD 622 until the Mongol sack of Baghdad in the thirteenth century; and (6) Italy, from the decline of Rome in the fourth century AD until the Golden Age of the Renaissance in the fifteenth century.

'Polities' Rather Than 'States'

'Polities' in our definition are entities with a significant measure of institutionalization and hierarchy, identity, and capacity to mobilize persons for value satisfaction (or relief from value deprivation). We regard the sovereign territorial states that are associated with the Westphalian settlement of 1648 as only one type of polity. All but perhaps the very earliest 'primitive' (pre) historical epochs have been characterized by layered, overlapping, and interacting polities – coexisting, cooperating, and/or conflicting. Indeed, a range of overlapping or embedded polity types may govern effectively, each within a specified (not necessarily exclusive) domain, over one or more issues. A polity's domain includes the persons who identify with it, the resources (including ideological resources) it has, and the issue(s) it affects. No polity is omnipotent, controlling all persons and resources with regard to all issues.

Although all polities have a territory of sorts – where the persons that identify with the polity are – that territory need not be clearly demarcated. A polity need not have a 'centre', though it is a disadvantage not to have one – or to have more than one, like the medieval papacy at one stage or the late Roman Empire. All of our historical cases suggest the utility of the distinction made by Sahlins (1989:4) between 'boundary' and 'frontier'. A boundary, like that of a Westphalian state, is a 'precise linear division within a restrictive, political context'; a frontier 'connotes more zonal qualities, and a broader, social context'. The linear boundary typified the Westphalian polity with its territorial view of society, reinforced by the European principle of contract and Euclidean conceptions of space. The idea of a zonal frontier allows for overlapping 'civilizations', with continuity regardless of changing linear boundaries. Nevertheless, just as there is a propensity among many international relations theorists to exaggerate the significance of Westphalian state boundaries, there is a tendency among them to ignore the extent to which many other polities do have well-defined boundaries.

Our cases reveal an enormous variety of polities. Those of the greatest significance in ancient *Mesopotamia* were cities, and loyalty to city consistently threatened to undermine empires. Once cities arose, many grew rapidly in size, population, and prosperity. Lagash, one of the largest Sumerian cities, had 30,000–35,000 residents. By comparison, during the sixth century Babylon – which was the centre of a much larger polity – alone had a population of 100,000. The Mesopotamian city was a genuine economic centre, not just a political and cultic core like the less-integrated 'village-state' model prevailing in China and some parts of Mesoamerica. Other key polities in the Mesopotamian case included large kingdoms (regional polities) and tribes, both inside and outside Mesopotamia. Temples, large private landowners, and merchants were important economic actors.

Mesopotamian tribes and cities afford excellent examples of overlapping and interactive polity types. Mesopotamian tribes included Bedouin nomads, whose only interest in civilization was an occasional raid for plunder, and others who became hired agricultural labourers, settled pastoralists, and/or mercenaries, and thereby acquired 'civilized' language and culture. Tribal organization included groups under individual shaikhs, as well as tribal federations, the names of which are associated with an entire people or ethnicity like the Chaldeans,[1] who nonetheless often fought among themselves and eventually became rulers of Babylon. If city polities were deeply embedded in Mesopotamian tradition, so were empires. Indeed, in the actual Mesopotamian context, there is ambiguity in both polity types. Some early cities were amalgamations of lesser cities, and various leagues of otherwise independent cities may have existed. There were fourteen known major cities in Sumer/Akkad during the Early Dynastic period. According to the Sumerian King-List, after kingship again descended from heaven following the flood, it was held in succession by a number of cities like Kish, each by implication exercising hegemony. The first Akkadian king, Sargon (2310–2273 BC), not only conquered rival cities, but also he and his grandson Naram-Sin (2246–2190 BC) created an empire that encompassed all of Mesopotamia. The Assyrian empire at its zenith in the seventh century BC reached as far as Egypt and Persia.

The city was the leading polity throughout much of the *Greek* experience, but there were also chiefdoms, alliances, hegemonical alliances, empires, and functional regimes for shrines and games. The city polity itself involved two main subtypes, the polis and the ethnos, and both exhibited considerable variety. Because Greek cities were so small, external relationships loomed large, and a wide range of informal and more institutionalized arrangements overarched the city polity. Alliances were influenced to some extent by historical ties, tribal identities, and constitutional preferences. Some alliances, such as the Spartan, evolved into hegemony, and that of Athens into a form of empire. The ethnos eventually provided a model for a series of federations, and regimes for shrines and games were important within their limited domains. Ultimately, however, no overarching polity threatening the freedom or independence of the individual city-state gained sufficient legitimacy to endure.

The *Mesoamerican* record reveals a rich variety of polities from families to empires. The patrilineal extended family was the basis of early Mesoamerican society, and kinship remained important. In many polities, including those of the classic Maya, a hereditary aristocracy emerged from the former heads of various lineages and came to control productive land, which client families worked. In central Mexico extended-kinship groups also retained a high degree of identity and autonomy. One can still see in

Teotihuacán the remnants of what were apparently apartment compounds in which such groups resided. These compounds resemble the urban residences of the *calpulli* of later Aztec times. Each *calpulli* worked a particular plot of land or engaged in the same craft, sent its members together into battle, educated young boys in its own school, and provided a shrine to honor its patron deity.

Beyond family and artificial kinship groups was tribe. Tribal groups overlapped not only with one another, but also with other polities. The Aztecs were confused about the legendary Toltecs, from whom they claimed descent. But who were the Aztecs? According to their chronicles, they were originally part of a group of seven Chichimec tribes that migrated over several generations from their original home, known as Aztlán, in western Mexico. One of their leaders was named Meci, from whom they acquired their own tribal name, Mexica. The name Aztec also came to refer to the imperial polity constructed by a triple alliance of the Mexica, the Acolhua, and the city of Tlacopán.

Long-distance merchant-trader was an important occupational-identity category. The best-documented long-distance merchant-traders were the Aztec *pochtecas*, who practiced their profession on a hereditary basis, lived in separate *barrios* in Tenochtitlán-Tlatelolco and probably elsewhere, married within their group, had their own courts and laws, and maintained their own shrines, priests, and sacrificial rituals. The *pochtecas* wore special dress and owed neither personal nor military service to the ruler, though they did pay tribute. The local guild was affiliated with a regional merchants' association stretching across the 12 towns in the centre of the Aztec empire.

Other Mesoamerican polities were local, subregional, or regional; and local and subregional identities and loyalties proved more durable than those associated with more inclusive polities. In the Valley of Oaxaca, widely spaced independent villages with dependent hamlets gave way to subregional centres, then to a single dominant regional polity, and finally to subregional centres again. At its peak, Monte Albán dominated the entire Valley of Oaxaca. In the Lowland Petén before 250 BC, Maya culture was one of scattered small villages. Over the next 500 years some six subregional fortress centres emerged.

Overarching Mesoamerican polities included alliances, empires, and a Mayapán 'confederation' that is difficult to distinguish from empire. The overlap between alliances and empire is even more pronounced. After the fall of the Toltecs and the weakening of residual Olmec control in the Basin of Mexico, three city polities – Azcapotzalco, Culhuacán, and Coatlichan – joined in an alliance dominated by the Tepanecs of Azcapotzalco. The newly arrived Aztec-Mexica eventually formed a triple alliance with Texcoco and Tlacopán that overthrew Azcapotzalco and inaugurated the Aztec Empire. That empire was only the last in a series of pre-conquest Mesoamerican empires, and at its peak ruled five to six million subjects.

The Spanish conquest added the Catholic Church to the list of Meso-american polities. No Indian temple priesthood ever matched the degree of autonomy, lands, and wealth the Spanish Church enjoyed. The Pope granted to Spain the *Patronato* charge of evangelizing the New World, and the King of Spain provided an enormous permanent income. The Church received land grants from the king and wealthy laypersons, and in time came to own or control much of the arable land in Mexico.

In ancient *China*, the family or clan was the basic socio-political unit, and China's ethical system was oriented toward the family rather than a supreme being (as in medieval Europe or Islam) or encompassing polity (as in ancient Greece). Since the patriarchal family was regarded as the taproot of other polities, no distinction was made between private and public spheres, and Chinese thinkers easily accepted hierarchy as an organizing principle. The family, rather than any larger polity, provided economic and personal security and was the source of personal and political values for individuals. Religious ideas, military organization, even agricultural labour mobilized from above revolved around the family. During the late Chou era, China consisted of a cluster of city polities, whose capital was home to a lineage that itself was a political entity.

Although Chou influence extended across much of northern China, as many as 200, small, walled cities and their environs, especially in the east, retained independence under vassal lords who acknowledged Chou suzerainty. The decline of the Eastern Chou left a number of competing polities in control of the north China Plain – some ten to fifteen by the eighth century BC. These sought to build alliances to protect themselves from the predatory policies of neighbours, and a novel approach to curbing instability was adopted in 651 BC, when these small polities designated the Ch'i ruler as hegemon of their confederation.

Nomadic tribes, ethnically similar to, but linguistically distinct from, the Chinese, constituted another polity type. Called *Hsiung-nu* by the Chinese, these nomads spoke a Turkish dialect. Horses provided them with mobility and allowed them to adapt to the grasslands of the northern steppe, which could not support the intensive agriculture that evolved in China's Yellow River basin. In the third century BC, even as China was being united, a *Hsiung-nu* tribal federation exercised authority across Mongolia from western Manchuria to the edge of the Pamir Mountains in Turkestan. *Hsiung-nu* mobility posed a permanent threat along the frontiers of cultural China and, at their peak, these nomads could put as many as 300,000 mounted archers in the field.

Notwithstanding the variety of polities in China, a strong sense of cultural unity developed early, and the Chinese regarded their civilization as superior to others. As a result, the ideal of an overarching Chinese polity remained strong even during eras in which it was a fiction. The first two historical dynasties, the Shang and Chou, actually controlled little beyond their capital cities and, under Chou feudalism, the centre was weak. Only with the triumph and consolidation of Ch'in authoritarianism after 221 BC did a genuine imperial polity emerge, and it was short-lived. Despite the myth of continuity from the Shang, it was not until the Earlier Han era (202 BC to AD 8) that a durable Chinese empire took root.

Islam began as a rebellion against Arab tribal practices, but the death of Muhammad triggered a struggle within the movement that led to clashes between tribal and statist practices, struggles among kinship groups, differing class-based perceptions, and strongly held religious beliefs. Three major polity types coexisted uneasily within the medieval tribal system: tribe, religious community, and empire. Tribal or clan loyalties dominated Arabia prior to the Prophet's revolution, and Muhammad sought to replace tribal attachments with loyalty to a Muslim community of believers. However, Muhammad's authority was putatively derived directly from Allah, and his actions were believed to have divine sanction that was unavailable to others. Ultimately, the identification of religious and secular symbols proved an insurmountable obstacle to institutionalizing 'statist' forms and practices.

Within Arab society, the extended family produced potent loyalties and was affiliated with a kinship group claiming a common ancestor that would afford protection and, if necessary, seek vengeance. The Islamic community was established by the Constitution of Medina that was written by Muhammad after his migration from Mecca to Medina in AD 622. Communal unity was to be based on religious belief rather than tribal affiliation, and tribal practices like blood feuds were to be abandoned. Muhammad's community was not a 'state' but an expression of Islamic solidarity against traditional tribal forms, and in contrast to tribal tradition viewed all individuals, whether or not blood kin, as equals. The Prophet's death triggered efforts to elaborate more centralized forms and brought to the surface old tribal loyalties and identities. Tribal customs alone were inadequate to govern an empire of such enormous size and diversity, and as power shifted from the Arabian periphery to the Syrian and later Iraqi heartland, the ruling elite grew hostile to tribal mores. The new government bureaucracy was taken over from Islam's imperial predecessors – the Byzantines and Sasanians. However, at no time did the caliphate exercise strong central control. Ultimately rival caliphates successfully challenged the centre.

After the decline of the Roman Empire, *Italy* also included a wide variety of polities. The two polities that occupied centre stage in the Middle Ages were an empire centred in Germany and a church in Rome. Both sought to inherit the mantle of the Roman Empire and exercise temporal authority over Christianity. Both the Holy Roman Empire and the papacy were actually territorial empires that sought to extend their territory and authority; their struggle waxed and waned for centuries, forcing other polities to take sides or play the two pretenders against each other. In the end, both had to cede primacy to the territorial princes whose allegiance they sought.

Tribes played a key role in Italy, especially in the decline of Rome. Like the Huns, most were clan federations. For some years after they invaded, the

Lombards ruled much of northern Italy. They, like the Goths who preceded them and the Carolingian Franks and Magyars who came later, found their ways of life transformed by the legacy of Rome, and tribe ceased to be a significant identity. Kinship ties persisted, however, and the rulers of Italian city polities were groups of families dubbed the patriciates. Many commercial and trading companies and banking houses were identified with particular families and *consorterie* (interfamily alliances and/or a family with its clients). Family rivalries complicated additional divisions – for example, Guelph versus Ghibelline, *popolo grasso* versus *popolo minuto* – and the resulting competition threatened public order in many cities. That was the immediate origin of the single *podestas* and *signori* whose appearance signalled the end of the communes' republican tradition. In the end, many cities installed family dynasties like the Florentine Medicis.

Italian towns and cities enjoyed greater autonomy from external authorities than German polities because feudal structures in Italy were weak. There was a growth of urban polities in much of Italy after AD 900. Many were on previous Roman foundations, while others developed around a local church or shrine, at the intersections of travel routes, or from clusters of villages or farms. Towns and cities helped fill the authority vacuum created by the absence of kings and the weakness of the Holy Roman Empire. Conceptions of urban communities began to change in the mid-twelfth century, when the term 'commune' came into fashion. A process of consolidation continued until the late fifteenth century, when most urban centres were overshadowed by Milan, Florence, or Venice.

Of importance, in addition to (and often overlapping) family groupings, were fraternities, guilds, companies, and banks. Fraternities and guilds served to advance economic interests, uphold standards, and regulate membership in a trade, and they also provided a sense of belonging in an urban setting. By the later thirteenth century trading companies and banks had evolved into powerful entities. Single-venture enterprises or family businesses developed into permanent firms, drawing capital from a variety of sources. Some Italian traders settled in foreign trading centres, where they formed local associations or 'nations' for mutual advancement and protection. Large banks established a symbiotic relationship with local and foreign governments as well as with popes, until it was difficult to determine who was beholden to whom.

A wild card among polities in Italy were the independent 'companies' of mercenary *condottieri,* who became arbiters of Italian politics between roughly 1340 and 1380. Conditions, both inside and outside Italy, helped account for the rise of the *condottieri*, including the progress of commerce and industry that undermined civic militias. Greater wealth made it possible to pay the high prices mercenaries demanded for their services. The Essex knight Sir John Hawkwood was the most famous mercenary general, waging war in the 1370s for the pope, Milan, and Florence. By the fifteenth century, the *condottieri* were largely Italian, and *condottieri* leaders like

Francesco Sforza countered adversity by capturing a city or group of cities that could serve as a permanent base.

Polities and Ideologies

Like Westphalian states, other polities attract loyalties and exercise authority. 'Authority' in our conception is effective governance, the ability to exercise significant influence or control across space over persons, resources, and issues. Authority is often not exclusive, and it need not be enshrined in formal law. Authority may even be regarded by many as illegitimate (like military 'authoritarian rule' in Latin American countries with democratic constitutions), although authority seen as legitimate is obviously more secure. Virtually all polities have means of disciplining or coercing persons within their domain, but individuals rarely accept authority just to avoid punishment. They expect benefits in exchange, including the psychological satisfaction associated with group identity and ideology. Identities can be imposed, but most are not; rather, they are embraced because they deliver what people want. Loyalty, too, is an exchange phenomenon that derives from perceived benefits.

Issues can arise that force choices among non-exclusive identities and loyalties. For example, Holy Roman emperors appointed bishop-barons as local imperial administrators because celibate clerics presumably could not found rival dynasties. This policy worked well until a reforming pope who came along insisted that bishop-barons put loyalty to church ahead of loyalty to emperor. Similarly, citizens and politicians in contemporary Europe are repeatedly forced to choose between the latest variant of supranationalism and their more familiar national loyalties. It is the sum of individual choices, over time, that strengthens some polities and undermines others.

Every polity needs a distinctive ideology, which helps to legitimize its authority, and that ideology is communicated and reinforced through a process of political socialization. The ideological source of supreme authority in Sumer was the leading god of the pantheon, Enlil, whose priesthood administered the temple Ekur at Nippur. When the Babylonians eclipsed the Sumerians, they elevated their own god Marduk to the top of the pantheon, and the Assyrians later did the same for Ashur. Athens and Sparta each cultivated a special ideological image–liberal democratic Athens versus disciplined oligarchic Sparta. Venice – formed by literally bridging what were circa AD 1200 some 60 neighbourhood parishes – rested on several reinforcing identities: Venice the Christian city of the apostle St Mark (versus less-favored patron saints); Venice founded by the last real Italian Romans and with a special relationship with Byzantium; and Venice of the Book of Gold noble families, whose stable rule earned the city the coveted appellation *la serenissima*.

The bridging analogy for Venice is fitting because the best ideology to legitimize a larger polity is one that is at once distinctive and yet makes use of ideological strands already within the expanded domain. Broad cultural norms can provide an ideological foundation for large polities. Mesopotamian and Chinese rulers made much of the common cultural heritage of their peoples, which contrasted with the supposed inferiority of neighbouring peoples. Mesopotamian empires appropriated a shared pantheon of gods, sacred shrines like Ekur at Nippur and the moon-god's abode at Ur, age-old sacred texts, and ancient titles like King of Kish – and thereby competed with city and other identities. The closest parallel in Greece was an overarching sense of Hellenism that sustained the alliance against Persia, the role of the oracle at Delphi and other shrines, and the Olympic Games. However, Greece was different from Mesopotamia and China in that there never developed a persuasive ideological justification for empire. Greece and Mesopotamia were similar in one respect: the primary identity in both regions continued to be cities.

Early on, China developed a powerful sense of cultural exclusivity, and the myth of a single unified kingdom governed by sage-kings persisted even in periods of anarchic localism. Religion – largely ancestor worship, and divination and shamanism – sanctified clan lineages in China, and larger polities drew sustenance from philosophies that were constructed on clan-based analogies. Constant war during the Warring States era eroded the most powerful clans, and loyalties to a variety of crisscrossing authority patterns, sealed by blood covenants, became common. The shift from ancestor worship to the universalism of Heaven under the Chou was gradual, retaining patriarchal authority and stressing ancestral protection.

When the Chou defeated the Shang, whom they had earlier served and to whom they were linked by marriage, they argued that theirs was the central kingdom, an extension of the Shang claim that they were at the centre of the universe, and proclaimed that the 'Mandate of Heaven' had been passed on because of Shang corruption. The effect was to replace pantheism and shamanism with a powerful abstract and universal principle. Thereafter, a belief that emperors enjoyed a 'Mandate of Heaven' helped legitimize an overarching polity and all Chinese dynasties, although it also acted as a constraint because of the assumption that an unpopular emperor's overthrow signalled the mandate's withdrawal.

Confucianist ideas, drawing analogies between ruler and father and emphasizing the role of virtue in acquiring the Mandate of Heaven, buttressed imperial stability based on conservatism and continuity. Confucius venerated the past, especially the peace of the early Chou, and stressed the need for continuity and social responsibility. He argued that political affairs should mirror a natural moral order. Confucian virtues were a direct extension of the ideal of filial piety, and Confucianism appealed to authorities because it emphasized the proper roles of individuals in society and the stability of the resulting hierarchy. The Confucian emphasis on ritual, manners, and deportment reflected beliefs that external forms could produce, or at least reinforce, virtue and that observing ritual was a bond with antiquity that increased legitimacy.

By contrast, Islamic ideology failed to sustain an overarching polity. The simplicity and egalitarianism of Islam made conversion easy and attractive, especially to those who had fared poorly under other polities. However, Muhammad's heirs did not enjoy the authority of a prophet. The caliphs received no revelations and, though they guarded the community and its traditions, they could not claim the legitimacy of one who was a messenger of Allah. For Muhammad, God was the source of authority and secular authority without religious sanction was inconceivable. Key questions remained: Did a caliph possess religious authority and, if so, what was its source? If a caliph lacked religious authority, what could be the source of his temporal authority? Were the tribal customs regarding caliph selection sufficient? Were caliphs infallible and, if not, could they be overthrown? Did legislation issue from the caliphs or the jurists, or was the Qu'ran its only legitimate source? Neither the Qu'ran nor Muhammad's prescriptions provided clear answers.

Tribal and class differences intensified disputes about these matters. A schism among Shi'a, Sunni, and Kharijite branches of Islam over the sources of political authority erupted with the fifth caliph, who assumed power after a civil war and the murder of 'Ali. For those who assumed the name *shi'at 'Ali* ('followers of 'Ali'), 'Ali's blood tie to the Prophet had been the basis of his authority, which could neither be surrendered to nor seized by others. 'Ali's followers believed that the line of succession should come through his sons, thereby preserving a portion of Muhammad's charismatic authority, and they resisted the resurgence of tribal traditions. Those who supported the Umayyads and accepted the legitimacy of the caliphs after 'Ali were known as Sunni ('standard practice' or 'normal and normative custom'). They viewed Muhammad as a tribal, as well as religious, leader and accepted much of pre-Islamic tribal tradition as a source of authority and practice. The Sunni tradition was a pragmatic concession to practical necessity and changing circumstances.

Nested Polities

A consequence of contact among polities is the nesting or embedding of some within others, as though one polity form were superimposed on another. One form may lose some of its separate identity and autonomy, but in the process the dominant polity may assume some of the characteristics of the one(s) it has incorporated. A nested polity is either the remnant of an earlier form or the incubus of one yet to come, depending on the direction of political evolution. Most polities are always changing or 'becoming', sometimes coming from or moving toward another polity type.[2] During some epochs change is tumultuous, and during others it is so slow as to be almost imperceptible. In Greece, the polis gradually established its domination over Dark Age chiefs whose source of authority was kinship and artificial kinship. However, kinship ties retained importance among aristocrats in different poleis and in the diplomatic institution of proxenia.³ Meanwhile, the polis became more complex internally and linked to various external polities – alliances, functional regimes, and informal empires.

In Mesopotamia, cities retained their identities and the loyalties of inhabitants even under local hegemons or after incorporation into larger polities. There was also residual tribalism. In Mesoamerica, the head of one Maya family (the Cocom) in the Yucatán succeeded in grouping Maya cities into a single regional 'confederation' polity under his leadership at Mayapán. The nesting was almost literal, insofar as the rulers of other polities were required to establish residence at Mayapán. Indeed, before the Spanish arrived, as we have stressed, Mesoamerica had a remarkable range of overlapping and nested polities, including extended-family and artificial kinship groups, merchants, tribes, villages, cities, subregional urban centres, regional polities, and empires.

Nesting was common in ancient China, too, especially when triumphant rulers surrounded themselves with officials co-opted from defeated lineages. Chou rulers, for example, appointed a Shang prince to govern the old Shang capital region and used Shang officials in local governments. Medieval Islam eroded, but did not eliminate, tribal solidarity. Tribal practices resurfaced almost immediately after Muhammad's death, when a tribal council selected his successor, and claimants to the caliphate had to demonstrate a familial relationship to the Prophet. Tribal favoritism was widespread, and nepotism during the reign of the third caliph roused discontent and was a factor in his assassination. The importance of tribal vendetta resurfaced when the clan Banu Umayya resisted 'Ali and sought to avenge kinsmen who were killed in a battle they fought against Muhammad.

Nesting is equally apparent in contemporary politics. For example, today's European states are in the midst of an awkward transition. None is fully responsible for its own defence; some economic functions have been 'EC-ized', and others have been surrendered to multinational firms and worldwide financial markets – not to mention the challenges of coping with a more organized and demanding citizenry. There has been such to-ing and fro-ing that there is no historical model that can do justice to the patterns of authority taking shape in modern Europe.

The impact of nested polities will be felt in the unique attributes of the successor polity and will show up in variations among institutions, ideas, and behaviour within each class of polity. Thus, even in this century, some state forms have been hard to distinguish from empires (the Soviet Union), tribal conglomerates (Rwanda and Kenya), religious movements (post-Shah Iran), multinational firms and banks (Japan Inc.), cities (Hong Kong and Singapore), or even coteries of families (El Salvador). Each polity reflects the impact of its own history and other polity types that are nested within it. We ignore nested polities at our own peril. Just as the imperial form assumed by the ninth-century caliphate contrasted with its Byzantine and Persian predecessors because of its tribal and clan patrimony, so contemporary Muslim states of the Middle East (or for that matter Israel with its Zionist roots) have little in common with European states of different parentage. And the facile assumption that all states are the same – with similar motivations or institutions – plays no small role in the errors policymakers make when they meddle in states with nested tribal or clan polities such as Somalia, Lebanon, and Iraq.

Polities do not evolve in a vacuum. The path that political evolution takes – toward centralization and larger polities, or toward decentralization and fragmentation – depends on factors that have a different impact in specific historical contexts. Thus, for almost every issue we can identify three generic polity forms: status quo, expansive, and contractive. The competition among status quo, expansive, and contractive polities is apparent in a range of economic issues. The European Exchange Mechanism (ERM) crisis in Europe illustrated the resistance of national bureaucrats to expansive polities. When the German Bundesbank failed to lower interest rates, pressures on other European currencies drove them down against the deutsche mark and encouraged wide swings in the frenetic financial markets. In no case was the limited capacity of Westphalian polities more clearly revealed than in their inability to insulate themselves from resulting speculation; not even the Bank of England had sufficient currency to defend the pound. The crisis may have been a setback for one expansive polity – the EU – but it reflected the power of others – globalizing business and financial firms – to operate across national borders.

The resistance of status quo polities was reflected more broadly in efforts to sabotage the Maastricht Treaty and in resistance to progress in the Uruguay Round of the GATT on both sides of the Atlantic. Unfortunately for Maastricht, recessionary conditions, long-standing resentments over regulatory decisions of the Brussels bureaucracy, fears of the erosion of national culture in a wider Europe, and the Yugoslav debacle undermined support among publics for political integration. It was the threat of an expansive polity – 'Fortress Europe' – that provided, in turn, one incentive for the negotiation of another – the North American Free Trade Agreement (NAFTA).

One of the United States' other NAFTA partners, Canada, confronts political difficulties of another kind as it faces the challenge of contractive nationalisms. Unlike Yugoslavia, the outcome of the struggle between status quo and contractive polities for the loyalty of Canadians remains in doubt. Polls suggest that most Canadians do not want an end to Canada, although national identity is weak. Were the country to divide, it is unclear along what lines – far West, agricultural heartland, French speakers, and Maritime provinces? – because Quebec is not the only distinct identity. Also uncertain is the eventual effect of NAFTA on the unity issue. NAFTA should increase general prosperity and thereby enhance the rewards of being Canadian. On the other hand, militant separatists argue that, with larger entities like NAFTA, membership in a Canadian national economy has lost much of its relevance. Canada is a victim of both fission and fusion.

As issues like this reveal, centrifugal and centripetal forces continuously tug polities in different directions. There is a 'tale of two tendencies' that characterizes historical change: the elaboration of larger networks of inter-action and interdependence, alongside the fragmentation of other collectivities into vulnerable and tiny units of self-identification.

Change, Stasis, and the State Concept

Richard Hooker is credited with observing that change 'is not made without inconvenience, even from worse to better'. What was true for the sixteenth century is no less true for the twenty-first, both for our hopeful, yet turbulent post-Cold War world and for the theories we use to make sense of that world. Today, there are many versions of 'the state' as well as numerous polities with only a fragile kinship to any historical state. A model of dichotomized – domestic versus international – political life fails to capture the trends we have highlighted. The state concept provides an illusion of stability and continuity that contrasts with a restless reality. The question is not whether the state exists and is observable, but to what extent it explains the things we need to under-stand. Although the state has many definitions, in international relations it is usually equated with the Westphalian model of a sovereign territorial entity enjoying a monopoly of authority within and legal equality without. Today this model serves as something of an ideal type that few actors approach.[4] In this usage, the European experience of a particular era is generalized to all times and places. In fact, the Westphalian state is just one type of polity, distinguished less by any criteria focusing on loyalties or resources than by a legal claim to legitimacy and the formal recognition of other members of the 'sovereign club' that it is what it claims to be. Unfortunately, there is no official certification board comparable to the community of states to pro-vide formal recognition for other polities.

Generalizing from the Westphalian model conveys the appearance of a world divided into neat territorial compartments, each governed by a single set of authorities who command the exclusive loyalties of those residing within its boundaries. In fact, history contradicts assumptions about the universality, exclusivity, or permanence of any polity. The record reveals the presence of constant pressure both toward larger and more inclusive polities and the fracturing of existing polities. Fortunately there are other, nonstatist ways to think about the world, including conceptualizing a single political arena consisting of a wide range of actors engaged in issue-specific beha-viour. The ways in which people organize themselves for political ends evolve along with everything else, and an intellectual map that focuses only on the interaction of two hundred 'states' captures only a slice of reality. Our alternate model extends beyond the familiar notion of 'pluralism' and paints a world of overlapping, layered, and interacting polities.

Today, as in the past, human beings identify themselves in a variety of poli-tically relevant ways and, as a result, are enmeshed in a multitude of authoritative networks, have loyalties to a variety of authorities, and distribute resources (including their time, labour, and money) among them. Each network has the capacity to mobilize adherents in the context of issues that touch their perceived interests or excite their passions. Each is a polity of sorts with a hierarchy (albeit sometimes minimal), ideology, frontiers, and resource base. Patterns of loyalties and resulting polities necessarily overlap, thereby blurring 'frontiers'. This overlap does not usually entail conflict. Particular polities tend to enjoy niches in the lives of adherents, and the loyalties they evoke are normally activated only in the context of specific issues. There is no inherent contradiction between an individual's national, religious, tribal, professional, or other affiliations. Tensions may arise, however, when authorities perceive conflicting interests in the same issue(s) and compete with one another to become the principal objects of affection for the same constituents. Clashes like those that pitted Chinese communism against the Chinese family during the Cultural Revolution or the Polish church against the Polish communist party in the 1950s exemplify such conflicts. Contests for loyalties and the changes in affiliation that they produce are the stuff of history.

Change is continuous as loyalties, like cards, are shuffled and reshuffled and people are seduced to follow new authorities on new political adventures (or misadventures). Rarely are contests sufficiently decisive to eliminate polities permanently; sometimes, as in the Chinese absorption of the Mongols or the Islamic absorption of Arab tribal loyalties, new polity types arise that synthesize the key features of old ones. Napoleon's effort to replace the sovereign Westphalian state by an empire of nations was finally rebuffed by the older states at the gates of Moscow, and efforts to build a new entity – the nation-state – succeeded, but only for a time. The murder of an Austrian archduke in 1914 highlighted the tension between the Westphalian state and nationalist passions, and the Wilsonian doctrine of national self-determination revealed the incompatibility of the two concepts as organizing devices. History has a habit of biting those who would ignore it, and it is hardly surprising that the end of the Cold War again pointed up the ill fit between 'state' and 'nation' in the Balkans, Africa, and elsewhere. In the words of Secretary of State Warren Christopher, if the fires of contemporary nationalism continue to burn unchecked, 'we'll have 5,000 countries rather than the hundred plus we now have'.[5]

Although the Westphalian polity triumphed in its collision with tribal polities in Africa and the New World between the fifteenth and twentieth centuries, no polity remains unchallenged or unchanged forever. Old loyalties remain, sometimes dormant, that may be triggered by events like the fall of communism in Eastern Europe. It is a challenge to any polity to cope with old memories, identities, and loyalties within its domain. While it is easy to make martyrs, it is almost impossible to eradicate an old identity. In this respect the world appears a 'living museum' of identities and loyalties in which some exhibits are currently on show, some are being refurbished, and still others are in cold storage. Polities survive only if they can co-opt those old memories, identities, and loyalties – those that once supported other polities – or fit them into their own ideologies.[6] Unless old authorities and ideologies are co-opted, they may haunt a new polity and later become the bases of rival political associations and faiths.

The manner in which the Westphalian polity evolved illustrates the fate of all polities. Its ideology – sovereignty – grew out of a particular historical context. That polity never stood alone as an identity but from the outset prospered, both as an idea and as a fact, to the extent it incorporated other identities. Some of these identities have remained actual and potential challengers to the present day.

The Westphalian State and the Challenge of Nationalism

Medieval conceptions of legitimacy rested on an assumption of the unity of Christendom, and monarchs seeking to extend their authority beyond their family holdings looked to the Catholic Church and/or Holy Roman Emperor to establish a divine right to rule. Legitimate rule proceeded only from God, though God's earthly intermediaries had to ratify the grant. The technical problem was that some saw the pope, and others the emperor, as God's certifying agent, but one or the other could usually be found to give the blessing, normally in exchange for a supplicant king's pledge of support in the Church–Empire rivalry.

The Westphalian polity emerged gradually, as divine-right monarchy in the early modern period merged with a concept of 'sovereignty' that reflected the influence of Bodin and Hobbes. Monarchs claimed authority to rule over a territory that included and extended beyond their own holdings. The authority of Church and Empire waned with the consolidation of local polities, and the stirrings of secular humanism in the Renaissance also undermined the influence of the Church. Henry VIII and Cardinals Richelieu and Mazarin sought to capture what remained of Church authority and link it to the monarchy, thus providing ideological glue for a new state polity.

Although even the most absolute of divine-right monarchs was never fully autonomous, kings consolidated their positions enough to give sovereign claims some substance. They extended their territory and acquired standing military forces, significant internal police capabilities, extensive bureaucracies, and growing tax revenues. Historical sociologists stress the role of continual warfare in consolidating the power of early modern kings. Historian McNeill also observes that the Hundred Years' War (1337–1453) 'disentangled the French and English kingdoms from one another geographically [and] endowed the French king with a standing army and a tax system capable of supporting an armed force that was clearly superior to any and all domestic rivals in peacetime'. 'Challenges to royal absolutism did not disappear until after a final flare-up in the seventeenth century.' Nevertheless, 'armed rebellion was decisively defeated in France with the suppression of the Fronde (1633); whereas in England, where absolutism had never taken firm root, a remarkably flexible parliamentary sovereignty emerged from the Civil Wars and Glorious Revolution of 1688' (McNeill 1986: 39).

Nascent national consciousness enhanced the authority of early kings, and their consolidating activities, in turn, lent greater credibility to the sovereign state. Moreover, for all the significance of the establishment of national churches, the theoretical justification for sovereignty became increasingly secular; for example, Hobbes's claim that the only alternative to a single source of absolute power was chaos. In addition, early writers on international law, such as Grotius and de Vattel, added an external dimension to sovereignty by positing the existence of a system of independent states that were not obliged to recognize any higher authority.

According to McNeill:

> what mattered for the later rise of nationalism was the pattern of town and rural life in France and England, where sufficient homogeneity between urban populations and the surrounding countryside was sustained between the eleventh and seventeenth centuries to make an extension of the ancient civic ideal of citizenship to the kingdom as a whole seem conceivable by the mid-eighteenth century.

Not that anything like homogeneity was ever achieved. In France, writes McNeill (1986: 38):

> Apart from German-speakers in Alsace-Lorraine, and Celtic speakers in Brittany, the gap between Langue d'oc and Langue d'oïl divided peasant France into significantly different communities. Indeed, one may argue that the incandescent quality of revolutionary propaganda in the crisis of 1793–94 was partly a deliberate effort to override such local divergences by insisting on the sacredness of the republic, one and indivisible.

Nonetheless, the French Revolution, following the birth of the American republic, had a major impact on notions of the relationship between nation and state. Tamir (1993: 60) argues that the 'false identification' of nation with state 'reflects the historical processes that accompanied the emergence of the modern nation-state'.

The belief that the state should be the 'institutional representation of the people's will' formed the basis of the American and French revolutions, marking a substantial shift in the type of legitimacy sought by political institutions from justifications based on divine or dynastic right to justifications grounded in popular voluntary consent.

The legacies of American and French revolutionaries in this regard were distinct and not necessarily compatible. The new America was a republic but had to weave a separate ethnos out of almost whole political cloth.

Except for being colonials, most white Americans had cultural roots in the former metropole. In later years, of course, the United States attracted immigrants of so many ethnicities that the only possible 'American' ethnos was one based on myths of individual liberty and democratic citizenship. The American experience points up the fact that democracy is a brilliant ideological invention, not least because it does not demand that citizens give up their ethnic, religious, or other loyalties, unless those threaten the democratic process itself. It is significant, for example, that rioting blacks in urban ghettos demand not a separate state, but a share of the pie promised by their status as Americans. Nevertheless, like any polity, a democracy must demonstrate a capacity to meet demands, and failure to do so invites the (re)surfacing of competing identities.

By contrast, the model advanced by the French Revolution was based on ethnos. 'Whereas in America the new state had created a nation, the French Third Estate, in its search for an autonomous source of political legitimation independent from that of the old royalist regime, "invented" a nation, presented itself as its true representative, and demanded the right to self-rule' (Tamir 1993: 61). Napoleon convinced the French that they should support him – not because he was a divine-right aristocrat, but because he was French, and they were French, and emperor and people together could do glorious things.

As Bismarck was to demonstrate, when state becomes entangled with ethnos, it may be only a short step to Hegel's romantic view of the state as a moral idea, the highest realization of self, to a side connection with Social Darwinism's survival of the fittest and Treitschke's ecstatic hymns of praise for the race. In this fashion, national identity – expressed through democratic or authoritarian political institutions – legitimated a state polity that could no longer rely on the pope's blessing. Ironically, it was Napoleon's spectacular effort 'to build a transnational empire on the strength of an aroused and mobilized French nation' that 'assured the idea and practice of the ethnically unitary nation-state of rather more than a century of florescence' (McNeill 1986: 52). European rivalries fueled by that idea only ran out of steam about 1945, after two world wars. Meanwhile, Woodrow Wilson (influenced by John Stuart Mill) had given the national idea a new currency by advancing the principle of 'national self-determination'. The twist was dangerous, especially because no one, including Wilson, could offer a consensual definition of 'nation', thereby inviting any dissident group to claim nationhood and demand its own state. The Versailles conferees tried to limit the principle to the Hapsburg and Ottoman empires, which, because of their polyglot character, were the worst places to start. The result set the stage for World War II and is echoed in current Balkan conflicts. The self-determination principle was also enshrined in the UN Charter, where it was invoked after 1945 in support of Third World independence movements. Decolonization proceeded despite the fact that the only unity in evidence in some cases was that imposed by arbitrary colonial boundaries. Now the self-determination principle lies like a ticking bomb, waiting for the next round of ethnic claimants.

Wilson's 'nation' was not the only challenger to the Westphalian polity. Another was the idea of 'class', as proclaimed by Marx and Engels and, later, Lenin and Trotsky. In their eyes, the state was an instrument of class domination, and when the proletariat seized the levers of power, it would wither away. Although the Soviet state only recently withered (for reasons unforeseen by Marxists), the 1917 Revolution saved the Russian Empire from the fate of the Hapsburgs by substituting class – the dictatorship of the proletariat – for a Westphalian-state Tsar.

The popularity and durability of the ideology of the Westphalian polity, ironically, owes much to European imperialism. There is a parallel here to McNeill's observation about Napoleon's campaigns and the growing popularity in the early nineteenth century of the ethnos model of identity. Later in that century, statist ideology followed the conquering flags of the Europeans. When the sun finally set on those empires in the mid-twentieth century, a host of new states appeared with the former colonial boundaries. They were sovereign entities like the European metropoles, but different from them in almost every other respect.

The Pressures of Change: Past and Present

The apparent contradiction between the expanding functions of the European Union (EU) and the centrifugal pressures of separatists like the Corsicans in Europe – the home of the Westphalian polity – illustrates the continuous and simultaneous pressure on polities to grow and fracture. An efficient solution is to create polities that can 'specialize' in meeting specific human needs and encourage citizens to divide their loyalties for particular purposes. It may make sense to look to large specialized polities to achieve economic efficiency while nourishing local loyalties to provide psychological satisfaction. Unfortunately, it is difficult to maintain those 'rational' boundaries, so different polities tend to collide.

The Westphalian polity is much admired because it seemed to be a successful multifunctional experiment – large enough to satisfy values requiring economies of scale, but small enough to satisfy values that demand intimacy. In fact, the Westphalian model, as noted earlier, was an ideal type that was linked to the success of only a few polities in creating a viable 'national' identity and institutions. Nearly everyone thinks of England and France, though France fleshed out its present boundaries only late in the nineteenth century and the United Kingdom still has problems with its Celtic fringe. But why should England and France be considered 'typical' when in fact most of Europe's states have always had to find ways to cope with dangerous identity fault lines? Flemish and French quarrel in tiny Belgium. Renewed constitutional invention may be needed there, as in Spain, which granted autonomy to various regions including Adains, Catalonia, and the Basque region.

Relatively late bloomers like Germany and Italy also have a claim to being considered 'typical'. Germany, like Italy, was forged in the late nineteenth century with Prussian power and Bismarck's *zollverein* providing the core. Nevertheless, the Holy Roman Empire model and spread of the German language and culture seriously complicated the problem of identifying 'natural' German boundaries. Italy, on the other hand, only *appeared* to create a viable state. Local and regional loyalties remained primary; some of the most dynamic sectors of the economy have never been integrated – or documented and taxed – and the Mafia established itself as the most effective authority in southern Italy and Sicily. And today, as the government wages inconclusive war on organized crime, the separatist Lombard League has emerged as a significant political force in the prosperous north.

The Westphalian polity prospered in Europe, but not in isolation. From 1945 until recently, Europe's security – the hallmark of sovereignty – has been bound up in NATO, and Cold War bipolarity kept the lid on change. Events in Yugoslavia and Brussels suggest that the fission and fusion of polities has not ceased, even in the cradle of state-centric mythology. The European Union has gradually extended its authority over matters historically regarded as within the exclusive preserve of states. Despite posturing in some quarters about loss of sovereignty, preserving 'national security' in traditional fashion is inconceivable without cooperation and institution-building – within the region and across the Atlantic. Although each step toward integration in Europe has preserved the legal nicety of countries 'voluntarily' surrendering sovereign rights, the fact is that borders have gradually diminished in significance and decisions are made in an EU context that used to be made only by national decision-makers.

None of this means that the Westphalian polity is disappearing. Instead, it is evolving into something different alongside new polities. As Peters and Peters explain, there are 'at least three large games being played' in Europe today. One is a 'coping with interdependence' game in which governments seek 'to extract as much as possible from the EC, while relinquishing as little ... as possible'. Another involves competition among European institutions themselves. The third is a bureaucratic game 'that is apparently becoming an important subtext for everything else happening within the EC'. Twenty-three directorates-general develop 'their own organizational cultures and approaches to policy', compete for 'policy space', and attempt to establish 'their own working relationships ... with relevant elements of national governments'. Peters and Peters (1992:107–07, 107n) add: 'There may also be still other games being played simultaneously, including those involving interest groups.' 'Firms, for example, may believe that they would find a less restrictive regulatory environment if the Community had greater control of environmental policy.' As with other polities, the future of 'Europe' rests on establishing authority in a particular domain, supported by identity and ideology. Whether Westphalian polities will become nested in the future remains to be seen.

The end of the Cold War, the reunification of Germany, the emancipation of countries in the East, and the crises over the ERM, and ratification of the Maastricht Treaty raise new questions about the relationship of states, the EU, and smaller ethnic polities. What ideological basis should be invoked to legitimize the outcomes of political bargaining on these questions? 'Federalism' has uncomfortable Anglo-Saxon overtones and seems to suggest a 'United States of Europe'. 'Confederation' implies little more than loose political association. 'Subsidiarity' – the idea that control should be exercised at the lowest possible level – has a Catholic and Continental ring to it. On the other hand, subsidiarity is attractive in theory to the British and others who seek a decentralized EU, but it is not clear how the principle might apply in practice. How are Member States to decide what the appropriate level for control actually is? Finally, 'consociationalism' draws on the experience of divided democratic polities like those of Switzerland and Holland, which preserve the segmental autonomy of internal minorities by demanding consensus if major changes in common tasks and decision-making are to be made. Like subsidiarity, consociationalism might reassure those who are dubious about the common EU enterprise, but the formula is close to the long-standing EU arrangement whereby each member has an effective veto.

In the end, no Westphalian polity exercises the degree of autonomy and control that sovereignty implies, and only a few even put on an impressive show. Far from possessing a Weberian monopoly of legitimate violence, states – especially but not exclusively in areas of the Third World – often are unable to preserve a modicum of domestic tranquility because governments themselves lack legitimacy. They are routinely challenged by malaise and insubordination, as well as by street demonstrations, corporate power, rural guerrillas, urban terrorism, ethnic conflict, religious fanaticism, party strife, drug cartels, and warlord gangs. All illustrate the collision of loyalties based on interest and sentiment.

The challenges to the Westphalian polity are also intensifying with an increase of 'turbulence' in global politics. The rising capabilities of citizens and a tendency to subgroupism are interacting in unpredictable ways. More and more persons and groups are travelling, negotiating business deals, transporting goods, offering services, moving money, listening to mass media, telephoning, sending faxes, and sharing electronic data – and ideas. Sovereign boundaries in these respects are not so much being altered as ignored or transcended. The developments that overarch states also have an impact within them. They promote democracy and capitalism, and a resurgence of ethnic identity. Ironically, largeness has helped foster smallness; sovereignty-eroding economic and political interdependence have encouraged fragmentation. Self-determination seems more than ever within reach, partly because others are demanding it, but also because of the EU and the NAFTA; the revitalization of international organizations; and the resources of transnational corporations, banks, and other institutions of global capitalism. French-Canadian separatists, Baltic republics, Croatians, and others do not have to go it alone; they have other potential relationships to replace those they choose to end.

Security in a Post-Cold-War World

The end of the Cold War and the broadening of the concept of security to include economics, environment, and ethnicity have made it easier for advocates of expansive and contractive polities to make their cases openly and persuasively, to reawaken old identities and compete successfully for human loyalties. Whatever the taboo regarding the alteration of sovereign boundaries, in fact they have lately been radically rearranged *from the inside* in the former Soviet Union and Yugoslavia. With ethnic conflict simmering in Central Europe and many parts of the Third World, one wonders what claims for self-determination will be advanced next. Will there be external intervention, especially by neighbours claiming kinship? At the very least, there will have to be new forms of autonomy invented for pockets of ethnicity. Then, when the smoke has cleared, there will be a need for new formulas to knit the pieces back together into larger polities for functional ends. This returns us to the units to be ordered, and here the going gets difficult. Certainly, the primacy of economic issues opens up a broad field of polities and interacting polities that, until recently, political scientists have been pleased to leave to analysts in management schools.

The real world of politics has always been one of layered, overlapping, and interacting polities. Our task as theorists is to explain that most defining characteristic of politics: the manner in which individuals come together (or are brought together) to behave collectively. We need to understand the sources and consequences of political change – the processes by which polities emerge, evolve, expire, and are sometimes resurrected. As we have emphasized, there are always trends toward larger political groupings along with the fracturing of existing polities. The Westphalian ideal seems remote from the solutions that must be found to accommodate contemporary mininationalisms or issues of global scope. It seems destined to remain a reassuring symbol, rather like the British monarchy before the latest scandals, while what is most important takes place among other polities in a variety of arenas. New polity forms are being born, even as others persist. This sort of thing has happened many times before, and it will not cease simply because Hegel, Fukayama, or someone else declares history to have ended.

Part IV

Toward a Post-international World

9 Beyond International Relations to Global Politics

Overlapping political space, shifting boundaries, and revised authority structures (2008)

Multiple identities, new technologies, the proliferation of new groups and institutions, the porosity of sovereign-state boundaries, and the increasingly diffuse nature of threats to survival and well-being all conspire to diminish the role of territoriality – geographic space and authority over that space – in world affairs. There is a growing gap between the distribution of effective authority and governance in global politics and the map of a world divided into exclusive territorial boxes.

Not for nothing has the word 'deterritorialization' begun to appear more often in scholarly and popular literature. However, like the word 'globalisation', it can be misleading, and thus it is well for us to be specific and upfront in this essay about what we are *not* saying. We are not saying that territory, geography, or the legal borders of sovereign states have suddenly become irrelevant. Geographical location and topography still provide opportunities and constraints. Some territory, not least one's home or homeland, can often be the object(s) of intense emotional attachment. Moreover, all human behaviour – even Internet access to cyberspace – happens in physical space, and even identities like perceived race or ethnicity have territorial referents (where others of one's kind are situated). Companies have their markets, religions their faithful, sports fans a hallowed stadium, and so on. Financial districts in global cities continue to exist partly because of a need for face-to-face networking and negotiations. Anyone who has stood in a long line at an airport waiting to show a passport knows that state borders continue to matter.

What we *are* saying is that such traditional legal borders are of decreasing significance because they are often transcended or incongruent with actual patterns of identities and authority in an increasingly globalizing world that is simultaneously buffeted by powerful forces of fission and fusion. Traditional governments are experiencing an acute crisis of legitimacy. Citizens perceive that too many of their leaders are hopelessly confused by the turbulent course of events and unable to deliver on their promises. Governments may be 'adapting' to the challenges of globalisation – as suggested by some analysts who are more sanguine than we about the future of the state – but the crisis of confidence seems to be widespread and endemic.

Meanwhile, the political vacuum is being filled, albeit inadequately and sometimes chaotically, by a host of nonstate actors. In this context, 'political space' offers a much more useful characterization of global politics than the customary nation-state map. The structure of political space or boundaries, including (but not limited to) sovereign ones, are the 'domains' of polities, that is the range of persons, resources, and issues over which polities enjoy effective influence or control and which underpin their claims to be moral communities. Put another way, the map reflects *the ways in which identities and loyalties among adherents to various polities are distributed and related.*

The Interstate System Besieged

Territoriality is only one principle for organizing political space. There have and continue to exist rival principles of political organization, for example kinship in the case of clan and tribal polities, and religion for theocratic polities. Unlike nation-states, which have claimed a monopoly on citizens' political identities and loyalties for several centuries, today's proliferating non-territorial polities are characterized by overlapping political space. That is a feature that may promote and intensify identity conflicts on certain issues, but, owing to potentially cross-cutting identities, may mediate and reduce conflict with respect to others.

Contemporary global politics is witnessing the growing detachment of authority from its territorial moorings. A series of accelerating trends are diminishing the significance of territory, reducing the relevance of distance in global politics, and altering the essential nature of political space. The dramatic events of 11 September 2001 ('9/11') brought home not only the realization that even the wide oceans no longer afford the United States protection from military threats, but also the fact that the status and role of sovereign territorial states as an elite set of polities is being challenged as at no time since the seventeenth century. Just as geography did not protect American citizens from apocalyptic terrorism, the *absence* of a territorial focus on the part of Islamic jihadists has seriously complicated America's War on Terror.

Although the attacks of 9/11 were directed against architectural icons of US economic power and the global economy, Al Qaeda, with its professed aim of recreating the medieval Caliphate, also implicitly threw down the gauntlet at the territorially-grounded state system. Part of the challenge of militant Islam is to the global authority structure based on the legitimacy afforded by sovereignty or, as James Caporaso expresses it, 'the ideological justification for ultimate control within a specific territory' (2000: 1). Recognizing that 'the state system has been eroding', former US Secretary of State George P. Shultz further characterized the threat posed by Al Qaeda as that of 'an extensive, internationally connected ideological movement dedicated to the destruction of our international system of cooperation and progress'.

The response in his view: 'First and foremost, we must shore up the state system' (Shultz 2004). We cannot but be reminded of King Canute commanding the invading waters to recede.

Paradoxically, the interstate system itself emerged from a lengthy period of religious violence in Europe. In their insightful and provocative analysis of the meaning of the Westphalian settlement, David L. Blaney and Naeem Inayatullah argue that the endorsement of sovereignty was a bold effort to localize the religious cleavages that had rent Europe *within* what Michael Mann calls the 'caged societies'(1986: 40) of states. Blaney and Inayatullah contend that 'the differences constituting each state as a particular political community are kept and managed within the boundaries of the state. This demarcation and policing of the boundary between the "inside" and "outside" of the political community defines the problem of difference as *between and among* states as *international* difference' (2000: 44–45). European-wide religious differences were mitigated by dividing the world into bounded political communities that would no longer confront one another across an unbridgeable ideological divide. 'A system of sovereign states', write Blaney and Inayatullah, 'appears, then, as an opportunity to separate and contain difference, to make possible a *modus vivendi* among externalized differences that works to secure internal sameness' (2000: 54).

Islamic militants seek to reproduce a pre-modern world that existed before Westphalian sovereigns more or less successfully snuffed out religious conflict. They labour to replicate the sort of violent, borderless, identity collision that marked the Thirty Years' War, although now with Islam as the main protagonist. Ironically, though vehemently opposed to the cultural consequences of globalisation, Islamic militants are the unwitting allies of globalisers who are eroding the capacity of states in numerous other ways.

The medieval Caliphate, like Al Qaeda itself, was based less on residence in a bounded territory than on Arabic and nomadic tribal traditions and norms that antedated Islam. From this perspective, there is no place for notions of sovereign equality, non-intervention, or a society of states with exclusive jurisdictions. As Islam originally evolved, government was subordinate to religion, and there could be no acceptance of any limits to the expansion of the Islamic 'community'. In Europe, by contrast, '[t]he merging of the state with a clearly bounded territory is', as Agnew and Corbridge (1995: 80) argue, 'the geographic essence of the field of international relations.' 'Even that body of work which takes "geography" seriously,' they continue, ' . . . usually sees geography as a body of fixed facts setting the environment for the actions of territorial states that are essentially the same today as 200 years ago and as much so in Africa as in Europe.'

This difference between the two perspectives is no mere historical curiosity, but a collision of entirely different basic organizing principles. Michael Barnett captures this collision when describing the Ottoman Empire, the Turkish heir to the Caliphate. 'Until the late nineteenth century, inhabitants of the Fertile Crescent existed within a variety of overlapping authorities and political structures. The Ottoman Empire, Islam, and local tribal and village structures all contested for and held sway over various features of peoples' lives.' It was 'great power intrusions' that:

> primarily were responsible for setting into motion the statist forces that created a disjuncture between where political authority was to reside and the political loyalties of the inhabitants of the region. Specifically, while the great powers established a new geopolitical map, the political loyalties of the inhabitants enveloped these boundaries and challenged the very legitimacy of that map. (Barnett 1995: 492).

Many Kurds under Turkish legal jurisdiction reject it to the present day.

It was the nature of the challenge to the very legitimacy of the interstate map – to the supremacy of territorial states, their exclusive right to use force legitimately, and the legal imprimatur of sovereignty that is rooted in defined and hard territorial boundaries –that explains the widespread support offered to the United States by other states after 9/11, as well as America's extraterritorial response to that challenge. Al Qaeda's rejection of, and contempt for, the basic norms on which interstate relations is based explains the willingness of many states to align themselves against the threat of non-territorial terrorists.[1] At the same time, it was precisely the George W. Bush administration's militant unilateralism especially with regard to Iraq – so out of step with a world that has now become unaccustomed to such a degree of sovereign hubris – that cost him even more widespread support and reduced the 'coalition of the willing' to a rather pitiful few.

Events such as 9/11 defy Kenneth Boulding's classic formulation that 'each nation's strength declines as it moves away from its home base' (1962: 230). For much of the history of global politics, Boulding's 'loss-of-strength gradient' fairly represented the relationship between distance and declining influence and authority. However, it is of diminishing relevance to contemporary global politics. Two reasons account for this: (1) The growing capacity of sovereign and non-sovereign actors to project influence and authority over vast distances, and (2) the proliferation of non-territorial polities with non-geographic boundaries.

Technology has literally shrunk distances, enabling the rapid and large-scale movement across national borders of persons, things, and ideas that collectively constitute globalisation. It is ironic, as van Creveld points out, that technology 'which between 1500 and 1945, was such a great help in constructing the state, has turned around and is often causing states to lose power in favor of various kinds of organizations which are either not territorially based, or lacking in sovereignty, or both' (1999: 337). Between the seventeenth and nineteenth centuries, technological innovations helped to institutionalize territorial states, secure their autonomy, and spread the legitimizing principle of sovereignty. Such was the case *until* the appearance of technologies that functioned best as networked systems – railways, telegraphs, and telephones – for which national frontiers were irrational impediments (van Creveld 1999: 378). Today, the microelectronic revolution is producing a step-level change in global politics by widening the gap between *territorial* and *political space*. While it may have been the case that, as Ruggie (1993: 143–4) argues, the 'central attribute of modernity in international politics has been a peculiar and historically unique configuration of territorial space', that 'historically unique configuration' is passing into history.

The relationship between the microelectronic revolution and the role of territory is controversial. Although technology can be used to reinforce state power, in many ways technological developments are undermining territoriality in global politics. Some of these developments, especially the Internet, contribute simultaneously to globalisation and localisation, and pose a severe management problem for states (Loader 1997: 9). Those like Paul Frissen who argue that the Internet reduces the role of territory contend that with 'distributed and relational databases it no longer matters where an organization or an administrative layer is located' and that the 'trend towards "deterritorialisation" produced by ICTs [information and communications technologies] ... undermines the legitimacy of a political system which is territory-bound' (Frissen 1997: 114–15). Others agree with Martin Dodge that 'the idea that the Internet liberates you from geography is a myth' (cited in 'Putting It in Its Place' 2001: 18). Dodge points out that the fibre-optic cables, 'server-farms', reliable electricity to run e-businesses, and a nearby telephone exchange that are necessary for a high-speed digital-subscriber line connection to work require a territorial location that is vulnerable to attack. To some extent, of course, both are correct.

The Medieval Alternative

At this juncture, additional historical perspective may be useful. The inter-state system that has been presumed to dominate global politics since Westphalia was imposed by Europeans and built on territory. International relations was a game played in two dimensions, built on what ethnologist Jonathan Boyarin calls 'close genealogical links between the "Cartesian coordinates" of space and time and the discrete, sovereign state, both associated with European society since the Renaissance' (Boyarin 1994: 4). Territory was the source of a sovereign's wealth, status, and power. More territory meant a larger population for the army, more land for crops and grazing, more taxes for military expenditures, and a larger home market to be protected and exploited by mercantilist policies. Most important, more territory afforded greater security from foreign invasion.

During Europe's dynastic era when public and private interests merged and sovereignty inhered in a ruler, territory was a mark of dynastic as well as national prestige and continuity. Following the Augsburg and Westphalian settlements, territory replaced religion as the basis of political legitimacy and as the mark of sovereign authority. Only sovereign actors could play the game of global politics, and territory defined sovereignty. Sovereign authority was based on a state's *exclusive* control of its territory and of those inhabiting that territory. The interstate world was divided into exclusive territorial holdings with 'mutually agreed upon spatial parameters, that is, borders' (Spruyt 1994: 17) that enclosed them.

However, a system based on exclusive authority over territory was neither historically necessary nor inevitable. Europe's Middle Ages provided an obvious alternative to interstate territoriality and the dominance of a single authority to make rules. Instead, medieval Europe consisted of a multiplicity of authorities that shared territorial space and claimed the right to make rules or share in their making for particular spheres of activity. That world, as described by John Ruggie (1983: 275), was:

> [a] 'system of segmented territorial rule', having 'none of the connotations of possessiveness and exclusiveness conveyed by the modern concept of sovereignty ... a heteronomous organization of territorial rights and claims – of political space'. Unlike the interstate world that later emerged, the medieval world was 'a patchwork of overlapping and incomplete rights of government', which were 'inextricably superimposed and tangled', and in which 'different juridical instances were geographically interwoven and stratified, and plural allegiances, asymmetrical suzerainties and anomalous enclaves abounded'.

Like the emerging global system, the medieval world was home to a wide variety of polity types. Within the Holy Roman Empire, even after 1648, there were, according to Krasner, at least four additional types of polities – 'ecclesiastical states, imperial cities, estates of imperial counts and knights, and secular states' (Krasner 1993: 247). Lacking a fully territorial conception of space, Europe's feudal system, like African and North American tribal polities, was, as Spruyt (1994: 40) argues, 'rule over people rather than land'. This is also the case with contemporary sources of authority ranging from Muslim *mullahs* to international regimes and the boards of transnational corporations (TNCs).

The similarity between medieval Europe and governance in contemporary global politics today makes it fashionable to suggest that we are experiencing a sort of 'new medievalism'. All five trends that Hedley Bull (1977: 264–76) identified as harbingers of a 'new medievalism' – regional integration of states, disintegration of states, the restoration of private international violence, the emergence of transnational organizations, and the technological unification of the world – are visible. More recently, Stephen Kobrin (1998: 369, 366) has argued persuasively that the declining relevance of 'the idea of geography as a basis for the organization of politics and economics' is one of several changes in global political economy that auger such a new medievalism.[2] The other changes he mentions are equally compelling divergences from interstate politics: 'space, geography and borders', 'the ambiguity of authority', 'multiple loyalties', 'transnational elites', 'distinctions between public and private property', and 'unifying belief systems and supranational centralization'. Although we ourselves continue to regard the concept of a new medievalism as regrettably Eurocentric, because it seems to ignore the rest of world history that did not lead to the exceptional era that constituted the European state system, we do accept the thrust of the argument.

Ruggie (1983: 274, 276)[3] maintains that an interstate system only became possible when the 'rediscovery from Roman law of the concept of absolute private property[4] and the simultaneous emergence of mutually exclusive territorial state formations, which stood in relation to one another much as owners of private estates do' produced 'a "legitimation crisis" of staggering proportions'. Like medieval Europe, today's world provides, as Krasner (1993: 253) says of the era during which the Westphalian state took shape, 'a political and geographic space within which a new political form' can emerge. Forms (plural) is a better way of expressing it, and in some cases it is also not so much a matter of emerging as reappearing. Thus our own description of a contemporary world where 'future shock' meets 'history's revenge.'

Just as the medieval system of competing loyalties and authorities collapsed under the weight of a legitimation crisis, so today's interstate system is confronted by what Rosenau calls a 'turbulent environment' (1990: 59) and 'a *world crisis of authority*' (1984: 246). The situation is bad enough among established and relatively prosperous states. The crisis is far worse in the developing world, where there is a divorce of nation and state, and spreading state-failure. An optimism of post-colonial nation-building has surrendered to the pessimism of disunity in the name of tribalism and ethnicity. Spreading disease, cynical misrule and rampant corruption, environmental catastrophe, and endemic but savage – and sometimes genocidal – violence are all features of failed and failing states. Such states lack at least three of the four elements of sovereignty identified by Krasner – effective control over its territory, capability to control borders, and exclusion of external actors 'from domestic authority configurations' (1999: 9). Thoroughly penetrated from without and lacking in even limited autonomy, all that remains is 'international legal sovereignty'.

The Declining Role of Territory in a Globalizing Economy

The interstate system with its territorial foundation accounts for progressively less of what is important in contemporary global politics. 'The absolutes of the Westphalian system – territorially fixed states where everything of value lies within some state's borders; a single secular authority governing each territory and representing it outside its borders; and no authority above states', as Jessica Mathews observes (1997: 50), 'are all dissolving.' Nowhere has this been truer than with respect to the global economy.

In this realm, the role of territory began to decline during the industrial revolution when capital and labour became more important in determining productivity and wealth. The declining importance of land as a source of wealth, except in the realm of natural resources, has accelerated in recent decades. 'Traders do not need to come to market any more because computer networks can take markets to traders, wherever they are', and 'American exchanges, such as Nasdaq, cannot be said to be based anywhere in particular. Nor can its new online brokers, such as E*Trade, whose services are directly available through any computer hooked up to the Internet' ('Capitals of Capital' 1998: 3, 5). The growing impact of transnational enterprises, microelectronic technologies, direct and indirect investment, and knowledge industries in wealth creation further diminishes the role of land in global economics, affording city-polities like Singapore and Hong Kong an importance not enjoyed since the Westphalian polities of Europe eclipsed the skill-centres of Italy's city-states.

Today, only one of ten largest states in terms of land area (the United States) ranks among the ten wealthiest nation-states as measured by per capita GNP (World Bank 2003: Table 1, 252–3). And today's 'global cities', like Italy's Renaissance cities were, are centres of global economic activity, financial skill, and wealth, linked increasingly to one another more tightly than to their own hinterlands. They are, as Saskia Sassen suggests, global centres tied together through a financial chain of production (Sassen 1994: 42–57), and the operations they host represent an 'embedding' of the 'global' in the 'national' (Sassen 1999a). Globalisation, she argues, 'is a reality' in global finance, especially in the relationship among 'the "big three" – London, New York, and Tokyo' (Sassen 1999b: 81). Thus, '[b]y the end of 1997, 25 cities controlled 83 percent of the world's equities under institutional management and accounted for roughly half of global market capitalization' (Sassen 1999b: 77).

For their part, non-territorial transnational corporations exercise immense economic clout. The combined sales of the world's 200 largest corporations account for over a quarter of global economic activity, and the value of their sales exceeds the *combined* gross national income of 182 of the world's 201 countries. These corporations have sales valued at almost twice those of the poorest four-fifths of the world's population (US$7.1 trillion to US$3.9 trillion), and one-third of world trade is conducted among units within corporations (Anderson and Cavanaugh 2000). As of 2004, fourteen corporations ranked among the world's 50 largest economic entities The value of Wal-Mart stores' sales for the year 2004 alone was greater than the gross national income of all but 17 countries or almost the equivalent of the gross national income of all of sub-Saharan Africa.[5]

Overall, the spreading authority of private firms has muddied the traditional distinction, albeit always tenuous, between 'public' and 'private' economic actors and issues. The editors of a volume on this topic argue that 'firms may draw more heavily on the capacities of the state in constructing private authority, or the state may delegate or confer authority', and that 'the emergence of private authority where none existed previously ... may involve a displacement of public authority and public institutions by private authority and private institutions' (Cutler, Haufler, and Porter 1999b: 335). Without question, part of the process involved in many states 'adapting' to globalisation has been to bow to the insistence of private economic actors that there must be changes in national legal systems and, in some instances, even more government regulation to serve their need for protection and competitiveness. One might well ask, in this relationship, whether the private tail is wagging the state dog?

Global and regional patterns of trade, investment, and financial speculation transcend sovereign boundaries and substantially ignore geographic distance. The globalisation of trade and financial markets has been made possible by the information revolution, and this globalisation reflects the contradiction between what Friedrich Kratochwil (1986: 42) calls 'the universal recognition of territorial sovereignty' and 'the erosion of boundaries through the increasing interdependencies of modern economic life'. Modern telecommunications permit instantaneous movement of financial data and trillions upon trillions of money – many times the amounts needed to support trade in actual goods – around the world. Electronic cash, for example, which does away with the need to move funds physically across national boundaries, poses problems for governments because of the 'disconnect between electronic markets and political geography' (Kobrin 1997: 75). These systems provide corporate executives with a means of communicating instructions to employees wherever they may be, and allow producers and service providers to generate advertising tailored to meet local tastes. Many major firms continue to reflect their national origins, but most analysts agree that genuinely global strategies and business cultures are steadily building.

In these ways, financial institutions and markets have been revolutionized and globalised by computers, microchips, and earth-orbiting satellites to the point where, as Miles Kahler (1995: xv) observes, '[c]ross-border economic integration and national political sovereignty have increasingly come into conflict, leading to a growing mismatch between the economic and political structures of the world. The effective domains of economic markets have come to coincide less and less with national governmental jurisdictions.' Global markets reflect, as David Held (1995: 127) argues, 'a clear disjuncture between the formal authority of the state and the spatial reach of contemporary systems of production, distribution and exchange which often function to limit the competence and effectiveness of national political authorities.'

When all is said and done, the boundaries of today's markets and states are less compatible than at any time since Westphalia, although some huge internal markets, like that of the United States, still account for more actual economic activity than foreign ones. The greater mobility and autonomy of sellers, purchasers, and the global markets they produce contribute to undermining the capacity of states to control their own economic fortunes.

Strange concludes from this that we are witnessing the 'retreat of the state' in which states have 'surrendered' to the very markets that they originally created. For Strange 'the reality of state authority is not the same as it once was' (Strange 1996: 84). Among the areas of traditional state responsibility in which state authority is ebbing, she cites maintaining the value of the currency, choosing the type of capitalism to be followed, correcting the cycle of booms and slumps, providing a social safety-net, taxation, controlling foreign trade, providing economic infrastructure, and protecting 'national champions' and monopoly privileges (Strange 1996: 73–82). Globalised capital flows, currency speculation, investment decisions, and markets dramatically complicate (and sometimes even dissolve) state capacity to set macroeconomic policy for citizens. National trade policies are routinely undermined by massive intra- and inter-firm trade, monetary policy by investment flows, corporate investment decision, corporate outsourcing, and offshore and joint ventures.

Asia's economic crisis at the end of the 1990s, like the financial contagion brought on by US problems with sub-prime mortgages in 2007, showed that in an interdependent world when financial instability shakes one country, tremors may spread outward like ripples in a pond regardless of geography. Neither physical location nor distance matters much. The resulting turmoil may be contagious, as speculators try to take advantage of currency fluctuations and withdraw funds not only from the country at risk but from others that are seen to have similar problems. This contagion effect – called the 'Tequila Effect' (Hausmann 1997: 54) – had been apparent as early as Mexico's 1994 economic crisis, and it reappeared as Southeast Asia's financial woes spread northward to currency and stock markets in South Korea and Hong Kong. The contagion then attacked Russia and leapfrogged all the way to Brazil.

Writing of the Mexican crisis, Moisés Naím described an economic world in which conventional geography played no role and in which the idea of a 'neighbourhood' assumed a new meaning. Financial markets, argued Naím:

> tend to cluster those countries perceived to be in the same 'neighborhood' and to treat them roughly along the same lines. This time, however, the neighborhood is no longer defined solely in terms of geography. The main defining criterion is the potential volatility of the countries; the contagion spread inside risk-clusters, or volatility neighborhoods. (Naím 1995: 125)

And when the 'volatility neighbourhood' is extensive, as it was in 1997–98, the entire global economic system may be at risk.

The Deterritorialization of Violence

For much of the past three centuries, wars have been waged over territory. However, the role of territory in war has ebbed in two principal ways. The first involves the declining ability of countries to invade and occupy one another, and the second concerns the declining impediment posed by geographic distance to force projection.

Today, territorial occupation may be a source of weakness rather than strength in the face of politically conscious and mobilized masses. Whereas Europe's imperial expansion was made possible through the co-optation and manipulation of small indigenous elites, the spread of political consciousness, often a result of modern media, greatly complicates efforts at occupying foreign territory.[6] In earlier centuries, it took only a relatively few Europeans to conquer India, Algeria, and Indo-China, but no number of highly armed European soldiers would suffice to retain imperial control by the time of the late twentieth century. Russia's experience in Afghanistan and Chechnya is a metaphor for the fate of unwanted occupiers everywhere. America's experience in Afghanistan and Iraq – rapid conquest of an enemy's conventional forces followed by a costly insurrection – likewise reflects the difficulty in controlling territory in an era marked by high levels of mass political consciousness and efficacy.

The role of geography in warfare has also waned. In recent centuries, geography helped determine what was possible and probable in military affairs. Until the use of railways in the 19th century, as Herman M. Schwartz points out, 'virtually all economic, social, and political life' took place within about 20 miles of market towns, and he cites Charles Tilly's observation that in 1490 the average radius of most European polities was only 50 miles or about the distance a band of men on horse could travel in a day (Schwartz 2000: 13). As a result, during much of this period, most land warfare was, in John Keegan's words, 'a short-term and short-distance activity'.

> For that there is the simplest explanation. When a body of men join together to perform a day's task, they will need at the very least to eat once between sunrise to sunset. If the task protracts beyond a single day, and the men move from the place where they keep their food, they will have to carry their meals with them. Since all but the most primitive operations of war entail protraction and movement, warriors necessarily burden themselves with rations as well as weapons. Experience ... has established that the soldier's load cannot on average be made to exceed seventy pounds' weight of which clothes, equipment, arms and necessaries will form at least half; as a daily intake of solid food by a man doing heavy work weighs at least three pounds, it follows that a marching soldier cannot carry supplies for more than ten or eleven days ...
>
> (Keegan 1994: 301)

If horses were used, the possible distance travelled increased, but so did the burden of movement owing to the need to bring fodder.

Developments at both ends of the military spectrum have degraded the role of distance in warfare. Both high-tech warfare and terrorism have reduced the security that geographic space once afforded. Over four decades ago, John Herz (1959) presciently concluded that military technology, especially aircraft and missiles, had developed to the point where the frontiers ('territoriality' or 'hard shell') of states – originally developed to provide physical protection for subjects – no longer served this end.

And the prospect of information war or cyberwar – the stuff of dreams or nightmares, depending on one's perspective – implies conflict 'beyond' territory, prompting Colin Gray (1997–98: 53, 54) to write of 'anti-geography' and phenomena that are 'placelessly "beyond geography"'. Paradoxically, although high-tech computer-based systems generate effects across vast distances, they themselves tend to be highly centralized and, like other centralized systems, create vulnerabilities that do not afflict decentralized systems. 'Instead of using explosives to kill and destroy', declares Steven Metz (2000: 185, 187), 'the warrior of the future' may be armed 'with a laptop computer from a motel room', and '[h]acking, virus-writing, and crashing data information systems – as well as defending against enemy hackers and virus writers – may become core military skills, as important as the ability to shoot.' Future war 'may see attacks via computer viruses, worms, logic bombs, and trojan horses rather than bullets, bombs, and missiles' (Metz 2000: xiii). Cyberwar might involve the electromagnetic destruction of an enemy's command, control, communication, and radar systems, deceiving an enemy's sensors, or obtaining access to an enemy's computers.

The incidence and seriousness of cyberattacks of various kinds began to expand after 9/11. Richard Love writes:

> Coinciding with the September 11 terrorist attacks, the rate of cyber-attacks in the United States ... increased by an estimated 79 percent in the last six months of 2001. Worldwide, cyberattacks grew at an annual rate of 64 percent in the first six months of 2002, with more than 1 million suspected attempted attacks and 180,000 confirmed successful attacks. Power and energy companies were heavily targeted; 70 percent suffered severe attacks, a rate more than twice the mean of all companies.
>
> (Love 2003: 195)

These, together with technology, financial services, and media firms, averaged more than 700 attacks per company in the last six months of 2001.

Cyberwar potential is ever more available, not only to states but also to other actors ranging from individuals to small networks. Cybertechnology is cheap and accessible. 'Most of what is needed to achieve information superiority in times of war', observes Martin Libicki (1999–2000: 39), 'is now available over the counter in the global marketplace.' The relatively simple 'I Love You' virus, created and disseminated globally by a single hacker in the Philippines, caused worldwide disruption, and, in September 2003, a virus temporarily shut down all of the US immigration authorities' capacity to check passports and process visas. Even more worrying, between 2004 and 2005, an individual or a small group in Europe successfully penetrated thousands of computer systems, including government and corporate sites (Markoff and Bergman 2005).

'Cyberattacks', argues Metz (2000: xiii), 'might erode the traditional advantage large and rich states hold in armed conflict. Private entities might be able to match state armed forces.' The diffusion of information technologies may be even more dangerous than the proliferation of weapons of mass destruction. 'Even the smallest of countries', Libicki (1999–2000: 35) explains, 'can make use of a single connection, a cheap computer, and a clever hacker to disrupt or corrupt any of the world's major information systems: funds transfer, transportation control, air traffic safety, phones, electric power, oil and gas distribution, and even military system.'[7]

Even as cyberspace has collapsed distance, some of today's high-tech weapons defy limitations imposed by physical distance on force projection. For example, American planning for weapons in space – 'Common Aero Vehicles', Hypervelocity rods', and lasers – previews the virtual disappearance of geography as a military factor (Weiner 2005). Of course, distance remains important in warfare, especially as regards logistics, but it has been significantly undermined by revolutions in communication, transportation, and delivery systems. Distance and topography are less and less critical when real-time contemporary knowledge of a field of battle allows precision-guided munitions to locate and destroy a factory in the Sudan, a terrorist camp in Afghanistan, or an automobile with terrorists in Yemen from vast distances. In the 1999 Kosovo conflict, the United States dispatched B-2 stealth bombers from Missouri to strike targets deep inside Yugoslavia. In a round trip taking nearly 30 hours the bombers were able to attack dangerous high-value targets and then return to their own bases safe in the continental United States. Pilots, according to one report at the time, were 'living at home while also acting as combatants in a war in a faraway land about which their neighbors know little' (Ricks 1999: A1). Predator missiles controlled from the US heartland have also been an important local asset in the war in Iraq.

Psychological Distance

Today, geographic distance is often less crucial than psychological distance, that is, the degree of dissimilarity between cognitive and normative frameworks, empathetic capacity, or ways of looking at, assigning meaning to, and coping with the world. Simply put, psychological distance reflects the extent to which peoples share concepts and interpret the world through similar lenses. Over half a century ago, Karl Deutsch discussed psychological

distance and propinquity in his research on social and political communication. At one point, he described how:

> [the] Swiss may speak four different languages and still act as one
> people, for each of them has enough learned habits, preferences, sym-
> bols, memories, patterns of landholding and social stratification, events
> in history, and personal associations, all of which permit him to com-
> municate more effectively with other Swiss than with the speakers of his
> own language who belong to other peoples.

Deutsch cited a Swiss newspaper editor who observed that:

> I found that my German was more closely akin to the French of my
> [French-Swiss] friend than to the likewise German (*Ebensfallsdeutsch*)
> of the foreigner. ... The French-Swiss and I were using *different words
> for the same concepts*, but we understood each other. The man from
> Vienna and I were using the *same words for different concepts*, and thus
> we did not understand each other in the least.
>
> (Deutsch 1966: 97, emphasis added)

Today, psychological distance is, at best, only modestly correlated with
geographical distance. Technological change and the advent of globalised
economic and cultural systems make it possible to maintain relative intimacy even at great geographic distance. It is both the material and psychological dimensions of this condition to which Immanuel Wallerstein (1996:
88) is alluding when he argues that '[c]oreness and peripherality, being
relational, are not always geographically separated. The two kinds of activity may well coexist within the same square mile.' Indeed, 'core' and 'periphery' increasingly are found cheek to jowl in the world's major urban
centres.

Global socio-economic processes produce yawning cognitive gaps, not
only between generational and age cohorts, but also between 'modern' and
'traditional' segments of society coexisting at the same time. At any
moment, different societies or social segments are located at different historical points, with institutional forms and identities from various epochs.
Time warps abound. Just as modern cities have become islands of modernity and postmodernity, so every continent is dotted with peoples and
places living in pre-modern settings and thus 'off the grid'. And the psychological distance between pre-modernity and postmodernity is infinitely
greater than that between peoples from different cultures who are living at
the same developmental moment.

Some of the biggest gaps and, therefore, the greatest psychological distances separate modernized urban elites from traditional agrarian peasants
(many of whom are living in transition in urban shantytowns) within the
same societies. In China, for example, political and social tensions are

intensified by the presence of modernizing and entrepreneurial elites in coastal cities, such as Shanghai and Hong Kong, amidst what remains a largely agrarian country. Increasingly, psychological distance separates the ideas and norms of communist party leaders in Beijing and advocates of state control of the economy from those of neo-liberal communists to the south. In India, Dalit labourers till fields not far from the offices of Bollywood producers and Bangalore high-tech tycoons. And in Turkey, there is a growing psychological chasm between secular and urbanized 'European' Muslims in Istanbul who look westward and seek admission to the European Union, even as masses of peasants in Anatolia turn their eyes towards the Middle East and Asia and are increasingly attracted to an Islamic worldview that Mustapha Kemal rejected over eight decades earlier.

Psychological distance is as much a product of time as of space, and psychological distance can be lengthened by time alone, regardless of geography. History is accelerating in contemporary global politics. Until the late twentieth century, people could expect that the world into which they were born would remain much the same during their lives. They spent most of their lives within the immediate vicinity in which they were born and raised, and the rhythm of their lives was predictable and measured. The world of children, including even the likelihood of traumatic events, resembled that of parents and grandparents. Generation 'gaps', if they existed at all, were limited. Today, in contrast, the lengthening of life spans and the acceleration of change mean that newborn children can anticipate not one, but several, generation gaps in their lifetime. Such gaps represent step-level 'jumps' in psychological distance and may be a source of social cleavages. Consider the tensions emerging between young and old in 'aging' Western societies with regard to the state's responsibility to provide social insurance for the elderly.

Additionally, different demographic patterns, combined with relative ease of migration across vast distances, have led to ever greater movement and mixing of persons from traditional societies with surpluses of young people located at earlier cognitive and technological epochs to and with modern societies with slowing population-growth rates, aging citizens, ballooning social security costs, and a need for unskilled labour. Such movements have already had profound consequences for Europe and North America in a variety of ways – growing social heterogeneity, cultural collisions and cultural fusion, remittances back home, 'people smuggling', political battles over immigration quotas, guest workers, and illegal migrants, and so forth.

Technology has fostered new and ingenious ways for manipulating psychological distance. The microelectronic revolution enables political entrepreneurs to mobilize and coordinate activities in cyberspace and organize transnational networks of political support. Such networks range from the multitude of NGOs that can promote issues on to the global agenda to shadowy terrorist and anti-government groups that use email and cellular and mobile phones to coordinate resistance.

Two cases illustrate how modern technology can be used to enhance political mobilization while overcoming the impediment of physical distance. The first illustrates how technology can be harnessed to organizing and coordinating individuals located far from one another. In April 1999, a previously little-known quasi-religious group called Falun Gong staged a massive silent protest around the Beijing compound housing China's communist leaders. China's leaders were caught off guard because Falun Gong had organized its activities in cyberspace by means of email, without arousing suspicion or alerting the country's extensive surveillance systems.

A second case illustrates how a geographically isolated group can use technology to break out of isolation. Few resistance groups have outdone Mexico's Zapatistas in their ability to exploit these new technologies to mobilize global support. The Zapatistas have remained in the impoverished Mexican province of Chiapas where they first emerged on 1 January 1994, but they have used cyberspace, videos, audios, and radio to attract support worldwide. As a result, the Mexican government has been unable to isolate or co-opt the group without attracting global attention. An 'Intercontinental Network of Alternative Communication' existing largely in cyberspace publicizes their views. (See 'Zapatistas in Cyberspace' nd.) At one point some 11 Internet lists and 56 pro-Zapatista websites existed, managed by groups such as Austria's *Mexiko-Plattform Österreich*, Spain's *Plataforma de Solidaridad con Chiapas de Madrid*, Switzerland's *Solidaridad Directa con Chiapas*, and France's *Comité de Solidarité avec les Peuples du Chiapas en Lutte*, and Germany's *Gruppe b.a.s.t.a.*

Overlapping Polities, Clashing Identities, and New Patterns of Authority

Political space, as we conceive it, is more likely to be defined by cultural and ideational factors than by accidents of geography, and, unlike citizenship, the identities that demarcate most polities reflect psychological rather than territorial space. Generational factors, as well as processes of uneven political, economic, and social development, also make it necessary to integrate a temporal dimension into our understanding of political space. New political communities lacking the imprimatur of sovereignty and without territory in the conventional sense are becoming important sources of political identity and loyalty.

Potential identity categories such as class, caste, religion, ethnicity, gender, and even civilization largely reflect non-territorial conceptions of political space in which identity groups occupy the same geographic locations and in which identities, loyalties, and authorities routinely overlap and intersect. Less and less do the boundaries that separate territorial states demarcate political spaces based on salient identities or on economic, social, or cultural interests. Each identity group has its own boundaries that in the face of localization and globalisation are ever less compatible with the territorial frontiers of states.

The complex universe of non-territorial polities that criss-cross one another and cut across the state boundaries makes it virtually impossible to differentiate between the 'domestic' and 'foreign' realms (or 'inside' and 'outside'). Comparative politics, as well as international relations, merge into global politics. As in medieval Europe, global politics today features complex jurisdictions, shared loyalties, and competing identities. The emergence of new loci of authority – subnational, transnational, and international – alongside of national authorities is producing a highly decentralized global political system that is symbolized by the market decisions of billions of consumers and sellers.

It is hardly surprising that Krasner (1999) finds the novel organization of political space in contemporary Europe difficult to fit in his state-centric universe.[8] According to Christer Jönsson, Sven Tägil, and Gunnar Törnquist (2000: 152), Europe 'is not held together in the manner it used to be. The image that emerges is one of a fragmented territory, an archipelago of self-reliant regions linked together through different types of networks'. The European Union is, in fact, a hybrid polity that is simultaneously growing upwards as greater authority in some areas is ceded to Brussels, downward as more decisions are given to and greater interaction takes place at the regional level, across as in efforts to legislate community-wide law, and beyond as new members are digested, additional ones wait in the wings, and the Mediterranean programme attempts to promote a special relationship with North Africa.

Michael Keating and Liesbet Hooghe (2001: 216–29) describe how overlapping authorities within the same territorial 'regions' in the European Union enjoying relatively autonomous political space is an even more complex conceptualization of political space. They point out that no 'homogeneous regional tier of government in the EU' has emerged:

> There remain a variety of levels of territorial mobilization: historic nations; large provincial regions; units in federal or quasi-federal states; cities and city regions. . . . In some cases, the regions can be identified with a structure of government. In others, civil society or private groups are more important in defining and carrying forward a regional interest.

Neither is there a 'new regional hierarchy', nor can policy-making 'be explained simply by inter-state bargaining'. Instead, 'national politics are penetrated by European influences through law, bureaucratic contacts, political exchange, and the role of the commission in agenda-setting. Similarly, national politics are penetrated . . . by regional influences.' In sum, what seems to be happening is 'a Europeanization and a regionalization of national policy making' coupled with 'a Europeanization of the regions and a regionalization of Europe'.

An Emerging Global Elite?

As we have discussed with respect to psychological distance, the consequences of technological change have affected some social strata more than others, everywhere altering the lives of modernized urban elites and middle classes far faster than rural populations or those at the bottom of the socio-economic ladder. 'Knowledge workers' in business, government, and universities have been disproportionately advantaged by the information revolution and the spread of microelectronic technologies (Strange 1996: 102). Differential access based on wealth and knowledge within societies, while enhancing communication among those in similar professions regardless of where they live, has had the opposite effect on communication between rich and poor regardless of geographic proximity.

An emerging global elite, associated with the globalisation of neo-liberal capitalism, can exploit the declining role of distance, while exercising authority over globalised economic and cultural systems. This elite, as Wallerstein (1996: 89) suggests, has 'no intrinsic commitment to product, to place, to country'. They speak English, holiday at the same resorts, and live behind high walls, in secure, luxury apartment buildings, or in gated communities. Integrated in the global economy, with similar tastes and norms – whether in Caracas, New York, or Karachi – the elite has little in common with the burgeoning underclass that has grown throughout the course of massive urbanization. The horizontal boundary that separates the former from the latter in the same societies is more difficult to cross than the borders that separate members of this elite residing in different countries.

Members of the elite can often see the underclass from their office windows and can neither avoid viewing it through car or taxi windows nor encountering it on crowded sidewalks. Under such conditions, physical proximity does not translate into psychological intimacy. Instead, the confrontation of modernity and traditionalism engenders anger, crime, and civil violence.

Today's globalised elite are both the products of globalisation and the evangelists for a global world. They constitute an insular moral community whose members are obliged to treat one another according to shared norms, rules, and standards that do not apply to 'outsiders'. Their sense of reciprocal obligation rests on a perceived bond of sameness and shared fates. Like the new global elite, Europe's ruling aristocracy in the eighteenth century constituted a moral community whose members were linked by a common conservative outlook and personal empathy, and their policies, though competitive, were limited by the dynastic principle that provided legitimacy to the system as a whole. Like today's elite, they followed the same code of etiquette and rules of precedence, spoke the same language (French) in preference to their national tongue, and had more empathy for 'foreign' aristocrats than for those of other classes in their own country. And, like the principled commitment of the new elite to globalisation, Europe's earlier transnational elite was dedicated to reciprocal obligations and a set of norms, chief of which were the balance of power and aversion to overthrowing other legitimate dynasts. Like the invisible hand of global competition that contemporary neo-liberals believe is raising the global standard of living, eighteenth-century leaders viewed the balance as a mechanism that transformed the interests of sovereign egoists into a common good.

Conclusion: The Challenge of Remapping Political Space

The interstate system was built on the distribution of territory among sovereigns who enjoyed exclusive authority over that territory. A combination of dramatic technological and ideational change has eroded the authority and capacity of states and of the interstate system more generally.

Of course, as we acknowledged at the outset, territory still matters, even if attachment to it does not always favour existing sovereign boundaries. Territory perhaps matters most in less advanced regions, especially a few unique concentrations of natural resources (for example, oil-rich regions in the Middle East and South Asia), durable strategic locations like the Straits of Malacca and the Golan Heights, and the putative 'homelands' of ethnic minorities like Kurds and Palestinians. Canada, Mexico, and Cuba still feel the proximity of their giant neighbour.

In addition, citizens in many, if not most, states still rely on their governments for physical protection and a minimum standard of welfare. Sovereign states are not disappearing, and most sovereign boundaries have remained unaltered on traditional maps. Indeed, with decolonialization and the collapse of the former Soviet empire, it could rightly be argued that there are more of them than ever before. Yet, paradoxically, it is also true that respect for state boundaries persists in no small part because they are hard to change and of decreasing significance anyway. The cost of war and occupation continues to rise. Additional territory does not typically translate into more power and wealth, or less territory into less power and wealth. Most important state-boundaries 'contain' less and less. They are routinely transcended by nonstate authorities, identities, and loyalties.

Theory will have to accommodate new maps of a world in which polities can form in cyberspace or can overlap in a single territory. Recognizing that territoriality is an insufficient basis for understanding political authority in global politics today, some scholars have begun to scramble for alternative conceptualizations of political space. Some of them highlight integrating and centralizing tendencies in global politics; others, fragmentation of authority. But the key theme is the need to shift from a static conception of political space to one that emphasizes variability and plasticity. Adopting such a dynamic map rejects the premise that history somehow culminated and ceased with the territorial state, enables us to appreciate present-day complexities, and provides a better guide to the road ahead.

10 War and Innocent Victims

The paradox of Westphalia (2008)

Although war has been with us virtually forever, the savagery with which it is fought, including the manner in which warriors have treated enemy soldiers and civilians, has varied dramatically. This essay argues that two key factors determine the degree of brutality involved in global violence are (a) the degree to which the principal identities and loyalties in global politics cross-cut or reinforce one another and (b) the capacity of the territorial state to manage and channel warfare and separate legitimate from illegitimate violence. Changes in these factors, we suggest, help explain the moderation of violence following Europe's religious wars and the later increase in violence of global politics, first in relations among states in the nineteenth and twentieth centuries and then in the emerging post-international world of our present century.

The sovereign European state, as it matured during the seventeenth century, sought to channel and to manage warfare to avoid the excesses of the Thirty Years' War. Prior to the state's formation, 'political, social, economic, and religious motives were hopelessly entangled', and 'civilians suffered terrible atrocities' (van Creveld 1991: 50). Although interstate wars of the period remained bloody affairs, they did witness the evolution of norms that restrained conflict against enemy civilians and provided for the lenient treatment of enemy soldiers. Thereafter, the erosion of cross-cutting identities and of state capability witnessed a progressive weakening of such norms. Post-international conflicts in recent decades reflect ever fewer restraints on violence or limits on the depersonalization of the 'other'. Paradoxically, this dilution of norms comes at a time when civilians enjoy greater legal protection than at any time in history.

Wars, Violence, and Moral Communities

Theorizing about identity reveals the cognitive underpinning of *us* and *them* as bases for political action and legal regulation. Common identity rests on a high degree of normative consensus, and durable identity groups become moral communities – communities of caring – in which members share an intersubjective consensus that they are obliged to treat one another according to shared norms, rules, and standards that do *not* apply to 'outsiders'. Members of moral communities have a capacity to empathize with one another and are sensitive to one another's needs. Such obligation holds communities together and provides boundaries of inclusion and exclusion. Regardless of the identity that forms the basis for community solidarity, perceptions of sameness provide legitimacy for communities of obligation based on reciprocity and fairness.

However, where there is 'sameness', there is also 'otherness'. Moral communities also function to define 'others' and provide justification for treating them differently. Race, ethnicity, and even gender are categories of identity that are significant, not because of some intrinsic objective content, but because of the significance attached to their difference in contrast with another or others. Frequently, that significance includes the putative superiority of one identity over another. By demarcating inclusion and exclusion on the basis of sameness and difference, moral communities draw boundaries of 'inside and outside' according to which justice presumably is distributed. And the existence of an 'other' for purposes of comparison explains why it is hard to imagine a cosmopolitan identity with humanity as a whole.

The absence of obligation to the 'other' was evident in Europe's relations with those whom it conquered. Just as violence among European Christians and Muslims was regarded as legitimate in the Middle Ages, so were few of the limitations on violence imposed by European states on one another extended to indigenous 'pagan' peoples. Since indigenous peoples, as Martin Van Creveld (1999: 41) observes, 'did not know the state and its sharply-drawn division between government, army, and people', they 'were automatically declared to be bandits'. The debate among lawyers and theologians eventually came to rest on the notion that a war conducted to Christianize a pagan people was a just war, and Europeans in the seventeenth century, while seeing themselves as a community of Christians who were subject to the limitations of international law, viewed the conquered peoples of the New World as outside that community and thus beyond the bounds of obligations that united Christians.

Only when Spanish missionaries and theologians like the Dominican Francisco de Vitoria and Bartolomé de Las Casas declared that the indigenous people of the Americas had rights, did their situation improve. Vitoria argued that under natural law the Indians were free people and had owned their land before the Spaniards arrived (Von Glahn 1996: 25–26), and he denied that they lacked the power of reason and were, therefore, naturally slaves. Instead: 'There is a certain method in their affairs', he wrote, 'for they have polities which are orderly arranged and they have definite marriage and magistrates, overlords, laws, and workshops, and a system of exchange, all of which call for the use of reason: they also have a kind of religion' (cited in Serra 1946: 58).

Similar boundaries between 'inside' and 'outside' exist in all cultural-historical contexts. The boundary between Europeans and non-Europeans, for example, was similar to the cultural divide perceived by the Han Chinese when they described those beyond the reach of the Middle Kingdom as barbarians. Ancient Greeks held similar views of those who were beyond the reach of Hellenism. The basic idea is also captured by the aggressive definition that militant Muslims give to *jihad*.

As in the *Conquista* and *jihad*, the collision between moral communities may trigger efforts to make the 'other' more like 'us'. This was implicit in colonialism that evolved from an ideology of a 'civilizing mission' or a 'white man's burden'. Administration of colonial peoples through the League of Nations system of mandates and the UN Trusteeship Council also reflected a patriarchal ward-guardianship relationship between Western and non-Western peoples based on European efforts to make the 'other' better, in effect, more European.

Since identities demarcate psychological rather than territorial space, they can, like the moral communities they underpin, be overlapping and intersecting, as well as exclusive. When identities overlap it is possible for those who are 'aliens' in relation to one community to be compatriots in another, thereby attenuating hostility. When wars take place, the level of violence and the degree to which depersonalization leads to mistreatment of enemy soldiers and civilians varies according to the degree to which adversaries have common or cross-cutting identities. Where foes retain some common, as well as conflicting, identities the possibility exists that shared norms may moderate violence. Under these conditions, leaders' goals are not rigidly ranked, and trade-offs are possible. Where shared identities are absent, there will be fewer limits on treatment of non-combatants. The psychological distance that separates foes is unrelieved by perceptions of similarity and linked fates.

The fewest normative constraints exist when a moral community is rent by civil war. Then, there are few restraints on the treatment of foes owing to a sense of 'betrayal' that each side ascribes to those with whom they had formerly enjoyed a shared identity. Such conflicts reflect a breakdown in the system of obligations and duties attaching to community membership and an end to the moral consensus that had sustained the normative order.

Thus, in Europe and in the Islamic community (*umma*), when religious 'heresies' threatened the unity of existing societies, limitations on violence were ignored. Religious dissidents such as France's Cathars were treated with the utmost brutality. Catharism, which arrived in Languedoc in southern France some time in the eighth century from the Balkans, was built on Manichaeism in which good and evil were locked in struggle. The Cathars' vows of poverty and purity and their criticism of the worldliness of the Catholic establishment led to church efforts in the twelfth century to end the heresy. In 1198, Pope Innocent III set out to extinguish Catharism, culminating in the slaughter of believers during the crusade of 1209. Later states treated internal foes much as the Church had treated the Cathars.

Christianity's Civil War

In medieval Europe, the strongest moral communities had been local, based on family and kinship, and political authority had been concentrated in the hands of a caste of warrior-gangster knights who could afford armour, war-horses, leisure to train, and the other trappings of their profession. Despite the efforts of the medieval Church by expedients such as the Peace of God to forge a larger moral community based on Christian unity, that unity proved a feeble barrier to the conflicts that set knights against one another and the class-based violence of knights against commoners. In addition, under the medieval system of overlapping property rights and obligations, it was virtually impossible to differentiate between internal and external wars; the very distinction between 'inside' and 'outside' was amorphous, as was the boundary between war and crime. Thus, war in Europe's Middle Ages resembled banditry or 'private' warfare with members of the military caste of knights raiding one another's lands, ravaging the land, and creating general insecurity. War 'was all but indistinguishable from simple brigandry' (Van Creveld 1989: 108).

Nevertheless, as the Crusades and codes of chivalry suggest, some sense of moral community could be encouraged under favourable circumstances, especially the presence of external foes. However, even this modest sense of common identity eroded with the gradual emergence of territorial principalities in Europe after the eleventh century and the declining authority of Church and Holy Roman Empire. The Reformation smashed what unity remained and produced a widespread authority crisis. Efforts to restore unity produced two centuries of religious strife, climaxing in the Thirty Years' War.

The initial stage of the Thirty Years' War centred on religious animosity, but, as its religious character faded after 1635, it pitted Sweden, France, and a number of German princes against the Habsburg rulers of Austria and the Holy Roman Empire. Undiluted by cross-cutting identities, the war featured savage violence and atrocities against civilians who were the main victims of 'the chaotic and roving warfare of the so-called wars of religion' (Palmer 1986: 94). The fate of the fortified German city of Magdeburg at the hands of imperial troops in which there 'was naught but beating and burning, plundering, torture, and murder', reflected the absence of limitations to violence that characterized the conflict (Robinson 1906: 211–12). The indiscriminate violence moved Hugo Grotius (1957: 21) to denounce the absence of 'respect for law, divine or human; it is as if ... frenzy had openly been let loose for the committing of all crimes'.

The Peace of Westphalia recognized that the dream of a united Catholic Europe was no longer realistic. The treaty between the Holy Roman Emperor and the King of France and their respective allies was a rambling document consisting of 128 articles of which only two – Articles 64 and 65 – introduced the contours of state sovereignty. Transcendental goals yielded to tangible ones as Calvinism was officially recognized, and the Peace of Augsburg, which the warring parties had failed to observe, was restored. The Peace of Westphalia recognized the sovereign authority of the German princes to govern their territory and make autonomous decisions about war and peace.

German lands lay in ruins, and the population of the Holy Roman Empire had declined from about 21 to 16 million during the war. Hence, the great princes of the time recognized that limits had to be placed on warfare, or they and their domains, too, could become victims of mindless destruction. This entailed differentiating between legitimate and illegitimate violence.

Transformation in military technology and the capacity of monarchical bureaucracies to manage violence against subjects, as well as foreigners, was necessary for the triumph of the territorial state and, in turn, for Europe to establish its commanding role in global politics. The Westphalian polity was militarily superior to rival political forms such as city-states, fiefdoms, tribes, confederations, and at least some empires owing to its social and political organization and economies of scale. The creation of the territorial state, as Murray (1997: 70–71) writes, 'based on organized and disciplined military power' was a product of the seventeenth-century military revolution that 'laid the basis for the modern state'.

The escalating costs of war increased 'the minimum size necessary to make political units militarily viable', (Van Creveld 1989: 108) and changes in warfare indicated 'to political elites and social groups which type of organization was most efficient, and they subsequently adopted the most competitive institutional form' (Spruyt 1994: 178), that is, the territorial state. Economic and social factors (growing markets, a prosperous, urban, commercial class, and the growing use of specie) as well as military innovations (crossbows, gunpowder, and the *trace italienne*) combined to erode Europe's medieval political and normative orders. Military technology and especially 'fortress warfare', writes Van Creveld (1989: 107–8), demanded 'financial muscle, bureaucratic organization, and technical expertise' that 'were to be found less in the feudal countryside than in the bourgeois-capitalist town economy'. Only kings could acquire the resources to wage sustained interstate war, while simultaneously pacifying their domains.

Political leaders sought to centralize authority to mobilize the human and material resources necessary to fight. To be efficient and effective, the centralizing power structures required that the dynastic courts and family-based organizations of medieval Europe give way to rationalistic, merit-based bureaucracies capable of coping with the financial, logistical, and operational exigencies of large-scale warfare, and able to pay soldiers on time and discipline them in both peace and war. Government revenues grew rapidly as the state-enhancing dimension of war introduced a 'ratchet effect' in which 'the rapid growth of government and massive tax increases that occur during war usually level off at postwar levels much higher than were in effect before the conflict' (van Creveld 1999: 14). Meanwhile, the costs of war reinforced the normative consensus that warfare should be limited.

Changing stakes were critical in this context. After 1648, interstate wars were waged largely over territory that, unlike religious dogma, was tangible and divisible, thereby limiting the scope of violence by facilitating compromise and shifting alliances. Territorial expansion provided the human and material resources for war, and geographic space afforded protection from enemy attack. And, so long as territory remained the principal focus of political ambition and 'territoriality ... the functional equivalent of property rights', (Gilpin 1981: 37) people were more likely to fight neighbours than others (a fact reinforced or countered by the relative level of technology).[1]

Centralization of authority and the normative demarcation between crime and war went hand in hand with a growing acceptance of a distinction between inside and outside the state. Even before the French Revolution, centralized authority was reinforced by the construction of national identities, manifested in the spread of national languages, cultural practices, and bounded histories that reinforced unity at home, while building barriers to the influence of 'outsiders'. Sovereign identities in turn provided the bases for the legitimacy of the new states, and this legitimacy partly depended on a state's exercise of a monopoly over 'right and proper' coercion. In other words, legitimacy rested on the ability of Europe's rulers to manage violence by demarcating the boundary between proper and improper violence and provide subjects with security, understood as the management of threats to civil order. This view was reflected in the ideas of Hobbes and Bodin, and those ideas had a profoundly moral end: to limit the harm of unlimited violence to political communities and create centralized authority to limit violence among subjects while protecting them from external predation.

Taming the Beast

The state evolved within the historical context of shifting identities and boundaries that redefined the moral community. For about a century and a half, Europe's princes succeeded in containing and isolating inhabitants in territorial states, and, as van Creveld (1991: 33–62) describes it, dynastic states developed a 'trinitarian' conception of warfare in which governments waged 'authoritative' warfare through their military establishment with the support of their people. This conception originated with Clausewitz (1976: 89) who described war as:

> a paradoxical trinity – composed of primordial violence ...; of the play of chance and probability within which the creative spirit is free to roam; and of its element of sub-ordination, as an instrument of policy, which makes it subject to reason alone. The first of these aspects mainly concerns the people; the second the commander and his army; the third the government.

Armies would be the instruments of their states and leave civilians alone; but, in return, civilians must not take up arms against the state. Individuals other than lawful state-agents who took up arms were criminals engaged in rebellion or worse. In this way, Clausewitz drew a distinction between war and crime.

The state constrained violence in two ways. First, growing state capacity and the institutionalization of military and police bureaucracies, augmented by control over print media, permitted repression or cooptation of rival identity groups *within* its boundaries and, for great powers at least, protection of subjects from foreign invasion. Specialized bureaucracies enabled Europe's states to mobilize large populations for interstate war while pacifying the intrastate arena, and citizenship provided the main signpost for differentiating between 'inside' and 'outside'.

European state-building entailed imposing top-down processes and a sovereign 'civic culture' on local identities and communities. States' boundaries, internalized in the form of identities tied to territory and citizenship, gradually took precedence over, and in some cases erased, local boundaries delineated by regional, religious, or ethnic affiliation. Civic identity was accompanied by obligations of subjects to the state, and this identity reinforced the claim that transborder violence should only be authorized and organized by the state.

Second, the vertical barriers of state frontiers and the identity cleavages they reflected were softened by horizontal identity links among rulers, thereby limiting violence *between* states. In other words, the boundaries that separated states were to some extent transcended by cross-cutting class identities of dynastic rulers. International law confirmed both the unique authority of states to wage legitimate war and the ways in which the agents of states should treat each other, with both conditions critical to managing violence and imposing order.

The first condition we listed is often summarized under the rubric of the sovereign state's monopoly of the means of coercion. But we must be careful about this generalization. In fact, states *never* actually exercised *complete* control over the means of coercion. Although transborder violence in Europe gradually came under states' control after 1648, their control of violence outside of Europe, as Janice Thomson (1994: 11) reminds us, was a process not achieved until the nineteenth century: 'the state, portrayed in theory as monopolizing coercion, is distinctively modern' and 'reflected a redrawing of authority claims such that authority over the use of violence was moved from the nonstate, economic, and international domains and placed in the state, political, and domestic realms of authority.' As recently as 'little more than a century ago, the state did not monopolize the exercise of coercion beyond its borders' (Thomson 1994: 143). States did so only when they found that it was necessary in order to overcome very specific problems that arose in the course of Europe's outward colonial expansion.

As for the second condition, the story of the ties that bound Europe's aristocracy in the seventeenth and eighteenth centuries is too well known to require retelling here. Ruling families were linked by a common conservative outlook and personal empathy, and their rivalries were limited by the dynastic principle that provided legitimacy for the system as a whole. They played and holidayed together, married one another, followed the same rules of etiquette and precedence, and spoke French in preference to their own national tongue. Their wars were bloody but limited, rarely involving symbolic or transcendent stakes and avoiding any threat to one another's thrones and, therefore, to the system itself. 'The interests of her Princes', wrote Rousseau (1970: 135), 'are united by ties of blood, by commerce, arts and colonies.' Andrew Linklater summarizes the effort to minimize the tension between identities/loyalties to individual European states and the larger conception of European society by arguing that the 'modern European state emerged within the confines of a single civilization united by the normative and religious power of Christendom' and that, as it sought to rid itself of the normative constraints of the past, 'the state was aware of the dangers of totally undermining earlier notions of an international society'. In putting forward 'the notion of a wider society of states', the state wished 'to enjoy the benefits of preserving an international society without incurring the risk that individual citizens would challenge the state's legitimacy by proclaiming their allegiance to a higher cosmopolitan ethic' (cited in Barnett 1995: 496).

Chief among the norms that governed the intercourse of Europe's sovereigns and reconciled the individual and collective interests of Europe's states was the balance of power. The balance was the means that theorists believed made the interests of sovereign egoists compatible with the welfare of a society of states. Europe had become, according to Friedrich von Gentz (1970: 283), adviser to Metternich, 'an extensive social commonwealth, of which the characteristic object was the preservation and reciprocal guarantee of the rights of all its members'. Almost the same reverence for the balance as the key pillar of a European society was voiced by British radical Henry, Lord Brougham (1970: 269, 273), who likened the balance to a scientific breakthrough 'as much unknown to Athens and Rome, as the Keplerian or Newtonian laws were concealed from Plato and Cicero'. In his view, the balance had acquired the status of a 'species of general law'. Thus, even as the Westphalian polity emerged, 'European', as a geopolitical and cultural identity, also came to serve as a basis for another level of moral community, the community of 'civilized nations'.

With the French Revolution and the Napoleonic Wars, and the transformation of dynastic into national states, the vertical barriers between nations hardened, and the identities that had bound rulers were eroded. Clausewitz's incomplete masterpiece *On War* was written at a moment when the era of limited war was already coming to an end. His trinitarian world was one in which reason, not passion, should link politics and warfare, which was, after all, only one of many tools in the hands of statesmen. As John Keegan (1994: 5) argues:

> War as the continuation of policy was the form Clausewitz chose to express the compromise for which states he knew had settled. It accorded respect to their prevailing ethics – of absolute sovereignty, ordered diplomacy and legally binding treaties – while making allowance for the overriding principle of state interest.

However, as Clausewitz observed, the Revolutionary and Napoleonic Wars, unlike previous wars, bore little relation to narrowly defined reason of state in which political objectives dominated the passions of violence. France's adventures portended limitless contests in which political objectives were forgotten or subordinated to military necessity. Jacobin and Napoleonic warfare featured enormous armies of energized conscript soldiers, identification of the fate of 'citizens' with that of *la patrie*, extinction of state independence, and removal of legitimate dynastic rulers.

Conscription, close-order drill, and nationalism were a recipe for slaughter on behalf of the state even as warfare deepened citizen identities. As Michael Mann (1986: 20) notes, 'through wars eighteenth-century states enormously increased their fiscal and manpower exactions, caging their subjects onto the national terrain and thus politicizing them'. Such warfare reflected the powerful impact of the wedding of two polities, state and nation.

This process, beginning in the late eighteenth century and deepening throughout the nineteenth century, witnessed the ending of the cross-cutting identities among rulers that had limited interstate violence for about a century and a half. The pathetic exchange of letters between Russia's tsar and Germany's emperor on the eve of world war confirmed this. Even as industrialization and modern technology increased state capacity for violence by providing unprecedented financial and logistical resources, the hardening of boundaries between states and the growth in state control over education and information had two consequences. First, they combined 'nationality' and 'citizenship' into a single unique identity at the acme of most people's loyalty hierarchies. Second, by reinforcing one another, state and nation extended psychological distance between peoples and facilitated greater depersonalization and dehumanization of the 'other' in wartime. The latter was further intensified by the changing content of nationalism – to include racial mythology associated with Social Darwinism – in the second half of the nineteenth century and early years of the twentieth.

Clausewitz's universe seemed a distant dream by 1914 when the 'logic' of mobilization timetables and the industrialized warfare of the day saw an entire generation die in the mud and trenches of France and Belgium. The Second World War added the intentional victimization of civilians. From the fire bombings of Rotterdam and Dresden and Coventry, to the Holocaust, to the nuclear destruction of Hiroshima and Nagasaki – the world seemed to have embarked on an epoch of 'absolute' war. Perhaps, the Second World War was one that was worth fighting, but there is no escaping the conclusion that the state system could no longer manage violence.

For all its protective restraint on domestic violence, the nation-state built the most formidable war machine in history and used it repeatedly with devastating effect against enemy armies and civilians alike, justified in part by the growing involvement of entire societies in war-making as a result of industrialization. The breakdown of the rules of trinitarian warfare was reflected in the increasing proportions of civilian to military war deaths.

The relative peace of the later Cold War suggested that maybe Clausewitz's world could be restored. Although what we were really witnessing was the growing obsolescence of territory as a source of security, nuclear deterrence seemed, to some observers, an elixir of peace. Clausewitz was resurrected to help civilian strategists make sense of nuclear weapons, perhaps the ultimate indiscriminate weapon and negation of war as a rational extension of politics. The idea was to develop strategies of deterrence and coercive diplomacy that would restore the political dimension to war (Schelling 1966: 2).

Warfare and the Erosion of the Modern State

States today are less able than at any time in the past three centuries to manage violence. As in the epoch following the breakdown of the medieval order and the rise of Europe's states, especially after 1648, global politics today is confronting what Rosenau (2003: 71–73) calls an 'authority crisis' of monumental proportions. During such periods, global life is unpredictable and dangerous, and norms and customs are in flux. Conflicting identities, many of which lack territorial conceptions of political space, clash and compete for loyalties, and individuals and collectivities may experience paralyzing dissonance as they choose among competing authorities.

State legitimacy and capacity have declined precipitously in many areas, and state-based identities are yielding pride of place to transnational religious and ethnic identities, especially in the developing world. Clausewitz's world bears little resemblance to one in which armies and peoples become indistinguishable and where combatants are militias or gangs with AK-47s and SUVs (sports utility vehicles). What Clausewitz's formulation 'made no allowance for at all', as Keegan (1994: 5) observes, 'was war without beginning or end, the endemic warfare of non-state, even pre-state peoples, in which there was no distinction between lawful and unlawful bearers of arms'.

As Table 3 reveals, the result has been a dramatic decline in interstate wars, but an upsurge in civil and trans-state violence, especially since the 1970s. These conflicts, as Stephen Metz suggests, can be divided into 'informal wars' where at least one side is 'a nonstate entity' and 'gray area wars' which 'combine elements of traditional warfighting with those of organized crime'. States on whose territories such wars are fought are characterized by 'economic

Table 3 Numbers of Wars between 1820 and 1997 (based on Sarkees, Wayman and Singer 2003: Table 1, 61)

Decade	Interstate Wars*	Civil Wars
1820–1829	8	7
1830–1839	5	11
1840–1849	12	9
1850–1859	14	8
1860–1869	13	14
1870–1879	14	9
1880–1889	15	3
1890–1899	20	9
1900–1909	10	7
1910–1919	14	11
1920–1929	8	12
1930–1939	11	8
1940–1949	8	9
1950–1959	9	20
1960–1969	9	16
1970–1979	10	26
1980–1989	4	19
1990–1997	1	24

stagnation, ungovernability, and violence'. Their 'armed forces will take the form of armed gangs, militias, the personal armies of warlords, and terrorist groups', and their populations 'experience near constant low-level organized violence' (Metz 2000: xii, 18, 20, 21).

As states weaken, the boundary between the domestic and foreign realms, as well as the distinction between legitimate and illegitimate violence, break down. Human-rights advocates who point to state sovereignty as an obstacle to assuring human rights and fair treatment of civilians in wartime are only partly correct. To the extent that sovereignty outlawed violence within states and international law limited violence among states and against civilians, there was an established normative framework protecting individuals against unrestrained violence. However, that framework functioned only so long as states had the capacity to impose it; eroding state capacity to enforce norms is ever more responsible for abuses against civilians. Norms based on inter-state efforts to regulate warfare have little impact on the unregulated violence that plagues the new millennium – terrorism, crimes against civilians, ethnic or communal conflict, and full-scale genocide.

The growing porosity of sovereign frontiers in recent decades has muddled the distinction among interstate and civil wars, for example, in Afghanistan, Bosnia, Iraq, and Congo. Civil wars and other forms of local conflict afflict between one-third and one-half of the world's societies. As a result, the problem of demarcating the boundaries of civic and moral obligation is regaining an importance for political theory not seen since 1648. As old identities and loyalties are revived and new ones emerge, often manipulated by demagogues, fanatics, or 'big men', moral communities other than states proliferate. Thus, Charles Taylor was elected president of Liberia in 1997 because residents believed it was the only way to end the brutal civil war that he himself had started to control the region's diamonds.

To the extent that political objectives are involved, they are generic – struggles to alter peoples' relationship with one another or with the state regarding the terms by which authority is exercised. Such violence revolves around struggles for the remains of states, for personal power, and for the opportunity to pillage natural resources. In these arenas, armies are more effective in threatening their own citizens than in containing domestic insurrection or defending national frontiers. Many of these wars are among uncontrolled and fragmented groups – or, in others cases, involve private armies (see Muthien and Taylor 2002: 183–99).

State-based identities become relatively less important, and sovereign boundaries succeed less and less in demarcating spaces or in 'nationalizing' people's activities, perceptions, and beliefs. People then have to make painful choices among conflicting identities and the moral communities that are constructed from them. Ethnic, religious, economic, and political rivalries long suppressed by strong states have resurfaced, and old conflicts that had been defined in Cold War terms have persisted under new labels. This is most apparent in regions where Europe planted its flags and disrupted existing patterns of authority. The potential for redrawing boundaries among identity groups inside countries encourages militants to pursue their ambitions and prompts others to adopt violence as a means of defence.

As states lose the capacity to protect citizens, they 'turn private security into a growth industry *par excellence* worldwide', (van Creveld 1999: 404). This recalls the seventeenth century when Europe's religious wars were waged by 'military contractors' in whose hands 'war itself was turned into a form of self-sustaining capitalist enterprise that promised riches and even principalities to the most successful practitioners' (van Creveld 1989: 108). Early Westphalian polities used mercenaries, privateers, and trading companies that had their own armies to extend state influence, and, like today, they 'robbed the countryside on their own behalf, even building fortified strongholds where they collected loot and held prisoners for ransom' (van Creveld 1999: 50, 51). About all the good that could be said for them was that their contracts did not include dying for ideological causes; warfare for them was literally all in a day's work rather than a brutal campaign against 'others' (indeed, they were often foreign 'others' themselves).

The trend towards 'outsourcing war' is spreading because 'the increasing inability of weak governments to counter internal violence has created a ready market for private military forces' (Shearer 1998: 70). The use of hired guns is not the sole prerogative of failed states. Even the US government employs private specialists in violence. Private US contractors working closely with government agencies aid the Colombian government in its fight against its domestic adversaries (Forero 2001), and in Iraq, mercenaries entered into partnerships with American troops when private security companies like Blackwater USA and Global Risk Strategies were hired by the US government to provide up to 20,000 armed personnel to protect installations and private contractors (see *The Economist* 2004: 22 and Barstow 2004: A1, A11). According to one observer, these companies 'are corporate endeavors that perform logistics, support, training, security, intelligence work, risk analysis, and much more. They operate in an open market, work for many employers at once, and boast of their professionalism' (Avant 2004: 21). Global Risk Strategies describes itself as a 'compact, flexible and client oriented Political and Security Risk Management Company' with directors from 'military, industry and commerce backgrounds' (Global Strategies Group nd).

Outsourcing in modern war also takes the form of employing technical specialists just as three centuries ago 'artillery and siege engineering were often handled by contractors rather than military soldiers' (Metz 2000: 19). Today, the high cost of training and maintaining a permanent corps of specialists provides incentives to subcontract for such help when needed. As the entrepreneurial work of Abdul Qadeer Khan suggests, there is no reason to assume that similar private assistance is unavailable to actors such as terrorists, *narcotraficantes*, or rogue governments.

At the other end of the spectrum of violence, we still have to cope with the consequences of past and continuing nuclear proliferation with its potential for indiscriminate violence. Weapons of mass destruction (WMD) in the hands of apocalyptic terrorists top the list of today's security concerns. The anthrax attacks on US citizens that began in the autumn of 2001 illustrate how even limited bio-attacks can sow near panic and bring bureaucratic institutions to a halt. In this respect at least, WMD – like terrorism – can become weapons for the weak.

One of the most seductive elements of the 'American Way of War' – the relative unwillingness to put soldiers at risk and the emphasis on reducing casualties – has its roots in a perception that citizens are more selective in their willingness to die for the state than in the past. Defending against – and then retaliating for – terrorist assaults on homeland targets is one thing; serving in the military and fighting in foreign wars without a powerfully convincing interest at stake is another. The trend began in the stalemates of Korea and Vietnam and deepened with the end of the Cold War and America's disillusioning experience in Lebanon, Somalia, and now Iraq.

Currently, American political and military leaders place extravagant hopes on high-tech warfare for limiting violence and 'collateral damage'. Such warfare was previewed in the 1991 Gulf War and was updated for the Afghanistan and Iraqi campaigns. It has been developed, in part, to dominate conventional armies, limit casualties on both sides, and avoid bogging down in 'quagmires' like Vietnam or Somalia. Still, high-tech warfare is hardly free of civilian casualties or consequences. As Thomas W. Smith (2002: 355) points out, humanitarian laws of war are being 'recast in the light of hi-tech weapons and innovations in strategic theory'; 'Most striking is the use of legal language to justify the erosion of distinctions between soldiers and civilians and to legitimize collateral damage.' Smith acknowledges that high-tech war 'has dramatically curbed immediate civilian casualties', but he finds deeply troubling the fact that 'the law sanctions infrastructural campaigns that harm long-term public health and human rights'. Nor does such warfare rule out the use of WMD. Looking down the road, one frightening possibility is that countries that cannot compete at the high-tech level may conclude that acquiring conventional weapons, such as tanks or jet aircraft, is futile and instead intensify their development of WMD to deter or intimidate the superpower.

Advocates of the new technologies argue that soldiers will not have to slog it out in mud, jungle, or desert or fight it out house to house. There will be no more Stalingrads, and civilians will again enjoy relative safety in warfare. But the endgame in Iraq and the War on Terror raise serious questions about the prospects for sanitized warfare waged in cyberspace rather than in mud. Neither high-tech wizardry nor Western armies are panaceas for 'low-intensity civil wars, with their complicated ethnic agendas, blurred boundaries between combatants and civilians, and loose military hierarchies' (Shearer 1998: 70).

Efforts such as those of civilian nuclear strategists during the Cold War and advocates of high-tech warfare to restore a Clausewitzian universe confront what is perhaps their greatest challenge in the growing importance of non-territorial identities that challenge the legitimacy of state authority. Precisely because the boundaries of cultural, ethnic, and religious communities often cut across and stretch beyond sovereign frontiers, they frequently compete with state-based identities. Dramatic shifts in identities and identity hierarchies, ranging from the collapse of communism to the spread of radical Islam, are having a profound impact on global life, especially the lifting of restraints on violence.

What is so dangerous about some of these identities is that, like the identities that dominated European society before 1648, they are transcendent in nature – involving fundamental belief systems – and have become the foundation for non-sovereign moral communities that regard the 'other' with contempt and loathing. Bargains and trade-offs are extraordinarily difficult under these conditions, and rigidity becomes a hallmark of relations among communities based on such identities.

Challenging globalisation and its promise of material welfare, and manipulated by political entrepreneurs, these identities promise millenarian rewards and discourage compromise with foes. To date, the emergence of new globalised elites has not been sufficient to cross-cut and soften the powerful surge of religious fundamentalism – including that of militant Islam, Orthodox Jews in Israel, Hindu militants, or evangelical Christians – that has caused upheavals in many societies. Where religious and territorial identities reinforce each other as in Kashmir, Palestine, Bosnia, Kosovo, and

Iraq, intersubjective realities leave little room for tolerance of or coexistence with rivals.

A Growing Normative Gap

The erosion of limits on violence in global politics and the virtual disappearance of the line between war and crime have produced a bloody paradox: individuals today are probably more fully protected by international law and humanitarian norms than ever before, yet civilians are at risk to a greater extent than at any time since the Thirty Years' War.[2] This suggests a second paradox: human-rights activists seek to limit sovereign claims against domestic interference and humanitarian intervention, even while the erosion of state authority and sovereign capacity are accompanied by growing wartime abuses against innocent civilians.

We have seen how war and crime were largely indistinguishable in medieval Europe and in Europe's wars of religion and how the state imposed this distinction on global politics. Industrialization and national mobilization doomed Clausewitz's ideal of trinitarian warfare, making civilians part of the war effort. Both sides self-consciously waged war against civilians. Thus, 65 per cent of the total fatalities in the Second World War were civilians (in contrast to 15 per cent during the First World War), and in today's 'low-intensity' wars', 'the wars of Ivory Coast, Somalia, Sudan, Liberia, East Timor, and the former Yugoslavia – civilians constitute 90 per cent of the dead' (Ehrenreich 1997: 206, 227). The 'circumstances of contemporary conflict imply much more interaction with civil society, and a greater difficulty in separating combatants from non-combatants' (Freedman 1998: 47–48). Although the weaponry in such warfare is not highly sophisticated, just about everybody who gets in the way of the combatants gets killed.

The upsurge in atrocities is accompanied by encompassing comprehensive legal protection for individuals and recognition that the 'law of nations' is no longer sufficient. Following the Holocaust, progress was made toward expanding the regulation of violence beyond norms pertaining to non-combatants and prisoners of war during a war, to the general protection of civilians against abuses of state coercion through the articulation of universal human rights. This innovation extended the international regulation of violence into the shielded realm of state domestic jurisdiction.

Nuremberg established the precedent of individual responsibility for actions undertaken even under the justification of superior orders or operational necessity. In addition to designating acts of aggression as the 'crime' of war, individual agents of states could be held accountable for a whole new category of crimes – crimes against humanity and, later, genocide – in the misuse of state coercive power. The creation of the category of crimes against humanity entailed recognition of the breakdown of distinctions between soldiers and civilians, and war and crime. Thus, the murder of millions of Jews, like later 'ethnic cleansing' in Bosnia and Kosovo and genocide in Cambodia and Rwanda, were regarded by the global community as criminal acts. In recent decades, whether in Bosnia or Congo, it has been difficult to distinguish between organized war 'as a real political instrument' and mindless savagery or crime. Thus, we have come full circle, with warfare that would have been more familiar to Grotius in the seventeenth century than to the leaders of states in the brief era that Clausewitz idealized.

Since 1945, UN conventions and international and regional human-rights tribunals and law have reinforced the Nuremberg precedent. All entailed violations of classical sovereignty. The fiftieth anniversary of the UN's Genocide Convention and the Universal Declaration of Human Rights was on 10 December 1998. 1949 witnessed four Geneva Conventions governing treatment of civilians and prisoners of war. The European Convention on Human Rights emerged in 1950, and the following two years brought conventions protecting refugees and women. In ensuing years, additional conventions were adopted to deal with a variety of human-rights issues: stateless persons (1954), slavery (1956), forced labour (1957), consent to marriage (1962), racial discrimination (1965), apartheid (1973), discrimination against women (1979), torture (1984), and the rights of the child (1989). In 1966, the Universal Declaration of Human Rights gained specificity in the International Covenants on Economic, Social and Cultural Rights/Civil and Political Rights.

In May 1996, the first international criminal court since Nuremberg – the International Criminal Tribunal for the former Yugoslavia – was convened in The Hague. The UN also set up an international tribunal to deal with the Rwandan genocide. An even more ambitious step was the conclusion in the summer of 1998 of a treaty to establish a permanent International Criminal Court (ICC) to try individuals charged with genocide, war crimes, and crimes against humanity. The United States was one of only seven governments at the meeting to vote against it and insisted – in response to concerns expressed by the Pentagon and conservative members of Congress – that the court's jurisdiction should be automatic only for those countries that had signed the ICC treaty. Meanwhile, regional institutions such as the American and European Courts of Human Rights allow individuals to bring complaints to them, and, in Europe, even the United Kingdom has agreed that citizens can use domestic courts to enforce the European Convention on Human Rights.

The end of the Cold War and the spread of democratic norms made it easier to ignore power considerations and to provide scope for human-rights concerns, and the new climate accelerated the efforts of international organizations to institutionalize human rights. An important precedent was set in 1980 in a suit brought against a former Paraguayan police chief in an American court. That court ruled that individuals could use American civil courts to enforce international human-rights standards against foreign leaders on US soil. Another landmark was the 1998 decision by two separate panels of British Law Lords that Chile's Augusto Pinochet, though a former head of state, was not immune from extradition and prosecution for crimes against humanity. A year after charges were brought against Pinochet, the International Criminal Tribunal for the Former Yugoslavia charged and requested the extradition of a sitting head of state, Yugoslavia's Slobodan Milosevic for crimes allegedly committed in Kosovo. The trial of two Libyans accused of bombing a US jetliner, finally held before a Scottish court in the Netherlands, provided an additional reminder that those who violate human rights will be held responsible *as individuals.*

NATO's 1999 intervention in Kosovo suggested that state sovereignty would not shield human-rights violators from humanitarian intervention (whether or not with UN approval), and NATO's willingness to intervene there is only one of several cases in which sovereignty has been ignored in the name of restoring regional peace and security. UN sanctions against South Africa, its intervention in Somalia and Cambodia, Nigeria's presence in Liberia and Sierra Leone, NATO's bombing of Serbia, and the indictment of individuals by the ICC for crimes in Uganda and Darfur all indicated the declining sanctity of sovereign immunity.

In effect, an abyss has opened between the language and intent of the UN Charter's protection of domestic jurisdiction and the position of former UN Secretary General Kofi Annan, who declared: 'As long as I am Secretary General', the United Nations, 'will always place human beings at the center of everything we do.' Although 'fundamental sovereignty, territorial integrity, and political independence of states' continue to be a 'cornerstone of the international system', sovereignty, Annan continued, cannot provide 'excuses for the inexcusable'(cited in Miller 1999: section 4, 4).

Both non-governmental organizations (NGOs) and interstate governmental actors (IGOs), aided by regional regimes or former colonial powers, have become deeply enmeshed in efforts to manage violence and, once violence ends, in assuming an active interventionist role in restoring peace, promoting reconciliation in post-conflict environments, and reconstructing state institutions. Suggestions, once unthinkable, are now heard about establishing paternal relations such as a UN 'conservatorship' (Helman and Ratner 1992–93: 12–18) or 'disinterested neo-colonialism'(Pfaff 1995: 2–6) in the case of failed states. Because what Krasner (2001: 7) calls 'Westphalian sovereignty' ostensibly precludes legal external interference in domestic politics, the norms regarding international responses to civil wars are less developed than those pertaining to interstate war, offering little more than guidelines for the variety of possible responses available to the global community. Norms regarding the right of a state to request assistance from other states to secure itself against attack or pursue a strategy of collective self-defence (thereby, legitimating the use of force with the assistance of third parties) have left civil wars an uncertain area of international law.

Conclusion: Clausewitz is History

Contemporary violence, especially the victimization of civilians, increasingly resembles warfare during Europe's brutal religious conflicts of earlier centuries. The emergence of powerful territorial states moderated this violence because of cross-cutting identities and state capacity to repress violence at home and manage it abroad. As the cross-cutting identities associated with Europe's ruling elite waned and 'nation' and 'state' fused, interstate warfare became increasingly indiscriminate. Industrialization, technological development, and malignant nationalism ushered in an epoch of unrestrained warfare between mobilized moral communities.

Recent decades have witnessed the erosion of the second pillar of eighteenth-century moderation, the capacity of states to impose order on their territory. States and even entire regions have become, like Germany during the Thirty Years' War, arenas of unrestrained violence and sources of booty. Elsewhere, the declining legitimacy of state authority and the challenge of millenarian religious and civilizational identities that promise transcendent rewards threaten greater violence against civilians despite the proliferation of legal protections for human rights.

A final, sad note might be that some states like the United States and (to a lesser extent) the United Kingdom that long have been renowned for high standards of political freedom and protection for persons accused of crimes now seem to have been convinced by terrorism at home and abroad to lower their standards. In the United States, the examples of the Guantánamo camps and recent proposals to 'clarify' the Geneva Convention offer ominous evidence that irregular warfare of ruthless nonstate 'others' is threatening to brutalize the behaviour of even those states that have prided themselves on being moral communities worthy of the name.

11 Superpower, Hegemony, Empire (2008)

'It is an ill wind that doesn't blow some good.' Notions of United States omnipotence have suffered some setbacks in the last few years. However, the George W. Bush administration's militant unilateralism has prompted academics and policymakers to reflect again on the concepts of superpower, hegemony, and empire – and that is surely all to the good.

In this essay, we consider each of these three concepts in succession, with particular attention to empire. Empire merits special attention not only because the controversy surrounding it in our contemporary post-international world, but also because empires have arguably been even more important than states throughout human history. Moreover, thinking about empire and related political forms forces us to venture beyond the traditional state-centrism of IR theory.

Superpower

Changing power rankings

It is instructive to observe how prevailing popular and scholarly conceptions of the main features of global politics and the roles and rankings of major actors have changed since the mid-twentieth century. The words 'superpower' and 'bipolarity' first entered popular discourse after the end of the Second World War when the Cold War developed between two nuclear and ideological rival blocs. In the 1970s and 1980s, with Europe and Japan literally back in business, there was considerable speculation about the 'decline' of the United States. Some believed Japan had a more vibrant economy and society and that the twenty-first century therefore might 'belong' to Japan. As Joseph S. Nye, Jr commented in 1990, the United States had shifted from being the world's largest creditor to a net debtor, and there was significant slippage in production, exports, and monetary reserve statistics as well. He noted that:

> By 1989, half the American people believed the nation was in decline. Only one in five Americans believed that the United States was the top

economic power, even though it remained by far the world's largest economy. After President Reagan's military build-up in the 1980s, only a fifth of the people believed that the United States was ahead of the Soviet Union in overall military strength

(Nye 1990:2).

In this context, Nye was a lonely voice arguing that the United States was still the dominant world power and 'bound to lead'. More prevalent were voices like Paul Kennedy's, who in 1987 stressed the 'relative decline' of the United States and warned of 'imperial overstretch' (Kennedy 1987). His theme of empire foreshadowed later characterisations.

The demise of the Soviet Union and the end of the Cold War brought a more optimistic assessment of the US position in global politics. The United States was described as the only remaining superpower, and Charles Krauthammer (1990/91), among others, asserted the existence of a 'unipolar moment' in global politics. Francis Fukuyama (1992) went still further to proclaim 'the end of history', the almost certain eventual worldwide triumph of democratic ideals, free-market capitalism, and related neoliberal economic policies. The 1990s was an era when scholarly and public concern focused on globalising trends of which the United States was a leading proponent and beneficiary. Few doubted US pre-eminence in world affairs, only perhaps whether the United States would assume the full burdens of leadership and manage to persuade its European allies and others to provide adequate help. Richard N. Haass's description of the United States as a 'reluctant sheriff' captured the spirit of the times (Haass 1997). The Gulf War experience in 1991 seemed to suggest that the United Nations, under American leadership, might at last be functioning with Security Council cooperation as its founders had hoped and that others were prepared to join in a 'coalition' (or 'posse', maintaining the sheriff metaphor) to maintain order in the world as required.

The context shifted yet again with the advent of the George W. Bush administration and the 'War on Terrorism' that followed the apocalyptic attacks of 11 September 2001. The attacks awakened the sleeping dragon of American patriotism and provided an atmosphere in which pugnacious neoconservatives in the Bush administration gained the upper hand in internal bureaucratic debates. Their vision was one of unabashed American global primacy and involved deep mistrust of international institutions and multilateralism generally; diplomatic pressures and military 'pre-emptive strikes' as needed to defeat terrorism and curb 'rogue states'; a determination to keep weapons of mass destruction out of the wrong hands; and a campaign to spread democracy in the name of the 'democratic peace'.

The Bush administration's posture generated a chorus of US triumphalism in some quarters and warnings from others about American 'hyperpower'. That status has been otherwise described as 'superpower', 'hegemony', and even 'empire'. Michael Mandelbaum, for instance, wrote:

In the league standings of global power, the United States occupies first place –and by a margin so large that it recalls the preponderance of the Roman Empire of antiquity. So vast is American superiority that the distinction bestowed upon it and its great rival, the Soviet Union, during the Cold War no longer applies. The United States is no longer a mere superpower; it has ascended to the status of a 'hyperpower'.

(Mandelbaum 2002: 61)

Stephen G. Brooks and William C. Wohlforth similarly concluded: 'If today's American primacy does not constitute unipolarity, then nothing ever will. ... [T]he United States has no rival in any critical dimension of power. There has never been a system of sovereign states that contained one state with this degree of dominance' (Brooks and Wohlforth 2002: 21, 23).

Realist Power Factors

Superpower and related notions rest firmly on traditional realist and neo-realist models of international relations. One measure of the influence of classical realism is that practically every undergraduate student of world politics finds a chapter in their introductory textbook listing the 'power factors' that contribute to the power of a state.

By any such list, the United States scores impressively. The United States has a large and growing population in a large country with many natural resources, which is strategically situated between two countries neither of which constitute a military threat, and is separated from the rest of the world by two vast oceans. Even in the age of missiles, supersonic aircraft, global markets, and Al Qaeda, that geographical separateness remains significant. Although it slowed somewhat in recent years, US economic growth has outstripped that of other developed societies, compensating for Japanese deflation and still slower growth in most of Europe. And no one doubts that US corporations have been the primary engines of economic globalisation. Brooks and Wohlforth (2002) point out that the US economy is twice as large as that of Japan, its closest rival (among individual states); and that California's economy alone is the fifth largest in the world, ahead of France and only a little behind the United Kingdom. American media, American technology, and American products project US cultural influence worldwide.

Realists, of course, stress military power, and the high-tech wizardry on display in the 2003 invasion of Iraq, combined with American conventional forces and nuclear capabilities, puts the United States in a category of its own. An overview published by *The Economist* in 2002 before the second Iraq War is fairly typical:

By almost any of the usual measurements of power, the United States lead over others is far greater than, for example, that held by Britain in 1870,

and constitutes a situation of apparently overwhelming dominance. The U.S. share of Global GDP is 31.2%, of Global Defense Spending 36.3%, of Global Spending on research and Development 40.6%, and of Global movie box office revenues [blockbusters of a different kind?] 83.1%
('Present at the Creation: A Survey of America's World Role' 2002: 4).

In 2003, US military spending of $399 billion was as much as the next twenty top-spending countries *combined*. Brooks and Wohlforth (2002: 22) note that the US spends more on military research and development (R & D) than the next six countries combined and, perhaps more significantly, that it purchases its military pre-eminence with only 3.5 per cent of its GDP. As Paul Kennedy observed, 'being Number One at great cost is one thing; being the world's single superpower on the cheap is astonishing' (cited in Brooks and Wohlforth 2002: 22). John J. Mearsheimer (2001), perhaps the most prominent traditional realist in academic circles, concludes that the United States is likely to remain pre-eminent for the foreseeable future, and only warns that there are likely to be continued 'struggles for power' among 'great powers' in different regions and that a rising China might pose a serious threat if it achieves hegemony in Northeast Asia.

Limitations of Realist Assessments

Despite their surface appeal, power factors lend themselves to unsophisticated generalisation that obscures far more than it clarifies. One consideration is that each of the power factors has a 'downside'. 'Homeland security' is more difficult in a large homeland, especially one with an open democratic society and long undefended borders. The United States's isolated geographic position complicates efforts to project military power to distant places like the Middle East without overseas bases. American economic activity depends heavily on consumer spending, and Americans' abysmal saving rate produces dependence on Japanese, Chinese, and European purchases of American government securities to pay for huge trade and spending deficits. Energy profligacy makes the United States especially vulnerable to events in unstable and sometimes hostile oil-exporting regions. Military spending itself can be an albatross, insofar as the old adage about guns not being butter still holds. High-tech and nuclear weapons are largely ineffective in dealing with irregular conflicts such as the Iraq insurgency. Patriotism and moral zeal may lead to hubris and foreign adventures that are pure folly. And so on.

More important is the fact that – as W. T. R. Fox used to say in his Columbia classroom – 'power is not like money in the bank that one can draw on equally for all purposes'. Power is a *relative* concept and relative to more than just the power of other states in a Mearsheimer-like calculation. Fox offered what he insisted was the only 'Compleat Power Statement': A, B, C have power over D, E, F with respect to issues G, H, I under prevailing conditions X,Y, Z. Thus the context for any exercise of potential power is crucial.

For all its star-rating on the power chart, there are often serious limits to the effective exercise of US power, as many a president has discovered to his dismay. For example, President John F. Kennedy placed a high priority on cleaning up his Caribbean neighbourhood by getting rid of both Fidel Castro and 'Papa Doc' Duvalier. Decades later (at this writing) an enfeebled Castro is still in power, while Papa Doc died in his bed (later than Kennedy) and was succeeded by 'Baby Doc'. Cuban and Haitian politics will likely continue to bedevil Washington for many years to come. The Johnson and Nixon administrations poured blood and treasure into saving Vietnam from the communists, only to suffer humiliating defeat. Successive administrations have pressured Israel and the Palestinians to make some sort of peace, which remains elusive to the present day. Will the current Bush administration (or any administration) be able to bring political stability and democracy to Afghanistan or Iraq or Lebanon? Certainly the prospects are not very bright. Can the United States turn back the rising tide of Islamic fundamentalism, or does Washington's 'War on Terrorism' generate more anti-American fanaticism than it suppresses?

Not only does the effectiveness of the exercise of power differ by target actor(s) and issue and prevailing circumstances, but also resources must be sufficiently mobilised in advance for use. Even for a putative superpower, resources are not unlimited, and opportunities and challenges for their deployment have a disconcerting way of arising simultaneously. Thus, as the second war with Iraq proceeded, administration hawks were talking up some sort of drastic action in response to nuclear programs in North Korea and Iran. What indeed are the deployment options for the United States, which has no conscription and depends – in the absence of a palpable threat of sufficient magnitude – on a volunteer military that is itself substantially in reserve? After 9/11, US public opinion rallied around the flag, but support for involvement in the Iraq quagmire rapidly waned and there is little support – and a woefully inadequate number of men and women under arms – for extending military operations to other foreign fields.

A country's reputation matters, and America's reputation has suffered dramatically since the Iraq War ('U.S. Image Up Slightly, But Still Negative' 2005). Even examplar realist Hans J. Morgenthau (1978: 154) recognized the importance of how a country is perceived by others. '[A] government', he wrote, 'must ... gain the support of the public opinion of other nations for its foreign and domestic policies.' 'The power of a nation, then, depends not only upon the skill of its diplomacy and the strength of its armed forces but also upon the attractiveness for other nations of its political philosophy, political institutions, and political policies.'

Morgenthau was writing at the height of the Cold War, but the message – as Nye points out – is even more relevant in an era of clashing cultures and increasing globalisation. 'Hard power' is no longer enough. 'By traditional measures', writes Nye, 'no sovereign state is likely to surpass us, and terrorists cannot defeat us.' However: 'Fewer issues that we care about will prove susceptible to solution through our dominant military power. Policy makers will have to pay more attention to the politics of credibility and the importance of soft power' (Nye 2002: 75–76).

As Nye (2004: 73) recognizes, the society of states is not all that matters in global politics any more. Issue outcomes in global affairs are typically controlled or influenced by various *polities* of different types. The sovereign state is only one polity type and is rarely if ever a unified actor. Moreover, in many issue contexts, the state may not be the most important polity involved. Other polity types include families, tribes, cities, firms, religious organizations, international governmental organizations, and nongovernmental organizations. To the extent that polities have effective control or influence over particular issues, they may be said to be 'authorities' in that domain. The key point is that governance by various polities can and does exist within, across, and beyond the jurisdiction of sovereign states. Focusing on capabilities in the abstract does not give adequate weight to the enormous store of day-to-day global governance that has little or nothing to do with the Washington leviathan. The same, of course, might be said against assertions about hegemony and empire.

Hegemony

Hegemony is another concept with a long history that is receiving renewed attention (see Lamy, English, and Smith 2005). Quite apart from its roots in the ancient Greek rivalries, hegemony has been stock-in-trade of Gramscian analysis that associates it with a powerful coalition of elites. Philip Cerny (2006) rightly asserts that 'the very definition of hegemony is contested and therefore that any analyst's use of [it] will inevitably be value-loaded in terms of both a choice of definition and the methodological implications of applying it to particular empirical phenomena'.[1] Such, of course, is true of any major concept – including all three we spotlight in this paper – but making sense of hegemony and assessing its usefulness presents its unique challenge.

The fundamental contest plainly lies in the distinction between hegemon and hegemony. R. Barry Jones (2001: 669), for example, defines hegemony as 'the occupation of a dominant position in any system'. Surely this is about as good a working definition as we can get, but it still begs questions: Is the hegemon a single state or something else? What 'system' are we considering? And is hegemony an attribute of an actor and/or the system as a whole? Cerny, for example, writes:

> Hegemony is not merely the fact of holding a disproportionately powerful position, but one where that dominant position is firmly embedded in, and indeed generated through, a wider system which gives it its very

meaning and effectiveness. In other words, hegemony represents a structural space or level that is only significant in the way it gives rise to, stabilizes, manages, shapes, expands, and/or controls the wider system in which it is embedded. Hegemony is a *state or condition of the system itself*, and not a property belonging to the hegemon.

(Cerny 2006)

Ah yes, but where is the hegemon, the supposed prime mover, in the midst of all this? We can see this analytical problem in Donald Puchala's persuasive assertion that:

the hegemony that prevails today over the workings of major international organizations, including the UN, is not the imposed will of 'the only remaining superpower' but more precisely the imposed will of the historical bloc herein identified as the West. It is a hegemony of ideas – liberal ideas – that decisively affects and patterns outcomes in global political, economic, military, social and cultural affairs.

In his view, the US role 'is that of an enforcer' and the UN serves 'to validate the liberal world order' and consign 'counter-hegemonic ideas and projects' to 'history's dustbin' (Puchala 2005: 581). Interestingly, in this formulation, the United States appears to be an instrument of collective action of the West, rather than the sort of isolated and militantly unilateral superpower or empire that critics of the Bush administration contend.

Once again, recalling our discussion of the dangers of generalising about the United States as a superpower, we encounter similar difficulties with hegemony. Not only does it present the knotty question of where the putative hegemon ends and the system begins, but also which hegemony are we talking about and indeed – much more important – which system? Is there but one, or – as we insist – does world politics consist of countless overlapping and nested issue systems with different clusters of actors that have varying influence over outcomes? Cerny (2006) seems to be moving towards this conclusion when he comments that 'hegemony is unlikely to be a homogeneous or holistic phenomenon. It is made up of component parts, such that any attempt to put those parts together into a synthesis with predictable implications for real-world behaviour is little more than guesswork [and] its application to the complex contemporary world is fraught with hazard.'

Empire[2]

Empire Is Back but Never Really Left

Perhaps even more than superpower and hegemony, empire is back in the popular media, talked about within the Washington Beltway and at US military academies, discussed in scholarly publications and conferences, and denounced by anti-globalisation protestors and Islamic militants. The stock of empire is definitely up. It began to climb with the Bush team's early unilateral rhetoric and actions and soared after the terrorist attacks of 11 September 2001, the subsequently declared War on Terror, and military interventions in Afghanistan and Iraq. Frederick Cooper (2003–04: 1) observes: 'Now the state is back, and in one instance in a form so powerful that public intellectuals call it an empire.' However, as Alexander Motyl (2006: 229–30) comments: 'That empire in general and American empire in particular should be so closely associated with the actions of just one American administration ... is good reason to be suspicious ... about the utility of the concept.' 'When a word comes to dominate discourse, it has become a cultural phenomenon. But is empire also real?' We will return to that key question shortly and also the matter of whether stock in the putative US empire is now overvalued.

Although the Bush neocons and their political allies put the idea of empire back in the spotlight, we really should not make too much of the novelty. That is because empires, like the poor, have been with us always. Our field's fixation on the Westphalian state has tended to obscure the fact that the *main* actors in global politics, for much of history, have been empires rather than states. 'Most people throughout history', declares Eliot Cohen (2004: 50), 'have lived under imperial rule. The current international system, with nearly two hundred independent states and not a single confessed empire, is a historical anomaly.' State construction and evolution during the Westphalian era itself was also inextricably linked with building, defending, and (sooner or later) losing empires. Ironically, it was the European empires that carried the idea of the sovereign territorial state to the rest of the world, an idea that came back to haunt them when European ideas about nationalism and national self-determination also spread to the colonies. A peculiar Western polity form and its supporting ideology thus was superimposed over older polities and identities that nonetheless were not erased completely.

Even before the latest Bush administration, the 'unipolar moment' of the lone superpower and attendant globalising trends helped give empire some currency during the last decade of the twentieth century. A book by Andrew J. Bacevich (2002) on American Empire argued that there is little difference between the US role in the world as conceived and practiced by the George W. Bush and earlier Clinton administrations, and indeed that both had their foundation on 'U.S. exceptionalism' and dreams of special mission that are almost as old as the country itself. (Unfortunately, Bacevich published his book in 2002, before the excesses of Iraq highlighted the striking differences between Clinton and Bush.) Another widely read book, *Empire* by neo-Marxists Michael Hardt and Antonio Negri, also in fact antedated the current Bush administration. 'This book', they declare, 'was begun well after the end of the Persian Gulf War and completed well before the beginning of the war in Kosovo. The reader should thus situate the argument at the midpoint between those two signal events in the construction of Empire' (Hardt and Negri 2000: xvii). Hardt and Negri make it clear that their version of empire includes far more than the United States and is roughly equivalent to 'globalisation' in its economic and other dimensions. More about Hardt and Negri shortly.

Long before the 'unipolar moment', the bipolar world of two superpowers could have been and sometimes was regarded as a Cold War contest of two empires. President Reagan publicly characterized the Soviet Union as the 'Evil Empire', which he contrasted with the 'Free World' that the United States led in the halcyon years before Washington had to depend upon ever-diminishing 'coalitions of the willing'. The political Left was loathe to call the Soviet sphere an empire, although it was happy enough to apply that label to US behaviour in Latin America and other parts of the world. Then, as Motyl (2001) observes:

> The sudden unraveling of the USSR was the puzzle that revived the interest in empire. The abrupt and peaceful end of a superpower manifestly had something to do with the Soviet Union's internal constitution. And yet, although multinationality, hypercentralization, and other features frequently associated with empire had long been evident to Soviet nationality experts, if not to mainstream Sovietologists, they were rarely conceptualized in imperial terms. ... Ironically, the Soviet Union 'became' an empire at the very moment it ceased to exist.

The Puzzling Concept of Empire

The knotty question, then, is how is empire to be distinguished from all the other related concepts, if indeed the term has any inherent or even useful meaning at all. What is the essence of empire? How does it compare with superpower, hyperpower, hegemony, multinational states, federations, confederations, markets, or regional organizations? How does it relate to concepts like 'imperialism', 'suzerainity', 'colonial', 'post-colonial', or even 'globalisation'? '"Imperialism", as a word,' bemoans Stephen Howe, 'has gone imperial; "colonialism" has colonized our languages ... They have come to be used, at the extreme, to describe anyone's, any group's, or anything's supposed superiority, or domination, or even just influence, over any other person, or group, or thing' (Howe 2002: 10–11). The task of being more precise is made all the more difficult by the fact that there is no consensus even in the scholarly literature about the definition of empire – quite the contrary.

For example, Hardt and Negri describe their 'Empire' of globalisation as 'a regime that effectively encompasses the spatial totality, or really that rules over the entire "civilized" world' and in which the 'United States does indeed occupy a privileged position'. However, they also insist that "*no-nation-state can today, form the center of an imperialist project.*" Paradoxically, they then conclude: 'Imperialism is over. No nation will be world leader in the way modern European nations were' (Hardt and Negri 2000: xiii–xiv). Instead, 'sovereignty has taken a new [capitalist] form, composed of a series of national and supranational organisms united under a single logic of rule' (Hardt and Negri 2000: xii). In their view, 'the concept of Empire presents itself . . . as an order that effectively suspends history and thereby fixes the existing state of affairs for eternity'; indeed, it 'is always dedicated to . . . a perpetual and universal peace outside of history'. Furthermore, their Empire 'operates on all registers of the social order' and 'not only regulates human interactions but also seeks directly to rule over human nature' (Hardt and Negri 2000: xiv–xv).

Most recent assessments of United States power and influence have been equally broad. '[T]he British Empire', according to historian Niall Ferguson (2002: xii), 'is the most commonly cited precedent for the global power currently wielded by the United States. America is heir to the Empire in both senses: offspring in the colonial era, successor today.' G. John Ikenberry (2002: 44) observes:

> [S]weeping new ideas of circulating about U.S. grand strategy and the restructuring of today's unipolar world. . . . At the extreme, these notions form a neoimperial vision in which the United States arrogates to itself the global role of setting standards, determining threats, using force, and meting out justice.

'Whether or not the United States now views itself as an empire', adds Dimitri Simes (2003: 93), 'for many foreigners it increasingly looks, walks, and talks like one, and they respond to Washington accordingly' and 'an understanding of America as an evolving, if reluctant, modern empire is an important analytic tool with profound consequences.'

Simes's assertion that the United States now 'looks, walks, and talks' like an empire again highlights the problem of establishing just what sort of a duck an empire is. Simes offers a general description. Empires, he argues, 'exercise great authority over large and varied territories populated by diverse ethnic groups, cultures, and religions. They rely on a broad range of tools and incentives to maintain this dominance: political persuasion, economic advantage, and cultural influence where possible; coercion and force when necessary.' They also 'expect neighboring states and dependencies to accept their power and accommodate to it', and they have 'unique responsibilities and rights' that allow them to play by different rules than 'ordinary states' (Simes 2003: 92).

When we try to be any more precise than that we run up against the paucity of *careful* definitions of 'empire' in the scholarly literature. Why have we so few? However much in retrospect we might want to regard the post-Second World War Cold War as a contest between rival empires, in fact, the retreat of the former European empires and birth of so many new states focused attention on sovereign states. For a time, research on other political forms languished, leading Motyl (2001: 1) to observe that 'empire, as a distinctly *political* system, has received scant attention from social scientists. ... Until recently, Michael Doyle's [mid-1980s book on empires] truly was a voice in the wilderness.' Motyl reviews Doyle's definition of empire and those of several other scholars: Doyle defined it as 'a relationship, formal or informal, in which one state controls the effective political sovereignty of another political society' (Doyle 1986: 45). David Lake (1997: 34) described the relationship as one where 'one partner cedes substantial rights of residual control directly to the other; in this way, the two polities are melded together in a political relationship in which one partner controls the other.' Geir Lundestad (1990: 37) suggests that 'empire simply means a hierarchical system of political relationships with one power being much stronger than the rest'. Alexander Wendt and Daniel Friedheim (1995: 695) describe 'informal empires' as 'structures of transnational political authority that combine an egalitarian principle of de jure sovereignty with a hierarchical principle of de facto control'.

These definitions are far from satisfactory. Re Doyle's definition: Cannot one 'state' include another state at least in its informal empire as the USSR controlled Poland after the Second World War? When does 'effective political sovereignty' become ineffective? If State A controls several functions of State B, but State B retains control of other functions, is the latter's sovereignty effective or ineffective? What is a 'political society'? Does US control of Texas make it an empire? The same might be asked of Lake's definition. Lundestad's definition makes it impossible to separate empire from hegemony. As for Wendt and Friedheim, how much de facto control tips the balance to a 'hierarchical principle'? Were there no informal empires before sovereignty appeared as a Westphalian norm?

How, then, *are* we to differentiate between empire and other political institutions and relationships? What is at stake is our ability to categorise the universe of political behaviour, systems, and institutions we purport to describe and analyze.

When all is said and done, we submit, there are four avenues to resolving the problem: empirical, ideal type, constructivist, and normative. Each of these approaches has its practitioners and utility, although admittedly *the four are not entirely distinct*. All are constructions in their way and all carry normative implications.

Empirical Essence

The first approach is empirical in that it seeks to craft ironclad definitions to distinguish empire from that which is not empire. Motyl (2001: 4) insists that productive analyses of empire cannot proceed unless there is agreement as to what empire is – and is not. He notes that 'political entities do not become – or stop being – empires merely because terminological fashion says so'. 'Concepts usefully apply to reality if and only if we can isolate their defining characteristics *and* find appropriate empirical referents.' To his credit, he produces a persuasive version of the just the kind of definition he has in mind. He writes:

> What distinguishes empires from centralized multinational political systems ... is structure. The nonnative state's elite located in the core coordinates, supervises, and protects the peripheral native societies, which ... interact with one another only via the core. Empires, then, are structurally centralized political systems within which core states and elites dominate peripheral societies, serve as intermediaries for their significant interactions, and channel resource flows from the periphery to the core and back to the periphery. As structured systems, empires need not have emperors, ideologies, and exploitative relationships to be empires; by the same token, nonempires may have these features without being empires.
>
> (Motyl 1999: 126)[3]

Motyl also accepts another characteristic of empires, that they may involve direct rule by administrators of the core stationed in the periphery or indirect rule by native administrators under the control of the core – and normally some combination of the two.

Motyl's essence of empire is thus a hub and spokes model. That may be as near to a consensus definition as we can find. As Howe observes: 'Most analysts ... seem to agree that an empire is formed ... out of a dominant "core" and a dominated, often economically exploited "periphery."' An empire, he adds, 'rules over territories outside its original borders', which relationship 'always involve[s] a mixture of direct and indirect rule' (Howe 2002: 18, 14, 15).

We should pause at this juncture to note that, whatever empirical definition is most appropriate today, 'empire' has not always had the same meaning, and the practice of empire has differed dramatically over the years. The word 'empire' originally derived from the Roman word *imperium*, describing the executive authority of the Roman magistrates, analogous to the much later word 'sovereignty'. So Machiavelli could begin his *The Prince* with the phrase: 'All the states and dominions which have had and have empire over men.' Empire also came to be associated early-on with a sort of Aristotelian dominion that might or might not have external possessions or even ambitions. Only with the advance of the modern European imperial projects were the earlier usages of empire overshadowed by the modern understanding of hub and spoke (see Morrison 2001: 2–3). Meanwhile, the practical nature of empire had changed. There was a general trend away from patrimonial territorial conquest and simple accumulation that characterized the earliest empires to later empires driven primarily by the development of modern capitalist economies at home and the search for materials and markets abroad.

As Motyl contends – and surely he is correct – the crucial differences between empire and hegemony and related concepts like superpower and hyperpower are that the latter relationships are not hub and spokes and not a matter of direct or indirect administrative rule. Using this distinction, Motyl takes Niall Ferguson to task for confusing empire and hegemony in his recent book *Colossus* (2004). Ferguson argues that the paradox is that the United States really is an empire but refuses to act like one, a claim Motyl regards as absurd. Either the United States is an empire or it is not, and if the US is a hegemon, which Motyl believes it is, surely it cannot be faulted for not acting like an empire (Motyl 2006: 235).

Be this as it may, does empire characterize the United States any better than superpower or hegemon? If it is an empire, where is the hub (core) and what are the spokes (periphery)? In terms of territorial possessions abroad, apart from various military bases and what one might hope will be a gradually phasing-out presence in Afghanistan and Iraq, what else is there but Puerto Rico, the US Virgin Islands, and Guam? But, one might object, what of the empire of capitalism in all its dimensions in the analyses of historian William Appleman Williams (1980), Marxists, neo-Marxists, and Gramscians? Is not the empire of capital the real empire? But that alleged empire is inherently private and substantially transnational. It is not identical to or congruent with the United States or the Bush administration, whatever the 'Washington Consensus' or the presence of business lobbyists in high places. In a sense, Hardt and Negri are closer to the mark, but they too falter on the lack of Motyl's core and also the requisite coordination to make for hegemony – not to mention the indeterminate nature of the periphery. Who speaks and makes the decisions that shape the world economy? It is a market system or complex process with myriad actors. Government bureaucracies and international institutions, influenced by major governments, but not without some autonomy, have a major role. However, a host of private actors with their own regional and global strategies are the primary players.

Ideal Type

Motyl wants us to be empirical, but that should not rule out more flexibility than he allows. For example, he takes to task Dominic Lieven, a writer he otherwise praises, for his 'ambivalence toward conceptual clarity', that is, his refusal to provide what Lieven terms a 'sharply precise, all encompassing concept of empire'. Motyl (2006: 244) insists that only such a precise concept could identify those imperial polities worth including in Lieven's book. Yet Lieven focuses his book (2001) on several empires – the British, Ottoman, Habsburg, and Russian/USSR – whose inclusion in a book on *Empire* can hardly be controversial to anyone but Motyl.

A second approach to the definitional questions regards empire and other political forms as no more than ideal types – perhaps distinguished as much or more by what they are not as by what they are. (It should be stressed that this sort of ideal type is different from the Weberian variety, which is what we have labelled an empirical essence.) From this second perspective – one that we adopt in our work on polities – imperial forms shade off into other polities along a continuum or perhaps in all directions. Here we are in company with one founder of 'the English School', Adam Watson, who has a particular interest in 'international systems' before the European state system. '[I]n my examination of past and present systems', wrote Watson (1992: 4), 'it has become increasingly clear to me that while systems of independent states certainly differ from suzerain or imperial systems, a simple dichotomy between them is inadequate to describe the actual realties. A system of absolutely independent states and a heterogeneous empire wholly and directly administered from one center, are theoretical extreme cases.' In practice, 'all known ways of organizing diverse but interconnected communities have operated somewhere between these two extremes'. In addition, a 'given group of communities ... changes and evolves' and in doing so becomes 'tighter or looser, and so move along the scale in one direction or the other'.

Potentially inherent in the ideal-type approach to empire is the obligation to specify the steps that are stages along the continuum or less-direct connections to other political forms. If there is one ideal type, what are the subtypes or variations? Some of the distinctions are obvious: land-based versus seaborne empires, empires of conquest and others only of trading posts, empires that are consolidated and others that simply go on moving like those of Alexander and Muhammad – and everything in between. But at some point in making all these distinctions we reach a stage of diminishing returns. Niall Ferguson for instance, lists eight characteristics of empires, any one of which may vary and so produce a significantly different empire. Motyl (2006: 234) jibes: 'A simple mathematical calculation shows that his menu results in 184,320 possible combinations!'

Social Construct

With so many different communities 'out there' that may or may not be empires, it should not be surprising that the third approach to dealing with the problem of definition accepts in constructivist fashion that empire is significantly and sometimes almost wholly a matter of perception. Simes's previously mentioned 'looks, walks, and talks' like an empire comes to mind. Kathleen D. Morrison (2001: 3) boldly refers to the 'pornography definition' of empire – 'I can't say what they are, but I know one when I see one'. Of course, the clear lesson to be drawn from the pornography debate is that it *is* a debate: What the Christian Right views as pornography is not the same thing as many of the rest of us do. So Niall Ferguson, to Motyl's disdain, regards the United States as an empire even though its citizens refuse to recognize that fact. Michael Mann terms the US an 'incoherent empire' or a 'failed empire', again raising the question of whether a polity can be something (that is, an empire) when it is actually not (Mann 2003, 2004). In any case, as we have stressed in connection with superpower, perceiving and labelling can have its own consequences and often dangerous ones. Nevertheless, having consequences is exactly what those of a normative bent intend.

Normative Concept

It is an easy shift from empire as perception to our final approach to the problem of definition, that is, empire as inherently a normative concept that is deliberately invoked to express approval or disapproval or to urge some particular course of political action. The very idea of empire has carried different positive and negative connotations over the years, and sometimes, as at present, to different audiences at the same time. At the height of the British Empire, most British citizens and many elsewhere in the world thought of empire as a wonderful thing, bringing order and civilization to 'benighted' peoples and encouraging global commerce. Then following the Second World War period, nationalist movements demanding self-determination insisted that empire is a bad thing, and critics of one or the other superpower were also liable to hurl the charge of 'imperialism' at one another. However, with the end of the Cold War and the spectacle of failed states, some commentators were willing to say that maybe some limited revival of imperialism or at least trusteeship might not be such a bad thing after all.

Niall Ferguson is in essence a fan of empire (especially the contemporary US version 'that dares not speak its name' (2006b: 70)), as are the Beltway neocons, and a British friend of ours is fond of saying he would welcome an American Empire as long as it were well-run (which he thinks it is not). Meanwhile, scholars like Michael Cox (2004) and Michael Mann fulminate against the so-called American Empire. In labelling the US role in the world as imperial, they are sticking out their tongue at the Bush administration and associating themselves with like-minded critics around the world of Washington's militarism, diplomatic heavy-handedness, and neoliberal economic policies.

Conclusion: Take What You Want

At the end of the day, depending on the approach to the definition adopted, one can have whatever superpower, hegemon, or empire one wants. But there are consequences, sometimes intended, that flow from the way one categorizes individual polities and political/economic relationships. Our own reading is that the grand imperial ambitions of the Beltway neocons have already died an ignominious death in the sands of Iraq and that 'imperial America' will soon have a quaint historical flavour. Anti-globalisation protesters will no doubt continue to identify with a vague neo-Marxist posture like that of Hardt and Negri, but will ultimately have to contend with glo-balising forces that are far broader than the United States and the world economy, and more complex and diffuse than Don Quixote's windmills.

Perhaps the most useful of all the definitional debates is the one about empires. As Cooper (2003–04: 2) suggests:

> The virtue of thinking about empire historically is that it cuts the nation-state down to size. We need not see history as a succession of coherent epochs: from empire to nation to post-nation globality. Recognizing the continuing importance of empires well into the twentieth century and the importance of political movements that sought to change as well as replace empires points to a more general issue of continued relevance: the *range* of possibilities for exercising power. In past as in future, communities may be imagined, but not all imaginings are national ones.

A similar perspective – albeit one that emphasizes the distinction between state and nation – guides our own analyses and is, we believe, the only viable orientation to studying global politics.

12 Post-internationalism and IR Theory (2007)

The concept of 'the international' calls to mind a time that extended until not so long ago when conventional wisdom held that the world was securely divided by territorial boundaries into sovereign, legally independent states. Those boundaries encompassed 'national' political systems, laws, societies, economies, and cultures. Relative peace and order were presumed most likely to prevail in that sort of 'domestic' context. By contrast, 'outside' was the 'anarchic', competitive, and often violent realm of 'the international'. In that realm, where each state pursued its 'national interest' defined in terms of 'power,' diplomacy involved mainly state-to-state intergovernmental negotiations, and international law and institutions were weak. At that time most IR theorists were self-styled 'realists' and they branded anyone who offered any other perspective an 'idealist' or 'utopian'.

The foregoing is a caricature of realist thought that nonetheless, we insist, captures the fundamentals of the realist vision. However, it is obviously not the full picture. It is important to put twentieth-century realism in its context. Realism drew its modern lessons from what E. H. Carr labelled the 20 years' crisis from 1919–39 and continued to flourish – despite its inability fully to comprehend the ideological nature of the contest – during the post-Second World War Cold War between the United States and its allies and the Soviet bloc. Perhaps not surprisingly in time of total war and under the shadow of nuclear annihilation, the preoccupation of the realists was with state security and conflict, to the neglect of almost everything else.

Moreover, some key realists themselves seemed to recognize that something was missing from their fundamental world view. For example, E. H. Carr (1962: 109) wrote:

> The theory of the divorce between the spheres of politics and morality is superficially attractive, if only because it evades the insoluble problem of finding a moral justification for the use of force. But it is not ultimately satisfying. ... [T]he attempt to keep God and Caesar in watertight compartments runs too much athwart the deep-seated desire of the human mind to reduce its view of the world to some kind of moral order.

'Exemplar' realist theorist Hans J. Morgenthau (1987: 154) wrote: 'The power of a nation . . . depends not only upon the skill of its diplomacy and the strength of its armed forces but also upon the attractiveness for other nations of its political philosophy, political institutions, and political policies.'

Far more significant is that even early on there were a few IR theorists who looked at the world with less state-centric lenses. For instance, one of the English School founders, Hedley Bull (1977), while largely comfortable with the realist tradition, famously insisted that states might well find it in their national interest to observe and advance international law, build international institutions, and encourage international cooperation. James N. Rosenau (1969) went even further to argue that there were 'linkages' between the 'domestic' and 'international' politics that constituted a feed-back loop of sorts. But most IR theory remained locked in a realist state-centric worldview that today – although still admired by some theorists and policy-makers, especially in the United States – seems reactionary and naïve, the foreign-policy equivalent of creationism in natural science.

Contemporary scholars are increasingly aware of the enormous variety of states, the important distinction between 'state' and 'nation', the fact that states even at the policy-making level are not unitary actors, the importance of international institutions and norms, and the probability that violence will be 'intrastate' or 'trans-state' rather than 'interstate'. It is also apparent that the present-day stage of global politics is crowded with countless actors of different types, whose complex interactions substantially determine the intermediate and longer-range course of particular dramas. Moreover, the flow of events not only reflects such relatively familiar background factors as diversity among world religions and petroleum resource scarcity, but also especially the breathtaking and accelerating pace and volume of 'globalisa-tion' in its multiple dimensions and related 'localisation' dynamics that include resistance to globalisation.

'Post-internationalism' or 'post-international' theory reflects the world-view described in the previous paragraph. This essay explains what post-internationalism is and how it relates to other IR schools, and suggests an agenda for future theory-building. Bad theory usually makes for bad policy, a fact manifest in the combination of neo-realism and 'neocon' liberalism that has dominated Washington in recent years. Happily, post-international insights are likely to refocus practitioners away from the Scylla of power balances and the Charybdis of democratic regimes toward a multiplicity of actors, identity politics, and changing conceptions of political space. Thus, post-international 'theory' is not only theoretical but also a practical way of thinking about the world and analyzing global political issues.

Is post-internationalism a 'theory' (in the IR professional sense) or 'merely' an analytical framework? The answer to the questions depends entirely upon the definition of 'theory' employed. If theory implies the capacity to establish cause and effect for everything of significance in global politics, post-internationalism falls short. But what established theory does not fall short if such is the standard? An example is realism, so widely accepted for many years as a theory as to have been a veritable paradigm. To be sure, post-internationalism advances a worldview and an analytical approach, but it also makes theoretical statements about the dynamics of global politics, actors, identities, and related matters.

Central Tenets of Post-international Theory

Departure from State-Centric IR Theory

Post-international theory arose out of dissatisfaction with the inadequacies and distortions inherent in traditional realist and neo-realist theories, especially their state-centric vision of the world. The post-international view is that – although sovereign states and their 'international' relations obviously remain important and are likely so to remain – the *state-centric world* accepted as a given by traditional theories never fully existed, certainly does not exist now, and will never exist.

Our initial break from a state-centric perspective came from recognition in the mid-1970s that leading textbooks were out of touch with the real world, especially regarding the proliferation of nonstate actors ranging from terrorists to transnational corporations (Mansbach *et al.* 1976). In the 1990s we developed a 'polities' model for analyzing global politics that emerged from empirical research on six pre-Westphalian systems (Ferguson and Mansbach 1996), and we revisited and extended that model in *Remapping Global Politics: History's Revenge and Future Shock* (Ferguson and Mansbach 2004). Interestingly, it was becoming clear that our perspective, generated independently, was converging with Rosenau's pioneering and prolific work (1990, 1997, 2003). Rosenau coined the term 'post-internationalism' to describe 'an apparent trend in which more and more of the interactions that sustain world politics unfold without the direct involvement of nations and states' (1990: 6; see also 1997: 38n and 2000: 219–37). He continues to refer to post-international and post-internationalism, although he now typically describes his personal 'paradigm' or 'worldview' in dynamic terms as one of 'turbulence' or 'fragmegration' (Rosenau 2003: 11–16). Our polities model (1996: 51–57, 383) similarly highlights 'integration' and 'fragmentation' or 'fusion' and 'fission'. But 'post-international' still seems to us to be the best shorthand characterization of contemporary global politics.

Continuity, Change, and Complexity

Post-international theory emphasizes continual change, but change that is much faster in some contexts than others. In some cases, change is little more than an addition to or extension of existing patterns and does not necessarily obliterate all that has gone before. At the other extreme, change may be transformative, producing dramatic alterations in the nature of political life (see Holsti 2002: 3–43). However, post-international theory does not hold that change is necessarily unilinear and contains no assumptions – stated or unstated – about 'progressive' versus 'retrogressive' change.

Rosenau (2002: 261–79) argues that there seem to be different 'temperaments' at work among theorists. Some are predisposed to look for continuities, while others are inclined to emphasize the degree to which the present is different from the past. Our own perspective stresses the critical importance of history, although we acknowledge all the subjectivity highlighted by constructivists that is inevitably involved in historical interpretation. (Is there any less subjectivity involved in interpreting the contemporary world? Probably not.) As Saskia Sassen (2006: 404) expresses it: 'One uses history as a series of natural experiments to raise the level of complexity.' The present is at once the same as and similar to the past in some respects, yet very different in others. *So exactly how is the present both similar to the past and also different?* Everyone would benefit if all theorists were obliged to answer both questions and marshal evidence before writing anything further.

Historical analysis makes us keenly aware of the resemblances between our twenty-first century world of fragmented authorities, shifting identities, and competing ideologies and pre-international epochs like the Hellenistic Age. It reminds us, too, of the persistence of many historical political forms, ideas, and loyalties that today constitute what we call a 'living museum'. Sometimes the past seems almost to 'haunt' or have its 'revenge' on the present. Different exhibits from that museum come out of the storage cabinets at various and often extremely inconvenient times.

Rosenau (1997: 22–23) also acknowledges historical precedents of non-state authority such as the Medici family and the Hanseatic League; diseases like the bubonic plague; and the information impact of the printing press, wireless, and telephone. But for him – and who could disagree? – 'there are ... major dimensions of the present era that have led to differences in kind and not just in degree when compared with earlier times'. It is thus perhaps fair to suggest that his emphasis is on transformative change, while ours is on *both* continuity and change that only when *regarded together* can capture and account for present-day complexity.

In sum, Rosenau (1997: 56–77) tells the story of a world where history is speeding up, a world characterized by a bifurcation of global structures, the proliferation of actors, technological revolutions, the globalisation of economic exchange, the presence of interdependence/collective-goods issues, the weakening of state authority, subgroupism, increasingly skilled individuals, and a widening income gap both within and across countries that reflects those who are benefiting from globalisation and those who are not benefiting (or are benefiting to a much lesser degree).

That, in general, seems to us to be an accurate description. Nonetheless, despite transformative change, there remain not only significant historical precedents but also, more important, *direct legacies from the past*. The contemporary world is experiencing *both* 'history's revenge' and 'future shock'. This conjunction, we believe, helps explain the 'multiple contradictions' that Rosenau discerns in what he terms 'a new and wide political space' in global politics that is 'the domestic-foreign frontier'. It is a world in which states remain, some of which are powerful, but in which sovereignty matters less and less despite leaders' assertions to the contrary. Boundaries have become sieve-like, and territory, though still capable of generating passionate feelings, is often transcended.

> Landscapes are giving ways to ethnoscapes, mediascapes, ideoscapes, technoscapes, and financapes.
>
> (Rosenau 1997: 4)

Given this condition of perverse and bewildering complexity, the central analytical challenge is, as Rosenau (1997: 5) expresses it:

> How do we assess a world in which the Frontier is continuously shifting, widening and narrowing, simultaneously undergoing erosion with respect to many issues and reinforcement with respect to others? How do we reconceptualize political space so that it connotes identities and affiliations (say, religious, ethnic, and professional) as well as territorialities? ... Under what circumstances does authority along the Frontier accrue to like-minded states, to global regimes, to transnational organizations, to subnational entities, or to coalitions of diverse types of actors?

Post-international theory *does* emphasize fundamental change in global politics, albeit strongly tempered by historical inheritance. Such theory breaks sharply and self-consciously with static models (see, for example, Gilpin 1981: 7). Post-international change is the product of simultaneous processes of fusion and fission of authority. The first is reflected in the growth of networks that connect and influence the behaviour of persons 'remote' from one another. Remoteness, of course, is a function of physical distance, technology, and, not least, mindset, but, unlike the past, geography has less impact upon psychological distance or proximity. Ancient empires were impossible to micro-manage from a distant centre owing to the limits of transportation and communication technologies, and contemporary networks would be inconceivable in the absence of much more advanced technologies. The second tendency is the fracturing of existing political units into islands of self-identification that localize and often specialize authority and encumber efforts to deliver collective goods.

Thus, some associations are falling apart even as others come together. 'The seeming contradictions between the forces spreading people, goods, and ideas around the world and those that are impelling the contraction of people, goods, and ideas within narrowed or heightened geographic boundaries' (Rosenau 1995: 3) are engines of change in the post-international model that Rosenau collectively describes as 'fragmegration.' The 'central argument' of one of his most recent books (2003: 3) is that 'the best way to grasp world affairs today requires viewing them as an endless series of distant proximities in which the forces pressing for greater globalisation and those inducing greater localisation interactively play themselves out'.

The normative implications of these processes remain decidedly confused. Political, economic, and cultural integration offer advantages of scale, but may consign fragmented and less competitive parts of world, for example, to relatively lower living standards. Disintegration or disaggregation of authority preserves local culture and offers the psychological satisfaction of smaller units, yet it may also result in marginalization and ethnic strife over battlefields like Kosovo or East Timor. The two processes of change are related. Centralization produces a desire for recognition of and respect for social, cultural, and political heterogeneity and spurs efforts to decentralize authority. Decentralization produces demands for economies of scale, greater functional capacity, and efficiency that can only be realized through the exercise of wider authority.

Polities, Global Governance, Identities, and Loyalties

Post-international theory sees the world as inhabited by countless actors of many different types that reflect different identities, are differentially engaged in countless issues, and (as we shall explain) exercise effective authority in particular domains and contexts.

Although Rosenau takes us a considerable distance away from state-centric formulations, he does not in one respect take us quite far enough. His model of global politics retains 'two interactive worlds ... : a multi-centric world of diverse, relatively equal actors, and a state-centric world in which national actors are still primary' (1990: 97–98). Of course, there are interstate interactions; yet fewer and fewer interstate interactions of importance are not mediated or affected by other, often non-territorial, polities. This is not simply the case of 'low politics' as was once thought (see, for example, Keohane and Nye 2001), where, for instance, giant transnational corporations and banks have become engines of modernization and economic inequality. It is increasingly the case of 'high politics' as well. Thus, Hizbullah has become a fulcrum among Israel, Lebanon, Iran, and the United States in a regional struggle for power, and the Horn of Africa is an arena of colliding militias, warlords, and religious militants. These are examples of stateless realism with a vengeance.

Just as states in the past 'captured' subnational and transnational groups, ranging from ethnic nations to religions to enhance their legitimacy and stability, today states are being 'captured' by tribal militias and religious groups, much as Marx thought the bourgeois state had been 'captured' by capitalists. Countries such as Afghanistan, Pakistan, and Somalia are little more than deceptive colours on archaic maps. The Iraqi state exists only in the myopic vision of the last defenders of the failed policies of the G. W. Bush administration, and the Lebanese state will need to be (re)constructed both literally and figuratively.

Accelerating change is producing an increasingly complex universe of actors in global/local politics. We call them polities, while Rosenau prefers the term 'spheres of authority' or 'SOAs'.[1] Polities are collectivities – territorial and non-territorial – with a significant measure of identity and institutionalization, a degree of hierarchy in their organization, and the capacity to mobilize persons and groups for political purposes (value satisfaction). Some entities more clearly meet these criteria than others. For instance, most states, international institutions, transnational corporations (TNCs), major NGOs, and criminal and terrorist organizations are polities. By contrast, most markets are not polities because they lack the requisite identity, institutionalization, and hierarchy. Like global issues, markets are not themselves actors but reflect background factors as well as the behaviour of many polities, often including corporations, banks, and financial funds, as well as the day-to-day actions of many individuals.

Polities coexist, cooperate, compete, and clash. They often overlap, layer, and 'nest' (Ferguson and Mansbach 1996: 48–49) and hence share some of the same 'political space' – territory, issues, identities, markets, and/or cyberspace. Polities are all 'becoming' in the sense that political evolution is constant, although they evolve at different rates and not necessarily in a unilinear fashion. Even older states in Europe, such as Germany, Italy, and Belgium, are still trying to establish a fully secure national identity. Consider also the complicated nesting of various states and traditional nations in the European Union. The challenge of forging a national identity and even preserving a modicum of political order is clearly far more desperate in many other countries.

In a post-international world, sovereign territorial borders are increasingly porous and routinely transcended by all the major currents of globalisation. For Stephen Krasner (1999: 4) this erosion of 'interdependence sovereignty' does not entail a weakening of the three other dimensions of sovereignty that he posits. However, the interconnectedness of these dimensions makes this dubious; for example, it is difficult to see how 'interdependence sovereignty' can be reduced without limiting 'Westphalian sovereignty' and vice versa.

The health of national economies responds as much, or more, to developments in the global economy as to the actions of central banks. For all the attempts to censor Internet content, more and more individuals around the globe daily access the information highway and use email and cellphones to communicate across vast distances. Movies and television and popular music have become both global and regional enterprises. Turbulent weather patterns exacerbated by global warming spare the citizens of no land. Diseases like SARS or bird flu threaten global pandemics and prompt transborder research cooperation. Despite recent tightening of border controls, owing in part to perceived terrorism threats, the movement of peoples proceeds apace and creates grave challenges of assimilation into national cultures. Groups of 'home-grown' Muslims in Britain watch Islamic television and respond to fundamentalist ideological appeals for jihad. And so on.

Post-international theory acknowledges the continuing importance of sovereign states in world affairs, but refuses to privilege them in analysis, overestimate their influence, and thereby fail to appreciate the often much greater influence exercised by a wide range of other actors or polities. The sovereign state, with its peculiar legal status as independent and sovereign, now appears to have been a contingent product of a particular time and place – early modern Europe (see, for example, Spruyt 1994). The territorial state model succeeded insofar as it did because it then provided a measure of security, encouragement for markets and long-distance trade, a reasonably dependable system of law and justice, and a national loyalty that helped to bridge the dangerous ethnic and religious cleavages of the times. Nonetheless, boundaries continued to shift, and the national construction of institutions and identities was by no means a foregone conclusion – and it remains a work in progress to the present day.

Contemporary IR theory has tended to lose sight of the fact that the most prominent political units throughout human history, apart from villages and cities, have not been states but empires. 'Much of what we call history,' argues Niall Ferguson (2006: 46), 'consists of the deeds of the 50 to 70 empires that once ruled multiple peoples across vast chunks of the globe.' Even the Westphalian era was at least as much about empires as it was about states. As the European states were themselves consolidating, they set off on campaigns of conquest in far-flung corners of the globe. It was those same empires that implanted the nation-state model over many older political forms, identities, and loyalties, with varying degrees of success. Ironically, the triumph of 'decolonization' in the post-Second World War era took place against a background of a Cold War between two rival superpowers that resembled informal empires. Indeed, some observers contend that a 'United States empire' still persists in the current so-called 'unipolar moment' that began with the collapse of the Soviet Union and its clients in Eastern Europe. That idea may now be sinking fast in the quagmire of Iraq.

In the post-international framework, each type of polity is only an ideal type and assumes many different forms in practice. There are, for example, many variations in the structures and processes of cities and empires, and the same is plainly true of sovereign states. The nearly 200 such sovereign states in the world today vary enormously in their size, political influence, governmental forms and institutions, bureaucratic rivalries, value systems, and actual autonomy. Also, the presence of countless other authorities and domains limits the influence or control even of states that by realist standards would surely be classified as 'great powers.' Some states are actually 'failing,' while many if not most are experiencing varying degrees of 'legitimacy crisis' (see, for example, Pharr and Putnam 2000). Most states lack adequate capacity to meet rising citizen demands, especially in a context of globalising trends.

Fragmentation is continually expanding the number and variety of states and other actors with which existing states must share the global political stage. In addition, as Rosenau points up, as access to education and information continually improve around the world, more and more 'skilled' individuals are assuming active political roles. By virtue of their immense personal resources, some individuals like Bill Gates, George Soros, and Ted Turner are actually super-empowered. Gates, for example, is worth about as much as the total national income of Bangladesh (Kroll and Fass 2006). However, ordinary citizens are better informed, ever harder to fool, and are demanding more of their leaders, at the same time as national governments are less able to deliver on their promises. This is a basic reason politicians of nearly all stripes stand so low in the public opinion polls in most countries.

The state is not likely to disappear as a political form because some national loyalties run deep, some states still do a reasonably effective job at their traditional tasks, and a few that started behind are catching up. Moreover, some actors other than the state (like organized crime and terrorist groups) are abhorrent to many citizens, corporations and banks are widely distrusted, and other actors are even less well organized than the state to deliver the things people and indeed global markets need and want. So as Sassen (2006) suggests, the crux of the matter is not whether states are 'winning' or 'losing' in a general sense, but what specific institutions, laws, and functions of particular states are being 'denationalized' or significantly constrained by globalising processes. For most states, that is a long and growing list.

The 'domain' of a polity – its 'reach' in political space – consists of the resources that it can command and the persons and groups who identify with it and comply with its directives. All polities are 'authorities' and 'govern' within their respective and often overlapping domains. Thus 'governance' exists within, across, and beyond the jurisdictions of sovereign states, 'Global governance,' in turn, refers to patterns of polity authority domains in the world and not only to forms of governance that are truly 'global.' It is important to understand that post-international theory defines authority and governance as effective influence or control. Authority need not be 'legitimate' to be effective, although almost every polity offers some sort of ideological justification for its existence and role. Moreover, those polities that are able to gain compliance without substantial coercion obviously tend, for that reason, to be all the more secure.

The central analytical question for post-internationalists is *who or what influences or controls what in global politics – and why?* With that question in mind, familiar conceptions of power, distribution of capabilities, international structure, territory, and boundaries in IR take on decidedly non-traditional dimensions. Power is a relative concept so that a polity's 'hard' or 'soft' power resources have limited significance in the abstract. Notwithstanding the loss of parsimony, what matters is which other polities that polity is attempting to influence regarding what issues and under what conditions. Territorial boundaries may be a help or hindrance in exercising influence, but issue systems typically transcend such boundaries, as often do the identities and loyalties of individuals. Much if not most of what happens or does not happen, routinely or otherwise, in the world by way of effective influence or control – that is, governance – has little or nothing to do with superpower, hyperpower, empire, hegemony, or indeed, with states. The current Bush administration's adventures in the Middle East offer ample evidence that a rogue superpower may turn out to be merely a mouse that roars or, at best, a bull in a china shop as far as accomplishing many of its major objectives is concerned.

A post-international approach presumes that another related assumption of traditional IR theory – that the world is fundamentally 'anarchic' – tells us little more than that there is no overarching supranational authority. Human affairs are largely governed, that is, 'ruled' on a day-to-day basis, by a multitude of individual polities that exist within, criss-cross, or transcend individual states. Some of these polities are internally dysfunctional or inclined to disruption and violence, but many, if not most, act individually and collectively in a peaceful, highly effective, patterned, and often pre-dictable manner. The news media record shocking events, perpetrated by nonstate or sometimes state actors or Mother Nature in the case of hurricanes and other natural disasters, but normally fail to record (because it is not 'news') the vast tide of human events that each day occurs with its accustomed and reassuringly benign rhythms. It is the actions of individuals and polities of many types that constitute that tide and – whatever palpable injustices persist – we must be aware and thankful that the prevailing condition is complexity and not utter chaos.

As noted earlier, each polity has its own domain and it is increasingly the case that domains overlap and authority is shared. This is the 'real world order,' one in which the transformation of the micro, macro, and micro-macro parameters specified by the post-international model has led to new patterns with a potential for stability as well as turbulence. Once again, disorder, serious instability, and violence are the exception rather than the norm, whether we are considering what we usually term 'politics,' markets, professions, or the neighbourhood garden club. Individuals and families affiliate with their local religious organizations, companies decide to invest in a particular market or to resist stricter environmental standards, a university changes its curriculum, refugees and illegal immigrants migrate across borders, labour unions form picket lines, the World Health Organization starts a new vaccination campaign, the US Federal Reserve raises interest rates, currency speculators push up or depress a particular currency, the British International Studies Association elects a president and governing board, and so forth. It follows that much of the disorder that prevails in the world has limited relevance to anarchy among states and everything to do with the capacity of nonstate polities to challenge states or operate beyond state control or under their radar.

The distribution and relations among identities and loyalties are central to post-international analysis. Every person has multiple identities. Although some identities can be imposed (for example, prisoners at Guantánamo), most are willingly accepted in exchange for psychological and/or material rewards. Loyalties are distinct from identities and flow only to those authorities and associated identities that provide tangible and/or intangible value satisfaction. Many identities and loyalties can coexist for long periods of time without serious conflict, but periodically contexts arise involving issues that force individuals to make invidious choices as to which identities/loyalties they will serve. Will gender trump religion as regards reproductive health or family planning? Will Islamism trump Arabism on the streets of Cairo (Slackman 2006; Giry 2006)? Does religion dominate citizenship among British Muslims (Caldwell 2006: 41–47, 62, 74)?

The territorial state is only one focus of human identity and loyalty, and often not the most important one. Once we use contextual analysis, states typically gain or lose on the affinity scale to the extent that they are viewed as serving the perceived interests of self or collectives like family, ethnic group, or religion that individuals normally hold dearer than their nation-state. Nested identities/loyalties, like nested polities, are part of what we have termed the world's living museum, and they are activated by issues that affect specific identity groups. When one polity incorporates another, identities and loyalties associated with the former polity are rarely obliterated entirely and, even when it appears that they have been, may eventually be resurrected or reconstructed. The post-Cold War explosion of tribal, ethnic, religious, and racial identities offers powerful evidence of the revival or reconstruction of old memories and loyalties. More importantly, many new polities continuously form and strive to enhance their identity and build the loyalty of their adherents.

As governments reveal themselves to be less and less capable of meeting citizens' expectations and aspirations, their legitimacy declines and alienation from them increases. The unmooring of individual loyalties from traditional institutions produces what Susan Strange (1996: 198–99) labelled 'Pinocchio's problem'. Once Pinocchio became a 'real boy,' he no longer had his puppet strings to guide him and, therefore, no authority to command his behaviour. In a world of decentralized authority, and lacking global governance, 'we too have Pinocchio's problem. Where do allegiance, loyalty, identity lie? Not always, obviously in the same direction. Sometimes with the government of a state. But other times, with a firm, or with a social movement operating across territorial frontiers.' No longer do national loyalties remain consistently dominant and, according to Strange, without such 'absolutes', 'each of us shares Pinocchio's problem; our individual consciences are our only guide'.

Notwithstanding 'Pinocchio's problem', it is also important to recognize that identities and loyalties are not entirely a matter of individual volition. There are social pressures and socialization, political culture, habitual ties that bind, any number of polities and less-coherent 'causes' that are actively bidding for our support and allegiance, and powerful external trends and individual circumstances that pressure us and limit our personal range of choices.

Confluence and Conflict with Other Theoretical Approaches

This chapter is obviously not the place for a comprehensive discussion and critique of other 'schools' of theory. In this section, however, we merely attempt to identify post-internationalism's key points of convergence and contest with several other well-known theoretical approaches.

Realism and Neo-realism

The question post-international theory poses – 'who or what influences what in global politics – and why?' – shares with realism and neo-realism a pre-occupation with identifying the sources and directions of the patterns of authority that we observe. However, the answers post-internationalists offer to the question are very different from those provided by realists and neo-realists.

Post-international theory eschews the realist assumption that the state is the primary or indeed only significant actor in global affairs. States remain important, most show no immediate signs of disappearing, and many are to some extent adapting to changing conditions. But the state and its bureau-cracies are only some of a host of influential polities motivated by a shifting mix of interests and passions (Hirschman 1977). Familiar distinctions between 'public' and 'private' begin to dissolve when we perceive that states may be captured by private interests and that private actors, like Hizbullah in Lebanon and Hamas in Gaza and the West Bank, also perform public-interest functions and substantially affect the public good (see Cutler *et al.* 1999: Hall and Biersteker 2002). Furthermore, states themselves rarely if ever 'act' in a unitary fashion. State decision-making is perhaps best understood when it is deconstructed. Almost all 'state' policies can and should be traced back to their wellsprings in the likes of bureaucratic infighting, particular personalities, legislative manoeuvring, interest group influence (increasingly transnational), and alliances with nonstate entities.

For post-internationalists – unlike classical realists, but as neoclassical realists like Jennifer Sterling-Folker (2005) acknowledge – 'national interest' is primarily a subjective construction. Power shifts, external threats, and opportunities for cooperation are substantially matters of perception. There are very few 'imperatives' emanating from the environment in which policy-makers and attentive publics operate. 'State survival' is only very rarely at stake, and the precise requirements of 'national defence' and effective foreign policies are often hotly debated. Morgenthau's famous dictum that states pursue their national interest defined in terms of power is seriously misleading. Power is rarely an end in itself, but a means to other ends, and in any event, as we have noted, is always contextual, relative to other actors, specific issues, and prevailing circumstances. Despite being a superpower or putative empire, the United States is unable to achieve even its highest priority objectives. Neoconservatives in the current Bush administration surely did not enhance American power by launching the Iraq war, nor did they heed Morgenthau's advice to make 'prudence' the touchstone for policy.

Krasner (1999) is correct in arguing that 'sovereignty' in practice has always been variable rather than absolute, although we do not accept his position that, therefore, the challenges states face in the contemporary era are not new. State 'sovereignty' is best seen as an aspiration, a legal status and claim of the right to exercise authority, but there is no guarantee that attempts to exercise it will be successful or be regarded as legitimate. Moreover, civil conflicts, terrorism, and criminal activities should dispel the Weberian myth that states have a monopoly on the legitimate use of violence.[2] Not all state violence is regarded as legitimate, and clearly some nonstate actors and their followers believe it is fine for them to kill and coerce too.

Post-internationalism rejects the classic realist tenet that the state is the main identity and allegiance for citizens. The key identities and loyalties in human existence are to self and family/clan, tribe or loved ones, to religion, to professions, to interest associations, to ethnicity (in some societies), even to sports teams, and so on – in short, to relationships and polities other than the state. The modern state came into existence partly through coercion, but primarily because citizens came to identify the welfare of the things they mainly cared about with support of and loyalty to the state. When that linkage weakens, crises of state authority ensue. Today, the state system is experiencing an authority crisis as politicians find it harder and harder to deliver on their promises, much as earlier transformations witnessed authority crises for dominant polities like the Catholic Church during the Reformation or the Roman Empire when confronted by Christianity and 'barbarian' tribal polities.

Post-international theory sees the growth of international and regional institutions, as well as the slow but steady advance of international law, as a natural result of states' efforts to achieve through some measure of collective action what their own territorial constraints make it impossible for them to achieve alone. Post-internationalists also reject the classic realist dictum that norms must yield to expediency in international relations (Morgenthau 1946: 175–91). Although norms may come into conflict with one another or may yield unanticipated outcomes, normative impulses permeate human individual and collective behaviour, including IR theory. They underpin ideology; they provoke passion; and, in fact, most actors regard them as crucial sources of legitimacy. In fact, even realists should be seen as preaching their own version of what 'ought' to be. National governments use the claim of 'national interest' to muddy the waters, but everything leaders say or do has inescapable normative overtones and repercussions.

Not surprisingly, post-internationalists have a broader view of international system structure than do neo-realists. The exemplar neo-realist, Kenneth Waltz, focused almost exclusively on the distribution of capabilities among states and resulting polarity that starkly contrasts with the issue-oriented and contextual world we described above. In a post-international world, innumerable polities of different types, as well as countless individuals, interact on particular issues that routinely cross or transcend state boundaries. Taking Strange's reference to Pinocchio a step further, an analogy might be dramas acted out in a marionette theatre: whenever the strings cards labelled for this or that drama are pulled, the marionettes whose strings are attached to those cards begin to 'act', while all the others remain motionless. Thus, one way of conceiving of the 'structure' of global politics consistent with post-international theory is as numerous issue systems. They carry names like 'Iran's nuclear program', 'justice for the victims of genocide in Cambodia', 'fish stocks in the Outer Banks', 'avian flu', 'human trafficking', 'economic collapse in Argentina', 'agricultural subsidies', 'intellectual pirating of movies and music', and so on. Issues can be discrete, but, like the polities that are engaged in them, often overlap and nest. Iranian nuclear ambitions are part of a larger non-proliferation issue-area and Cambodia and Darfur are part of a bigger issue of genocide and war crimes, and the like.

In addition, there is a disturbing absence of attention in the neo-realist universe to the structural implications of the distribution of subjective factors such as expectations and affect. Thus, from a post-international perspective, it is critical to map the distribution identities and loyalties and/or, like Rosenau, the orientations of individuals to various 'global worlds', which is his main theme in *Distant Proximities*. He is at pains to point out that those orientations – may we add, rather like our marionette example – may shift even as individuals find themselves engaged in different issues. In short, issues arise that generate different attitudes and behaviour, even as they increase or decrease the salience of particular identities and loyalties.

Among realists, we applaud the search of structural realists like Barry Buzan, Charles Jones, and Richard Little (1993) for 'deep structures' in the international system, which appear to us to have the potential of revealing a world of polities. We do, however, disagree with Buzan's and Little's position (2000) that each historical epoch produces a dominant polity type and that the dominant type in the modern era has been the state (see, also, Denemark *et al.* 2000). Much of human affairs have proceeded apart from the state, and arguably the state's share has further diminished in recent decades. 'Dominance' or 'hegemony' depends on the issue.

We may also consider structure in global politics in terms of differential engagement in prevailing patterns including globalizing trends. Thomas Friedman (2005) is no doubt correct that for some business elites and companies, the world is decidedly 'flat'. For Richard Florida (2005: 48–51) – considering such things as concentrations of population, energy consumption, and patents and copyrights – the world is 'spiky'. Sassen (2001) and others have somewhat similarly looked at the world as a landscape of 'global cities' – 'scattered territorialities' (Sassen 2006: 54) whose connections are providing much of the dynamism for globalisation and are themselves being transformed by it.

Last but not least with regard to structure is the distribution of winners and losers from prevailing patterns. This is a normative dimension. Marxists have traditionally been preoccupied with matters of equality and justice, as are many of today's post-positivists, and these are concerns that must not be lost despite the abject failure of Marxism as a political project. Plainly, there are 'haves' and 'have nots' and lots of 'in-betweens' in the contemporary globalizing world, whether one is focusing on political human rights or economic welfare. There are also, evidently, close connections among this sort of structure, identities and loyalties, and actual or potential conflicts.

Liberal Institutionalism, International Society ('The English School'), Constructivism, Critical Theory, and Postmodernism

International institutions have proliferated in recent decades and have become increasingly important and familiar polities in global politics. Unfortunately, over the years much of the scholarship that has sought to wrestle with the growing impact of international institutions and law has had a strong state-centric realist bias. This was true of the early work of liberal institutional theorist Robert Keohane (1984), Hedley Bull (1977) of the English School, and most recently the specific version of constructivism advanced by Alexander Wendt (1999). Wendt's phrase that 'anarchy is what states make of it' (1992: 391–425) is an example. Nonetheless, all of the foregoing theorists, in their different ways, tried to make the useful point that states engaged in 'international society' might well perceive their interests to be served as well or better by international cooperation than by conflict.

The early approach to explanation, on the one hand, gave too little attention to increasing levels of interdependence that make it all the more likely that states will find institutions and rules well-nigh indispensable and, on the other hand, to the significant autonomy won by some institutions after their creation. Keohane's later work (2002), for example, stresses the 'thick networks of interdependence' involving both states and other actors and also the facts that institutions themselves 'matter' and have their distinct sources of legitimacy. Similarly, non-state-centric constructivists, notably Friedrich Kratochwil (1989), Nicholas Onuf (Kubálková *et al.* 1998), and John Ruggie (1998), also have systematically explored the reasons for the importance of international law, constitutive principles, and less formal rules in world affairs.

The recent work of Michael Barnett and Martha Finnemore (2004), who characterize international organizations (IOs) as bureaucracies that exercise 'rational-legal' authority 'in their domain of action', has significantly advanced our understanding of IOs. Barnett and Finnemore note that IO constitutions and mandates frequently require extensive interpretation and indeed that exercising initiative to sort out problems is exactly what states often want IOs to do. That said, IOs still have to be wary of powerful states, but many IOs have far more room for initiative than they usually get credit for. Indeed, IOs have their own sources of authority that derive from their reputation for serving noble purposes and also technical expertise. Barnett and Finnemore suggest that in fact IOs have identifiable 'pathologies' that derive from their bureaucratic nature and hamper their ultimate performance.

Such efforts to give IOs their due merit approval, but should not be allowed obscure the fact that the spotlight should also fall on a much broader range of polities on the global stage. Onuf's brand of constructivism helpfully emphasizes 'polities' on the level of basic individual relationships all the way up to 'complex relations, practices, institutions, "structures", or social arrangements that are called states and IR'. Onuf paints a picture of a 'staggering complexity and constant change' within the interwoven patterns of overlapping social arrangements' (Kubálková *et al.* 1998: xi).

In this connection, it is worth recalling Bull's (1977: 264–76) additional speculations about the possible eventual emergence of a 'new medievalism' in the global system. This idea remains highly provocative because all the trends that he identified three decades ago as foretokens of a 'new medievalism' are even more apparent today. Bull was certainly on the right track, but there were always two difficulties with that characterization. First, the concept has unfortunate Eurocentric overtones since 'the Middle Ages' are too often seen merely as the prelude to the European state system. Second, 'the new medievalism' is too limited with respect to time frame since the sort of dispersed authority patterns Bull saw threatening have actually been a feature of most of world history. Some of the interesting work of various scholars on 'world system history' is assisting to make this clear (see Denemark *et al.* 2000). Arguably it was not the Middle Ages but the Westphalian era in Europe that was exceptional, although the post-international lens perceives plenty of dispersed authority in the Westphalian era as well.

Post-internationalists do share with constructivists and postmodernists a concern with the 'socially constructed' dimensions of global politics, including the importance of identities as promoting interests and conditioning human behaviour. It is interesting and significant that Rosenau (2003: 405–20) now speaks of himself (perhaps facetiously) as a 'pre-postmodernist', partly because he is now keenly aware of the ways his own personal assumptions and motivations over the years have shaped his approach to theorizing and partly because part of his enterprise in later years has effectively deconstructed some parsimonious theories and concepts. That is a mission we have also undertaken.

Post-international theory merges to some extent with critical theorists and postmodernists with respect to the elusiveness of concepts and language generally and about the inherently normative nature of all scholarship. However, post-internationalism parts company with extreme relativists among the postmodernists and some critical theorists epistemologically because it still regards the theoretical quest as being essentially an empirical enterprise. We insist – and here we are in accord with Wendt and most constructivists – that there *is* an objective 'reality' 'out there', however hard it is to analyze objectively because of inadequate information and 'the spectacles behind the eyes' we all wear. The subjective dimension of political life – ideas, norms, identities, even language – consists of empirical referents and, though more difficult to scrutinize than the objective dimension, is also 'out there.' This does not mean that we retain any lingering faith – unlike Rosenau – in the eventual triumph of 'scientific' analysis (Ferguson and Mansbach 2003). We are more comfortable in the company of 'soft' social scientists and humanists than strict 'scientists' (which Rosenau himself today is not) and rational-choice gamers.

A Post-international Research Agenda

Fathoming the emerging post-international world requires a very long historical perspective. Many of the dynamics and patterns we now observe are by no means unprecedented, although some are entirely new. But which are which? One might expect the past to be far 'simpler' in many respects – and it was in some ways – but it was also remarkably complex in others. Interdependence, overlapping polities, and competing identities have been prominent features of world politics for millennia, including the three centuries of the 'Westphalian moment'. Revisiting these features in other settings and epochs and examining how they played out in the past suggests useful lines of investigation for the present (see Ferguson and Mansbach 2002: 87–111).

The authors of this essay are now engaged in two major projects. One focuses on *pre-international* polities in the ancient Mediterranean area and another on empires old and new. Making sense of the successive transformations that characterized a pre-international epoch, including its eventual evolution into international relations, will provide insights into the fundamentals of political change as well as the range of political forms and allegiances that still have relevance for our contemporary world. One of the reasons we have chosen to zero in on the ancient Mediterranean area for one project is the abundance of information on that evolving historical system and also its direct influence on later European political institutions and ideas.

Analyzing empires (not confined to ancient Mediterranean area) is an important reminder that territorial states with legally fixed boundaries are not the only polities in human history with a claim to primacy. Like states, empires have come in all shapes and sizes. Some observers suggest (in our view, erroneously in any empirical sense) that an American empire persists to the present day. Empires at once illustrate the nesting that so often characterizes polities, as well as the critical lesson that any central polity finds its influence severely limited. Successful empires profited from an understanding of their limitations and dependence on the domains of other polities. The same, of course, has been true for states.

Another dimension of a broader post-international research agenda must focus on the origins, evolution, nesting, and possible demise of identities and loyalties. This is a relatively new frontier. To what extent are long-standing notions of self and others remaining constant or shifting in response to broad systemic changes? Answers to this question are crucial to understanding the viability of existing political forms and possible future patterns of political association.

A fourth promising and almost limitless direction for research revolves around political issues. For each issue of concern, what general trends in global and local environments open space for and condition the behaviour of individuals and collectivities? What polities of various types are engaged in the issue? What are their sources of influence and/or control, how legitimate are they seen to be, and to what extent are they successful in realizing their potential? What are the normative implications of the patterns observed, including value allocations with regard to each issue? What policy prescriptions for which polities might lead the way to more desirable outcomes?

The research agenda we have outlined for ourselves and recommend to others is clearly an ambitious one, but in our view must be pursued if we are fully to comprehend our post-international world. There is really no alternative unless we are to content ourselves with a context-limited and state-centric neverland.

Notes

1 Between celebration and despair

1 'Structuration theory' is most clearly identified with the work of British sociologist Anthony Giddens.
2 We use the terms 'post-structuralists', 'post-positivists', and 'postmodernists' interchangeably as the relevant theorists themselves often do, emphasizing different aspects of their arguments.
3 Confusion between 'state' and 'government' is one explanation for the propensity to exaggerate the importance of sovereignty.
4 This Enlightenment metaphor is associated both with Voltaire and William Paley, once fellow and tutor at Cambridge University and later Archdeacon of Carlisle.

2 Values and paradigm change in global politics

1 By norms, we refer to considerations that are viewed as ethically compelling.
2 The following discussion is partly based on Mansbach and Vasquez, 1981: 57–60.
3 Among the key values that have been represented as universal are wealth, security, order, freedom, peace, status, health, equality, justice, knowledge, beauty, honesty, and love. See Lasswell and Kaplan,1950: 55–6; and Gurr 1970: 24–6. All are subjective constructs that express human aspirations for self-improvement.
4 Efforts to identify relatively permanent value hierarchies are at best elusive and, at worst, probably wrong-headed.
5 It is, thus, a paradox that so many scientists employed realist assumptions. Whether this was due to cognitive reconciliation of opposites or simple unconsciousness is not clear.
6 This view underlies the realist claim that perceptions of relative rather than absolute gain dominate policy.
7 The distinction between these two emphases reflects the problem of private versus collective benefits.

4 Historical perspectives on contemporary global politics

1 Working title: *Preinternational Polities*.
2 As Finley (1986: 22) reminds us, we need to be careful not to be too smug about our scientific advances. Fifth-century Athenians were about as equipped in terms of tools and manpower as Schliemann and Sir Arthur Evans to dig at Mycenae or Knossos, and certainly had the intelligence to link whatever they might have found to myths of Agamemnon and Minos. 'What they lacked was the interest.'

On the other side of the coin: 'Thucydides and his contemporaries knew the full corpus of lyric and elegiac poetry, but they made less use, and less skilful use, of this material for historical analysis than we make of the few scraps that have survived in our time.'

3 Stephen J. Kobrin (2000) quotes Stein, with equal appropriateness, to describe contemporary cyberspace.

4 The discussion of the debates addressed in this and the following paragraph rely in part on Freeman (1996: 5–6, 10–11).

5 A point made by Freeman (1996: 5–6) – and by McNeill himself in the 2nd edition (1991) of *The Rise of the West*.

6 It is important to specify *sustained* concern when making such a statement. Remote areas like Afghanistan or Quemoy/Matsu have obviously been of intense concern to the US for limited periods of time. Moreover, US Manifest Destiny policies and the Cold War probably had more impact upon the course of US-Cuban relations at any given time than Cuba's mere proximity to the United States.

7 Buzan and Little offer an unusually comprehensive and thoughtful survey of what they term 'systemic thinking in world history' (Buzan and Little 2000: Chapt 3).

5 The web of world politics

1 Such groups may lack the primary commitment to self-preservation we ascribe to state actors. They might be insensitive to the kinds of retaliatory threats that have been a mainstay of order in a decentralized world system. What this means is that they fall outside the scope of the logic of deterrence – a fact with profoundly destabilizing implications.

2 Only states have territoriality, another commonly cited attribute of international actors.

8 The past as prelude to the future?

1 The Chaldean label encompassed at least three distinct tribes: the Bit-Dakuri, the Bit-Amukani, and the Bit-Yakin.

2 Polities acquire one another's characteristics not only by nesting, subordination, and conquest, but also by contact at the periphery.

3 Whereby a citizen of one polis who was resident in another might act as a sort of consul, representing the interests of the citizens of his home polis.

4 A second usage, favoured by historical sociologists, equates the state with *any* institutionalized authority. It could be a democratically elected government, a military dictator and his cronies, a medieval monarchy, an Inca hierarchy, or the Ottoman Empire.

5 *New York Times*, 7 February 1993, pg. 1.

6 The manner in which Romans and Persians tolerated cultural and religious parochialism and early Christianity embraced symbols ranging from the Isis cult to Germanic paganism illustrate the value of co-optation.

9 Beyond international relations to global politics

1 For the impact of norms on state behaviour against renegades, see Löwenheim (2003).

2 Gidon Gottlieb (1993: 37–38) also offers the medieval analogy as an alternative to a territorially organized world.

3 Ruggie, 'Continuity and Transformation in the World Polity', pp. 274, 276. Ruggie is citing Perry Anderson (1974) *Lineages of the Absolutist State*, London: New Left Books, pp. 37–38. We must be careful about following Ruggie too

closely on the relationship between 'property' and 'sovereignty' because there are differences in the Anglo-American and continental traditions of defining private property. Continental thinkers have often viewed 'private' property as owned and managed by the state; whereas Anglo-American scholars have emphasized a tradition of individual ownership.

4 Bruce Bueno de Mesquita (2000: 101) argues that the revenue from vacant bishoprics enjoyed by kings under the terms of the Concordat of Worms (1122 AD) was 'a property right that adhered to the king as sovereign over the territory of the See' and that this right represented 'the beginnings of the state'.

5 We use total sales to measure TNC wealth and gross national income to measure national wealth. Gross national income is the value of all production at home plus income from abroad. Data from World Bank (2003: Table 1).

6 Van Creveld (1999: 349) sees as the Franco-Prussian War of 1870–71 as the 'turning point in the process that eventually made the annexation by one state of territory belonging to others into a legal and practical impossibility'.

7 Libicki (1999–2000: 41) also points out that what he calls the 'globalisation of perception', or everybody's ability to know what is going on in the world, can create world opinion to protect small states from large ones.

8 Krasner (1999: 235) writes: 'There is no commonly accepted term for the European Union. Is it a state, a commonwealth, a dominion, a confederation of states, a federation of states?'

10 War and innocent victims

1 The best summary of empirical analysis on the relationship among territoriality, contiguity, and war is to be found in Vasquez 1993: 123–52.

2 For a grim portrayal of the war, see Hans Jakob Christoph von Grimmelshausen, *The Adventurous Simplicissimus* (1669).

11 Superpower, hegemony, empire

1 Cerny carefully reviews the range of definitions in the literature.

2 Special thanks to Phil Cerny, Magali Gravier, and Alexander Motyl for their helpful advice on the subject and literature of empires.

3 For a fuller discussion, see Motyl 1999: Chapter 7, and 2001: 4–5.

12 Post-internationalism and IR theory

1 As Rosenau (2003: 295) sees it, 'an SOA can be an issue regime, a professional society, an epistemic community, a neighborhood, a network of the like-minded, a truth commission, a corporation, business subscribers to codes of conduct ... , a social movement, a local or provincial government, a diaspora, a regional association, a loose confederation of NGOs, a transnational advocacy group, a paramilitary force, a credit-rating agency, a strategic partnership, a transnational network, a terrorist organization, and so on across all the diverse collectivities that have become sources of decisional authority in the ever more complex multi-centric world'.

2 It always was something of a myth as Janice E. Thomson (1994) argues convincingly. See also Oded Löwenheim (2007).

Bibliography

Agnew, John and Stuart Corbridge (1995) *Mastering Space: Hegemony, Territory and International Political Economy*, London: Routledge.

Anderson, Benedict (1983) *Imagined Communities: Reflections on the Origin and Spread of Nationalism*, London: Verso.

Anderson, Sarah and John Cavanagh (2000) 'Top 200: The Rise of Global Corporate Power', *Corporate Watch*. Online Available at <http://www.globalpolicy.org/socecon/tncs/top200.htm>.

Ashley, David (1997) *History Without a Subject: The Postmodern Condition*, Boulder, CO: Westview.

Ashley, Richard K. and R. B. J. Walker (1990) 'Speaking the Language of Exile: Dissident Thought in International Studies,' *International Studies Quarterly*, 34: 3 (September), pp. 259–68.

Avant, Deborah (2004) 'Mercenaries', *Foreign Policy*, 143 (July/August), 20–28.

Bacevich, Andrew J. (2002) *American Empire: The Realities and Consequences of U.S. Diplomacy*, Cambridge, MA: Harvard University Press.

Barnett, Michael N. (1995) 'Sovereignty, Nationalism, and Regional Order in the Arab States System', *International Organization*, 49:3 (Summer), pp. 477–510.

Barnett, Michael N. and Martha Finnemore (2004) *Rules for the World: International Organizations in Global Politics*, Ithaca, NY: Cornell University Press.

Barstow, David (2004) 'Security Companies: Shadow Soldiers in Iraq', *New York Times*, 19 April.

Bell, J. Bowyer (1971) 'Contemporary Revolutionary Organizations,' in Robert O. Keohane, and Joseph S. Nye (eds), 'Transnational Relations and World Politics,' special edition of *Internal Organization*, 25:3 (Summer), pp. 503–18.

Bell, Peter D. (1971) 'The Ford Foundation as a Transnational Actor,' in Robert O. Keohane, and Joseph S. Nye (eds) 'Transnational Relations and World Politics,' special edition of *Internal Organization*, 25:3 (Summer), pp. 465–78.

Biersteker, Thomas J. (1989) 'Critical Reflections on Post-Positivism in International Relations' *International Studies Quarterly*, 33:3 (September), pp. 269–79.

——and Cynthia Weber (1996) (eds) *State Sovereignty as a Social Construct*, Cambridge: Cambridge University Press.

Binford, Lewis R. (1983) *In Pursuit of the Past: Decoding the Archaeological Record*, London: Thames and Hudson.

Black, Anthony (1992) *Political Thought in Europe 1250–1450*, Cambridge: Cambridge University Press.

Blaney, David L. and Naeem Inayatullah (2000) 'The Westphalian Deferral', *International Studies Review*, 2:2 (Summer), pp. 29–64.

Bosworth, A. B. (2003) 'Introduction: Some Basic Principles', in Ian Worthington (ed.) *Alexander the Great: A Reader*, London: Routledge, pp. 1–16.

Boulding, Kenneth E. (1962) *Conflict and Defense: A General Theory*, New York: Harper & Row.

Bourdieu, Pierre (1984) *Distinction: A Social Critique of the Judgment of Taste*, trans. Richard Nice, Cambridge, MA: Harvard University Press.

Boyarin, Jonathan (1994) 'Space, Time, and the Politics of Memory', in Jonathan Boyarin (ed) *Remapping Memory: The Politics of TimeSpace*, Minneapolis: University of Minnesota Press, pp. 1–37.

Bozeman, Adda B. (1960) *Politics and Culture in International History*, Princeton: Princeton University Press.

Bradley, James (with Ron Powers) (2000) *Faith of Our Fathers*, New York: Bantam, 2000.

Brierly, J. L. (1963) *The Law of Nations*, 6th edn, New York: Oxford University Press.

Brooks Stephen G. and William C. Wohlforth (2002) 'American Primacy in Perspective', *Foreign Affairs*, 81:4 (July/August), pp. 20–33.

Bronowski, Jacob (1978)*The Origins of Knowledge and Imagination*, New Haven, CT: Yale University Press.

Brougham, Henry Brougham (1970) 'Balance of Power', in M. G. Forsyth, H. M. A. Keens-Soper, P. Savigear (eds) *The Theory of International Relations: Selected Texts from Gentili to Treitschke*, New York: Atherton Press, pp. 260–74.

Bueno de Mesquita, Bruce (2000) 'Popes, Kings, and Endogenous Institutions: The Concordat of Worms and the Origins of Sovereignty', *International Studies Review*, 2:2 (Summer), pp. 93–118.

Bull, Hedley (1977) *The Anarchical Society*, New York: Columbia University Press.

Burke, Peter (1986) *The Italian Renaissance: Culture and Society in Italy*, Princeton: Princeton University Press.

Burnham, James (1943) *The Machiavellians: Defenders of Freedom*, Chicago: Henry Regnery.

Burton, J. W. (1968) *Systems, States, Diplomacy and Rules*, New York: Cambridge University Press.

Buzan, Barry and Richard Little (2000) *International Systems in World History: Remaking the Study of International Relations*, Oxford: Oxford University Press.

——and Charles Jones (1993) *The Logic of Anarchy: Neorealism to Structural Realism*, New York: Columbia University Press.

——(1996) 'Reconceptualizing Anarchy: Structural Realism Meets World History', *European Journal of International Relations*, 2:4, pp. 403–38.

Caldwell, Christopher (2006) 'After Londonistan', *New York Times Magazine* (23 June), pp. 41–47, 62, 74.

'Capitals of Capital' (1998) *The Economist* (May 7). Available at: <http://www.economist.com/surveys/displayStory.cfm?story_id=168334>.

Caporaso, James A. (2000) 'Changes in the Westphalian Order: Territory, Public Authority, and Sovereignty', *International Studies Review*, 2:2 (Summer), pp. 1–28.

Carr, E. H. (1962) *The Twenty Years' Crisis, 1919–1939*, New York: St. Martin's Press.

Cartledge, Paul (1993) *The Greeks*, rev. edn, Oxford: Oxford University Press.

Castells, Manuel (2000) *The Rise of Network Society*, 2nd edn, Oxford: Blackwell.

Cerny, Philip G. (2006) 'Dilemmas of Operationalizing Hegemony', in Mark Haugaard and Howard H. Lentner (eds) *Hegemony and Power: Force and Consent in Contemporary Politics*, Lanham, MD: Lexington Books, pp. 67–87.

Chadwick, John (1976) *The Mycenaen World*, Cambridge: Cambridge University Press.

Clausewitz, Carl von (1976, rev. 1984) *On War*, Michael Howard and Peter Paret (eds and trans.), Princeton: Princeton University Press.

Cohen, Eliot A. (2004) 'History and the Hyperpower', *Foreign Affairs*, 83:4 (July/August 2004), pp. 49–63.

Cooper, Frederick (2003–04) 'Modernizing Colonialism and the Limits of Empire', in *Items and Issues* (Social Science Research Council), 4:4 (Fall/Winter). Available at: <http://www.ssrc.org/publications/items/current.page>.

The Compact Edition of the Oxford English Dictionary (1971), New York: Oxford University Press.

Cox, Michael (2004) 'Empire, Imperialism, and the Bush Doctrine', *Review of International Studies*, 30:4 (October), pp. 585–608.

Crone, Patricia (1980) *Slaves on Horses: The Evolution of the Islamic Polity*, Cambridge: Cambridge University Press.

Cox, Robert W. (1986) 'Social Forces, States and World Orders: Beyond International Relations Theory,' in Robert O. Keohane (ed.) *Neorealism and Its Critics*, New York: Columbia University Press, pp. 204–54.

Cutler, A. Claire, Virginia Haufler, and Tony Porter (eds) (1999a) *Private Authority and International Affairs*, Albany, NY: State University of New York Press.

——(1999b) 'The Contours and Significance of Private Authority in International Affairs', in A. Claire Cutler, Virginia Haufler, and Tony Porter (eds) *Private Authority and International Affairs*, Albany, NY: State University of New York Press, pp. 333–76

Dabashi, Hamid (1989) *Authority in Islam: From the Rise of Muhammad to the Establishment of the Umayyads*, New Brunswick, NJ: Transaction Press.

Dahl, Robert A. (1967) *Pluralist Democracy in the United States*, Chicago: Rand McNally.

'Dangerous Work' (2004) *The Economist* (10–16 April), p. 22.

Denemark, Robert A., Barry K. Friedman, and George Modelski (eds) (2000) *World System History: The Science of Long-Term Change*, London: Routledge.

Dessler, David (1989) 'What's at Stake in the Agent-Structure Debate?' *International Organization*, 43:3 (Summer), pp. 441–73.

Deutsch, Karl W. (1966a) 'External Influences on the Internal Behavior of States,' in R. Barry Farrell (ed.) *Approaches to Comparative and International Politics*, Evanston, Ill: Northwestern University Press.

——(1966b) *Nationalism and Social Communication*, 2nd edn, Cambridge, MA: MIT Press.

Dijink, Gertjan (2001) 'The US as a Non-State or The Silent Language of History and Geography in International Relations', paper presented to the ECPR Pan-European Conference on International Relations, Canterbury, UK.

Dodds, E. R. (1964) *The Greeks and the Irrational*, Berkeley: University of California Press.

DomŌnguez, Jorge I. (1971) 'Mice that Do Not Roar: Some Aspects of International Politics in the World's Peripheries,' *International Organization*, 25:2 (Spring), pp. 175–208.

Doyle, Michael (1986) *Empires*, Ithaca, NY: Cornell University Press.

Easton, David (1965) *A Framework for Political Analysis*, Englewood Cliffs, NJ: Prentice-Hall.

Ehrenreich, Barbara (1997) *Blood Rites: Origins and History of the Passions of War*, New York: Henry Holt & Co.

Elton, G. R. (1967) *The Practice of History*, London: Fontana Press.

Evans, Peter B. (1971) 'National Autonomy and Economic Development,' in Robert O. Keohane, and Joseph S. Nye (eds) 'Transnational Relations and World Politics,' special edition of *International Organization*, 25:3 (Summer), pp. 675–92.

Feld, Werner (1970) 'Political Aspects of Transnational Business Collaboration in the Common Market,' *International Organization*, 24:2 (Spring), pp. 209–38.

Ferguson, Niall (2002) *Empire: The Rise and Demise of the British World Order and the Lessons for Global Power*, Oxford: Oxford University Press.

——(2004) *Colossus: The Price of America's Empire*, New York: Penguin Press.

——(2006a) 'Empires with Expiration Dates', *Foreign Policy*, 156 (September/October), pp. 46–52.

——(2006b) 'The Next War of the World,' *Foreign Affairs*, 85:5 (September/October), pp. 61–74.

Ferguson, Yale H. and Richard W. Mansbach (1988) *The Elusive Quest: Theory and International Politics*, Columbia, SC: University of South Carolina Press.

——(1989) *The State, Conceptual Chaos, and the Future of International Relations Theory*, Boulder, CO: Lynne Rienner, 1989.

——(1991) 'Between Celebration and Despair: Constructive Suggestions for Future International Theory,' *International Studies Quarterly*, 35:4 (December), pp. 363–86.

——(1996) *Polities: Authority, Identities, and Change*, Columbia, SC: University of South Carolina Press.

——(2002) 'Remapping Political Space: Issue and Non-Issues in Analyzing Global Politics in the Twenty-First Century', in Yale H. Ferguson and R. J. Barry Jones (eds) *Political Space: Frontiers of Change and Governance in a Globalizing World*, Albany, NY: State University of New York Press, pp. 87–111.

——(2003) *The Elusive Quest Continues: Theory and Global Politics*, Upper Saddle River, NJ: Prentice-Hall.

——(2004) *Remapping Global Politics: History's Revenge and Future Shock*, Cambridge: Cambridge University Press.

Fernández-Armesto, Felipe (1997) *Truth: A History and a Guide to the Perplexed*, London: Bantam.

Field, James A., Jr. (1971) 'Transnationalism and the New Tribe,' in Robert O. Keohane, and Joseph S. Nye (eds) 'Transnational Relations and World Politics,' special edition of *Internal Organization*, 25:3 (Summer), pp. 353–72.

Fine, John V. A. (1983) *The Ancient Greeks: A Critical History*, Cambridge, MA: Harvard University Press.

Finley, Moses I. (1981) *Early Greece: The Bronze and Archaic Ages*, rev. edn, New York: Norton.

——(1983) *Politics in the Ancient World*, Cambridge: Cambridge University Press.

——(1985) *The Ancient Economy*, 2nd edn, London: The Hogarth Press.

——(1986) *The Use and Abuse of History*, London: The Hogarth Press.

Florida, Richard (2005) 'The World Is Spiky', *Atlantic Monthly* (October), pp. 48–51.

Forero, Juan (2001) 'Role of U.S. Companies in Colombia Is Questioned', *New York Times*, 18 May.

Freedman, Lawrence (1998) *The Revolution in Strategic Affairs*, Adelphi Paper 318, New York: Oxford University Press.

Freeman, Charles (1996) *Egypt, Greece and Rome: Civilizations of the Ancient Mediterranean*, Oxford: Oxford University Press.

Friedman, Thomas L. (2005) *The World Is Flat: A Brief History of the Twenty-First Century*, New York: Farrar, Straus and Giroux.

Frissen, Paul (1997) 'The Virtual State: Postmodernisation, Informatisation and Public Administration', in Brian D. Loader (ed.) *The Governance of Cyberspace: Politics, Technology, and Global Restructuring*, London: Routledge, pp. 110–25.

Fukuyama, Francis (1992) *The End of History and the Last Man*, New York: The Free Press.

Giddens, Anthony (1984) *The Constitution of Society: Outline of the Theory of Structuration*, Cambridge: Polity.

Gilpin, Robert (1981) *War and Change in World Politics*, Cambridge: Cambridge University Press.

Giry, Stéphanie (2006) 'France and Its Muslims', *Foreign Affairs*, 85:5 (September/October), pp. 87–104.

Global Strategies Group (nd) 'Global Risk Strategies,' Available at: <http://www.globalrsl.com/>.

Gottlieb, Gidon (1993) *Nation against State: A New Approach to Ethnic Conflicts and the Decline of Sovereignty*, New York: Council on Foreign Relations Press.

Gray, Colin S. (1997–98) 'RMAs and the Dimensions of Strategy', *Joint Forces Quarterly*, (Autumn/Winter), pp. 50–54.

Green, Peter (1989) *Classical Bearings: Interpreting Ancient History and Culture*, Berkeley: University of California Press.

Grotius, Hugo (1957) *Prolegomena to the Law of War and Peace*, New York: Bobbs-Merrill.

Gurr, Ted Robert (1970) *Why Men Rebel*, Princeton: Princeton University Press.

Haass, Richard N. (1997) *The Reluctant Sheriff: The United States after the Cold War*, New York: Council on Foreign Relations Press.

Hale, J. R. (1971) *Renaissance Europe 1480–1520,* London: Fontana.

——(1977) *Florence and the Medici: The Pattern of Control*, London: Thames and Hudson.

——(1985) *War and Society in Renaissance Europe 1450–1620*, London: Fontana.

Hall, Rodney Bruce (1999) *National Collective Identity: Social Constructs and International Systems*, New York: Columbia University Press.

——and Thomas J. Biersteker (eds) (2002) *The Emergence of Private Authority in Global Governance*, Cambridge: Cambridge University Press.

Hammond, N. G. L. (1986) *A History of Greece to 322 B.C.*, 3rd edn, Oxford: Clarendon.

Hardt, Michael and Antonio Negri (2000) *Empire*, Cambridge, MA: Harvard University Press.

Hausmann, Ricardo (1997) 'Will Volatility Kill Market Democracy?' *Foreign Policy*, 108 (Fall), pp. 54–67.

Held, David (1995) *Democracy and the Global Order: From the Modern State to Cosmopolitan Governance*, Stanford, CA: Stanford University Press.

Helman, Gerald B. Helman and Steven R. Ratner (1992–93) 'Saving Failed States', *Foreign Policy*, 89 (Winter), pp. 3–20.

Herz, John H. (1959) *International Politics in the Atomic Age*, New York: Columbia University Press.

Hirschman, Albert O. (1977) *The Passions and the Interests: Political Arguments for Capitalism before Its Triumph*, Princeton: Princeton University Press.

Hitti, Philip K. (1956) *The Arabs: A Short History*, Chicago: Henry Regnery Company.

Hodder, Ian (1986) *Reading the Past*, Cambridge: Cambridge University Press.

Hollis, Martin (1994) *The Philosophy of Social Science: An Introduction*, Cambridge: Cambridge University Press.

Holmes, George (1975) *Europe: Hierarchy and Revolt, 1320–1450*, London: Fontana.

Holsti, K. J. (2002) 'The Problem of Change in International Relations History', in Yale H. Ferguson and R. J. Barry Jones, eds, *Political Space: Frontiers of Change and Governance in a Globalizing World*, Albany, NY: State University of New York Press, pp. 23–43.

Hostovsky, Charles (n.d.) 'How to Speak and Write Postmodern.' Obtained from hostovsk@geog.utoronto.ca.

Hourani, Albert (1991) *A History of the Arab Peoples*, Cambridge, MA: The Belknap Press of Harvard University Press.

Howe, Stephen (2002) *Empire: A Very Short Introduction*, London: Oxford University Press.

Huntington, Samuel P. (1996) *The Clash of Civilizations and the Remaking of World Order*, New York: Simon & Schuster.

Hyde, J. K. (1973) *Society and Politics in Medieval Italy: The Evolution of the Civil Life, 1000–1350*, London: Macmillan.

Ikenberry, G. John (2002) 'America's Imperial Ambition', *Foreign Affairs*, 81:5 (September/October), pp. 44–60.

Jervis, Robert (1997) *System Effects: Complexity in Social and Political Life*, Princeton: Princeton University Press.

Jones, R. J. Barry (2001) 'Hegemony', in *Routledge Encyclopedia of International Political Economy*, London: Routledge.

Jönsson, Christer, Sven Tägil and Gunnar Törnquist (2000) *Organizing European Space*, London: Sage.

Kahler, Miles (1995) *International Institutions and the Political Economy of Integration*, Washington, DC: The Brookings Institution.

Keating Michael and Liesbet Hooghe (2001) 'By-Passing the Nation State? Regions and the EU Policy Process', in Jeremy J. Richardson (ed.) *Policy Making in the European Union*, London: Routledge, pp. 216–29.

Keegan, John (1994) *A History of Warfare*, New York: Vintage Books.

Kennan, George F. (1951) *American Diplomacy 1900–1950*, Chicago: University of Chicago Press.

Kennedy, Paul (1987) *The Rise and Fall of the Great Powers: Economic Change and Military Conflict from 1500 to 2000*, New York: Random House.

Keohane, Robert O. (1984) *After Hegemony: Cooperation and Discord in the World Political Economy*, Princeton: Princeton University Press.

——(1988) 'International Institutions: Two Approaches' *International Studies Quarterly*, 32:4 (December), 379–96.

——(2002) *Power and Governance in a Partially Globalized World*, London: Routledge.

——and Joseph S. Nye (2001) *Power and Interdependence*, 3rd edn, New York: Longman.

Knorr, Klaus and James N. Rosenau (1969) 'Tradition and Science in the Study of International Politics,' in Klaus Knorr and James N. Rosenau (eds) *Contending Approaches to International Politics*, Princeton: Princeton University Press, pp. 3–19.

Kobrin, Stephen J. (1997) 'Electronic Cash and the End of National Markets', *Foreign Policy*, 107 (Summer), pp. 65–77.

——(1998) 'Back to the Future: Neomedievalism and the Postmodern Digital World Economy', *Journal of International Affairs*, 51:2 (Spring), pp. 361–86.

——(2000) 'There's No There, There: Gertrude Stein and the Governance of Cyberspace', paper presented to the International Studies Association (ISA) annual meeting.

Kornhauser, William (1959) *The Politics of Mass Society*, Glencoe, IL: Free Press.

Krasner, Stephen D. (1993) 'Westphalia and All That', in Judith Goldstein and Robert O. Keohane (eds) *Ideas and Foreign Policy: Beliefs, Institutions, and Political Change*, Ithaca, NY: Cornell University Press, pp. 235–64.

——(1999) *Sovereignty: Organized Hypocrisy*, Princeton: Princeton University Press.

——(2001) 'Problematic Sovereignty', in Stephen D. Krasner (ed.) *Problematic Sovereignty: Contested Rules and Political Possibilities*, New York: Columbia University Press, pp. 1–23.

Kratochwil, Friedrich V. (1986) 'Of Systems, Boundaries, and Territoriality: An Inquiry into the Formation of the State System', *World Politics*, 39:1 (October), pp. 27–52.

——(1989) *Rules, Norms, and Decisions: On the Conditions of Practical and Legal Reasoning in International Relations and Domestic Affairs*, Cambridge, Cambridge University.

——and John Gerard Ruggie (1986) 'International Organization: A State of the Art on the Art of the State,' *International Organization*, 40:4 (Autumn), pp. 753–75.

Krauthammer, Charles (1990/91) 'The Unipolar Moment', *Foreign Affairs*, 70:1 special issue *America and the World 1990/91*, (winter), pp. 23–33.

Kroll, Luisa and Allison Fass (eds) (2006) 'The World's Billionaires', *Forbes*. Available at: <http://www.forbes.com/billionaires/>.

Kubálková, Vendulka, Nicholas Onuf and Paul Kowert (1998) *International Relations in a Constructed World*, Armonk, NY: M. E. Sharpe.

Kuhn, Thomas S. (1970) *The Structure of Scientific Revolutions*, expanded edn, Chicago: University of Chicago Press.

Kumar, Krishan (1995) *From Post-Industrial to Post-Modern Society: New Theories of the Contemporary World*, Oxford, UK: Blackwell.

Lakatos, Imre (1978) *The Methodology of Scientific Research Programmes: Philosophical Papers* I, Cambridge: Cambridge University Press.

Lake, David A. (1997) 'The Rise, Fall, and Future of the Russian Empire', in Karen Dawisha and Bruce Parrott (eds) *The End of Empire? The Transformation of the USSR in Comparative Perspective*, Armonk, NY: M. E. Sharpe, pp. 30–62.

Lamy, Steven, Robert English, and Steve Smith (eds) (2005) 'Hegemony and Its Discontents: A Symposium', *International Studies Review*, 7: 4 (December).

Lapid, Yosef (1989) 'The Third Debate: On the Prospects for International Theory in a Post-Positivist Era,' *International Studies Quarterly*, 33:3 (September), pp. 235–54.

Larson, A. *et al.* (1965), *Sovereignty within the Law*, Dobbs Ferry, New York: Oceana.

Lasswell, Harold J. and Abraham Kaplan (1950) *Power and Society*, New Haven, CT: Yale University Press.

Le Goff, Jacques (1988) *Medieval Civilization*, trans. Julia Barrow, Oxford: Blackwell.

Lewis, Bernard (1993) *The Arabs in History*, New York: Oxford University Press.

Libicki, Martin (1999–2000) 'Rethinking War: The Mouse's New Roar', *Foreign Policy*, 117 (Winter), pp. 30–43.

Lieven, Dominic (2001) *Empire: The Russian Empire and Its Rivals*, New Haven: Yale University Press.

Lippmann, Walter (1955) *The Public Philosophy*, New York: Mentor.

Loader, Brian D. (1997) 'The Governance of Cyberspace: Politics, Technology and Global Restructuring', in Brian D. Loader (ed.) *The Governance of Cyberspace: Politics, Technology, and Global Restructuring*, London: Routledge, pp. 1–22.

Love, Richard A. (2003) 'The Cyberthreat Continuum', in Maryann Cusimano Love (ed.) *Beyond Sovereignty: Issues for a Global Agenda*, Belmont, CA: Wadsworth/ Thomson, pp. 195–218.

Löwenheim, Oded (2003) ' "Do Ourselves Credit and Render a Lasting Service to Mankind": British Moral Prestige, Humanitarian Intervention, and the Barbary Pirates', *International Studies Quarterly*, 47:1 (March), pp. 23–48.

——(2007) *Predators and Parasites: Persistent Agents of Transnational Harm and Great Power Authority*, Ann Arbor, MI: University of Michigan Press.

Lowenthal, David (1985) *The Past Is a Foreign Country*, Cambridge: Cambridge University Press.

Lundestad, Geir (1990) *The American 'Empire'*, Oslo: Norwegian University Press.

Mandelbaum, Michael (2002) 'The Inadequacy of American Power', *Foreign Affairs*, 81:5 (September/October), pp. 61–73.

Mann, Michael (1986) *The Sources of Social Power, Vol 1: A History of Social Power from the Beginning to A.D. 1760*, Cambridge: Cambridge University Press.

——(1993) *The Sources of Social Power, Vol. 2: The Rise of Classes and Nation-States, 1760–1914*, Cambridge: Cambridge University Press.

——(2003) *Incoherent Empire*, London: Verso.

——(2004) 'Failed Empire', *Review of International Studies*, 30:4 (October), pp. 631–53.

Mansbach, Richard W., Yale H. Ferguson, and Donald E. Lampert (1976) *The Web of World Politics: Nonstate Actors in the Global System*, Englewood Cliffs, NJ: Prentice-Hall.

——and John A. Vasquez (1981) *In Search of Theory: A New Paradigm for Global Politics*, New York: Columbia University Press.

——and Franke Wilmer (2001) 'War and the Westphalian State of Mind', in Mathias Albert, David Jacobson, and Yosef Lapid (eds) *Identities, Borders, Order*, Minneapolis: University of Minnesota Press, 2001, pp. 51–71.

Marcus Aurelius (1993) *Meditations*, trans Maxwell Staniforth, in Bernard Knox (ed.), *The Norton Book of Classical Literature*, New York: Norton.

Markus, Robert (1990) *The End of Ancient Christianity*, Cambridge: Cambridge University Press.

Markoff, John and Lowell Bergman (2005) 'Internet Attack Called Broad and Long Lasting by Investigators', *New York Times* (10 May). Available at: <http://www.nytimes.com/2005/05/10/technology/10cisco.html>.

Martin, Raymond (1989) *The Past Within Us: An Empirical Approach to Philosophy of History*, Princeton: Princeton University Press.

Matthews, Jessica (1997) 'Power Shift', *Foreign Affairs*, 76:1 (January/February), pp. 50–66.

McGowan, Patrick J. and Howard B. Shapiro (1973), *The Comparative Study of Foreign Policy: A Survey of Scientific Findings*, Beverley Hills, CA: Sage Publications.

McNeill, J. R. and William H. McNeill (2003) *The Human Web: A Bird's Eye View of World History*, New York: Norton.

McNeill, William H. (1963) *The Rise of the West: A History of the Human Community*, Chicago: University of Chicago Press.

——(1979) *A World History*, 3rd edn, Oxford: Oxford University Press.

——(1986) *Polyethnicity and National Unity in World History*, Toronto: University of Toronto Press.

——(1997) 'Territorial States Buried Too Soon,' *Mershon International Studies Review*, 41, Supplement 2 (November), pp. 269–74.

Mearsheimer, John (2001) *The Tragedy of Great Power Politics*, New York: Norton.

Metz, Steven (2000) *Armed Conflict in the 21st Century: The Information Revolution and Post-Modern Warfare*, Carlisle, PA: Strategic Studies Institute.

Miller, Judith (1999) 'Sovereignty Isn't So Sacred Anymore', *New York Times*, 18 April.

Moravcsik, Andrew (1997) 'Taking Preferences Seriously: A Liberal Theory of International Politics,' *International Organization*, 51:4 (Autumn), pp. 513–53.

Morgenthau, Hans J. (1946) *Scientific Man vs. Power Politics*, Chicago: University of Chicago Press.

——(1978) *Politics Among Nations: The Struggle for Power and Peace*, 5th revised edn, New York: Knopf.

Morris, Ian (1987) *Burial and Ancient Society: The Rise of the Greek City-State*, Cambridge: Cambridge University Press.

Morrison, Kathleen D. (2001) 'Sources, Approaches, Definitions', in Susan E. Alcock, Terence N. D'Altroy, Kathleen D. Morrison and Caria M. Sinopoli (eds) *Empires: Perspectives from Archaeology and History*, Cambridge: Cambridge University Press, pp. 1–9.

Motyl, Alexander J. (1999) *Revolutions, Nations, Empires: Conceptual Limits and Theoretical Possibilities*, New York: Columbia University Press.

——(2001) *Imperial Ends: The Decay, Collapse, and Revival of Empires*, New York: Columbia University Press.

——(2006) 'Is Everything Empire? Is Empire Everything?' *Comparative Politics*, 38:2 (January), pp. 229–49.

Murray, Williamson (1997) 'Thinking About Revolutions in Military Affairs', *Joint Forces Quarterly*, (Summer): 69–76.

Muthien, Bernedette and Ian Taylor (2002) 'The Return of the Dogs of War? The Privitization of Security in Africa', in Rodney Bruce Hall and Thomas J. Biersteker (eds), *The Emergence of Private Authority in Global Governance*, Cambridge: Cambridge University Press, pp. 183–99.

Naff, Thomas (1981) 'Towards a Muslim Theory of History', in Alexander S. Cudsi and Ali E. Hillal Dessouki (eds) *Islam and Power*, London: Croom Helm Ltd.

Naím, Moisés (1995) 'Mexico's Larger Story', *Foreign Policy*, 99 (Summer), pp. 112–30.

Nettl, J. P. (1968) 'The State as a Conceptual Variable,' *World Politics*, 20:4 (July), pp. 559–92.

Norwich, John Julius (1982) *A History of Venice*, New York: Knopf.

Novick, Peter (1988) *That Noble Dream: The 'Objectvity Question' and the American Historical Profession*, Cambridge: Cambridge University Press.

Nye, Joseph S. (1990) *Bound to Lead: The Changing Nature of American Power*, New York: Basic Books.

——(2002) *The Paradox of American Power: Why the World's Only Superpower Can't Go It Alone*, Oxford: Oxford University Press.

——(2004) *Power in the Global Information Age: From Realism to Globalization*, New York: Routledge.

Onuf, Nicholas G. (1989) *World of Our Making: Rules and Rule in Social Theory and International Relations*, Columbia, SC: University of South Carolina Press.

——(1995) 'Levels,' *European Journal of International Relations*, Vol. 1, No. 1 (March), pp. 35–58.

——(1998) 'Constructivism: A User's Manual,' in Vendulka Kubálková, Nicholas Onuf, and Paul Kowert, *International Relations in a Constructed World*, Armonk, NY: M. E. Sharpe, pp. 58–78.

Ortega y Gasset, José (1948) *The Dehumanization of Art and Other Essays on Art, Culture and Literature* Princeton: Princeton University Press.

Palmer, R. R. (1986) 'Frederick the Great, Guibert, Bülow: From Dynastic to National War', in Peter Paret (ed.) *Makers of Modern Strategy*, Princeton: Princeton University Press.

Peters, B. and G. Peters (1992) 'Bureaucratic Politics and the Institutions of the European Community,' in Alberta M. Sbraglia (ed.) *Euro-politics: Institutions and Policy-making in the 'New' European Community*, Washington, DC: Brookings Institute.

Pfaff, William (1995) 'A New Colonialism?' *Foreign Affairs*, 74:1 (January/February), pp. 2–6.

Pharr, Susan J. and Robert D. Putnam (eds) (2000) *Disaffected Democracies: What's Troubling the Trilateral Countries*, Princeton: Princeton University Press.

Plumb, J. H. (2004) *The Death of the Past*, Houndsmill, Basingstoke, Hampshire: Palgrave Macmillan.

'Present at the Creation: A Survey of America's World Role' (2002) *The Economist* (29 June), p. 4.

Puchala, Donald J. (1991) *'Woe to the Orphans of the Scientific Revolution,'* in Robert L. Rothstein (ed.) *The Evolution of Theory in International Relations.* Columbia: SC: University of South Carolina Press, pp. 39–60.

——(2003) *Theory and History in International Relations*, New York: Routledge.

——(2005) 'World Hegemony and the United Nations', in Steven Lamy, Robert English, and Steve Smith (eds) 'Hegemony and Its Discontents: A Symposium', *International Studies Review*, 7: 4 (December), pp. 571–84.

'Putting It in Its Place' (2001) *The Economist* (11 August). Available at: <http://www.economist.com/printedition/displaystory.cfm?story_id=729808>.

Refrew, Colin and Paul Bahn (1991) *Archaeology: Theory, Methods and Practice*, London: Thames & Hudson.

Reynolds, Susan (1984) *Kingdoms and Communities in Western Europe, 900–1300*, Oxford: Oxford University Press.

Ricks, Thomas E. (1999) 'For These B-2 Pilots, Bombs Away Means Really Far, Far Away', *Wall Street Journal*, (19 April), p. A1.

Robinson, J. H. (ed.) (1906) *The Destruction of Magdeburg, Readings in European History*, 2 vols, Boston: Ginn, pp. 2, 211–12. Available at: <http://history.hanover.edu/texts/magde.html>.

Roberson, Barbara Allen (1988) 'The Islamic Belief System,' in Richard Little and Steve Smith (eds) *Belief Systems and International Relations*, Oxford: Basil Blackwell.

Rosenau, James N. (ed.) (1969) *Linkage Politics: Essays on Convergence of National and International Systems*, New York: Free Press.

——(1984) 'A Pre-Theory Revisited: World Politics in an Era of Cascading Interdependence', *International Studies Quarterly*, 28:3 (September), pp. 245–305.

——(1986) 'Before Cooperation: Hegemons, Regimes, and Habit-Driven Actors in World Politics', *International Organization*, pp. 849–94.

——(1990) *Turbulence in World Politics: A Theory of Change and Continuity*, Princeton: Princeton University Press.

——(1994) 'New Dimensions of Security: The Interaction of Globalizing and Localizing Dynamics,' *Security Dialogue*, 25:3 (September), pp. 255–81.

——(1995) 'Multilateral Governance and the Nation-State System: A Post-Cold War Assessment', paper presented to the first meeting of a Study Group of the Inter-American Dialogue in Washington, DC.

——(1997) *Along the Domestic-Foreign Frontier: Exploring Governance in a Turbulent World*, Cambridge: Cambridge University Press.

——(2000) 'Beyond Postinternationalism', in Heidi H. Hobbs (ed.) *Pondering Postinternationalism*, Albany, NY: State University of New York Press, pp. 219–37.

——(2002) 'NGOs and Fragmented Authority in Globalizing Space', in Yale H. Ferguson and Barry Jones (eds) *Political Space: Frontiers of Change and Governance in a Globalizing World*, Albany, NY: State University of New York Press, pp. 261–79.

——(2003) *Distant Proximities: Dynamics beyond Globalization*, Princeton: Princeton University Press.

——and Ernst-Otto Czempiel (eds) (1992) *Governance without Government: Order and Change in World Politics*, Cambridge: Cambridge University Press.

Rousseau, Jean-Jacques (1970) 'Abstract of the Abbé de Saint-Pierre's Project for Perpetual Peace', in M. G. Forsyth, H. M. A. Keens-Soper, P. Savigear (eds) *The Theory of International Relations: Selected Texts from Gentili to Treitschke*, New York: Atherton Press, pp. 131–77.

Ruggie, John Gerard (1983) 'Continuity and Transformation in the World Polity: Toward a Neorealist Synthesis'. *World Politics*, 35:2 (January), pp. 261–85.

——(1993) 'Territoriality and Beyond: Problematizing Modernity in International Relations'. *International Organization*, 47:1 (Winter), pp. 139–74.

——(1998) *Constructing the World Polity: Essays on International Institutionalization*, London: Routledge.

Rummel, R. J. (1976) 'The Roots of Faith,' in James N. Rosenau (ed.) *In Search of Global Patterns*, New York: Free Press.

Russett, Bruce M. (1972) 'A Macroscopic View of International Politics,' in James N. Rosenau, Vincent Davis, and M. A. East (eds) *The Analysis of International Politics*, New York: Free Press, pp. 109–24.

Sahlins, Peter (1989) *Boundaries: The Making of France and Spain in the Pyrenees*, Berkeley, CA: University of California Press.

Sarkees, Meredith Reid, Frank Whelon Wayman, and J. David Singer (2003) 'Inter-State, Intra-State, and Extra-State Wars: A Comprehensive Look at Their Distribution over Time, 1816–1997', *International Studies Quarterly*, 47:1 (March), pp. 49–70.

Sassen, Saskia (1994) *Cities in a Global Economy*, Thousand Oaks, CA: Pine Forge Press.

——(1999a) 'Embedding the Global in the National: Implications for the Role of the State', in David A. Smith, Dorothy J. Solinger, and Stephen C. Topik (eds) *States and Sovereignty in the Global Economy*, London: Routledge, pp. 158–71.

——(1999b) 'Global Financial Centers', *Foreign Affairs*, 78:1 (January/February), pp. 75–87.

——(2001) *The Global City*, 2nd edn, Princeton: Princeton University Press.

——(2006) *Territory, Authority, Rights: From Medieval to Global Assemblages*, Princeton: Princeton University Press.

Saunders, J. J. (1965) *A History of Medieval Islam*, London: Routledge and Kegan Paul, 1965.

Scheidel, Walter and Sitta von Reden (eds) (2002) *The Ancient Economy*, Edinburgh: Edinburgh University Press.

Schelling, Thomas C. (1966) *Arms and Influence*, New Haven: Yale University Press.

Schwartz, Herman M. (2000) *States Versus Markets*, 2nd cdn, New York: St. Martin's.

Serra, Antonio Truyol (ed.) (1946) *The Principles of Political and International Law in the Work of Francisco de Vitoria*, Madrid: Ediciones Cultura Hispanica.

Shapiro, Michael J. (1989) 'Textualizing Global Politics,' in James Der Derian and Michael Shapiro (eds) *International/Intertextual Relations*, Lexington, MA: Lexington Books, pp. 11–22.

Shearer, David (1998) 'Outsourcing War', *Foreign Policy*, 112 (Fall), pp. 68–81.

Shultz, George P. (2004) 'A Changed World', Foreign Policy Research Institute (March 22). Available at: <http://www.fpri.org/enotes/20040322.americawar.shultz.changedworld.html>.

Simes, Dimitri K. (2003) 'America's Imperial Dilemma', *Foreign Affairs*, 82:6 (November/December), pp. 91–102.

Singer, J. David (1969a) 'The Global System and Its Sub-systems: A Developmental View,' in James N. Rosenau (ed.) *Linkage Politics*, New York: Free Press.

——(1969b) 'The Incompleat Theorist: Insight Without Evidence,' in James N. Rosenau and Klaus Knorr (eds) *Contending Approaches to International Politics* (Princeton: Princeton University Press), pp. 63–86.

——and Michael G. Wallace (1970) 'Intergovernmental Organization in the Global System, 1815–1964: A Quantitative Description,' *International Organization*, 24:2 (Spring), pp. 239–87.

Slackman, Michael (2006) 'And Now, Islamism Trumps Arabism', *New York Times* (20 August), sec. 4, p. 1.

Smith, Anthony D. (1991) *National Identity*, Reno: University of Nevada Press.

Smith, Steve (1996) 'Positivism and Beyond,' in Steve Smith, Ken Booth, and Marysia Zalewski (eds), *International Theory: Positivism and Beyond*, Cambridge: Cambridge University Press, pp. 11–44.

Smith, Thomas W. (2002) 'The New Law of War: Legitimizing Hi-Tech and Infrastructural Violence', *International Studies Quarterly*, 46:3 (September), pp. 355–74.

Sprout, Harold and Margaret Spout (1969), 'Environmental Factors in the Study of International Politics,' in James N. Rosenau (ed.) *International Politics and Foreign Policy*, rev. edn, (New York: Free Press), pp. 41–56

Spruyt, Hendrik (1994) *The Sovereign State and Its Competitors: An Analysis of Systems Change*, Princeton: Princeton University Press.

Sterling-Folker, Jennifer (ed.) (2005) *Making Sense of International Relations Theory*, Boulder, CO: Lynne Rienner.

Strange, Susan (1996) *The Retreat of the State: The Diffusion of Power in the World Economy*, Cambridge: Cambridge University Press.

Tamir, Yael (1993) *Liberal Nationalism*, Princeton: Princeton University Press.

Thomson, Janice E. (1994) *Mercenaries, Pirates, and Sovereigns: State-Building and Extraterritorial Violence in Early Modern Europe*, Princeton: Princeton University Press.

Thucydides (1972) *History of the Peloponnesian War*, trans. Rex Warner, rev. edn, London: Penguin.

Tickner, J. Ann (1997) 'You Just Don't Understand: Troubled Engagements Between Feminists and IR Theorists,' *International Studies Quarterly*, 41: 4 (December), pp. 611–32.

Tilly, Charles (ed.) (1975) *The Formation of Nation-States in Western Europe,* Princeton: Princeton University Press.

Tung, W. L. (1968) *International Law in an Organizing World,* New York: Thomas I. Crowell.

'U.S. Image Up Slightly, But Still Negative' (2005) *Pew Global Attitudes Project* (June). Available at: <http://pewglobal.org/reports/display.php?ReportID=247>.

Vallier, Ivan (1971) 'The Roman Catholic Church: A Transnational Actor,' in Robert O. Keohane, and Joseph S. Nye (eds) 'Transnational Relations and World Politics,' special edition of *International Organization,* 25:3 (Summer), pp. 471–502.

van Creveld, Martin (1989) *Technology and War* New York: Free Press.

——(1991) *The Transformation of War,* New York: Free Press.

——(1999) *The Rise and Decline of the State,* Cambridge: Cambridge University Press.

Vasquez, John A. (1993) *The War Puzzle,* Cambridge: Cambridge University Press.

Vital, David (1969) 'Back to Machiavelli,' in Klaus Knorr and James N. Rosenau (eds) *Contending Approaches to International Politics,* rev. edn, Princeton: Princeton University Press, pp. 140–57.

von Clausewitz, Karl Maria (1976), *On War,* Michael Howard and Peter Paret (eds), Princeton: Princeton University Press.

von Gentz, Friedrich (1970) 'Fragments upon the Present State of the Political Balance of Europe', in M. G. Forsyth, H. M. A. Keens-Soper, P. Savigear (eds) *The Theory of International Relations: Selected Texts from Gentili to Treitschke,* New York: Atherton Press, pp. 277–301.

von Glahn, Gerhard (1996) *Law Among Nations,* 7th edn, Boston: Allyn and Bacon.

Walker, R. B. J. (1989) 'History and Structure in the Theory of International Studies' *Millennium,* 18 (1989), pp. 63–83.

——(1993), *Inside/Outside: International Relations as Political Theory,* Cambridge: Cambridge University Press.

Wallerstein, Immanuel (1974) *The Modern World System: Capitalist Agriculture and the Origins of the European World-Economy in the Sixteenth Century,* New York: Academic Press.

——(1979) *The Capitalist World-Economy,* Cambridge: Cambridge University Press.

——(1984) *The Politics of the World-Economy: The States, the Movements, and Civilization,* Cambridge: Cambridge University Press.

——(1996) 'The Inter-State Structure of the Modern World-System', in Steve Smith, Booth, and Matysia Zakewski (eds) *International Theory: Positivism and Beyond,* Cambridge: Cambridge University Press, pp. 87–107.

Waltz, Kenneth N. (1959) *Man, the State, and War,* New York: Columbia University Press.

——(1967) 'The Politics of Peace,' *International Studies Quarterly,* 11:3 (September), pp. 199–221.

——(1979) *Theory of International Politics,* Reading, MA: Addison-Wesley.

—— (1986) 'Reflections on Theory of International Politics: A Response to My Critics', in Robert O. Keohane (ed.) *Neorealism and Its Critics,* New York: Columbia University Press, pp. 322–54.

Watson, Adam (1992) *The Evolution of International Society,* London: Routledge.

Watt, W. Montgomery (1973) *The Formative Period of Islamic Thought,* Chicago: Aldine Atherton, Inc.

——(1974) *The Majesty That Was Islam,* London: Sidgwick & Jackson.

——(1988) *Islamic Fundamentalism and Modernity,* New York: Routledge.

Weiner, Tim (2005) 'Air Force Seeks Bush's Approval for Space Weapons Programs', *New York Times* (18 May). Available at: <http://www.nytimes.com/2005/05/18/business/18space.html?hp&ex=1116475200&en=d2e1785def9a54d0&ei=5094&partner=homepage>.

Wendt, Alexander E. (1987) 'The Agent-Structure Problem in International Relations Theory,' *International Organization*, 41:3 (Summer), pp. 335–70.

——(1992) 'Anarchy Is What States Make of It: The Social Construction of Power Politics', *International Organization*, 46:2 (Spring), pp. 391–425.

——(1995) 'Constructing International Politics,' *International Security*, 20:1 (Summer), pp. 71–81.

——(1999) *Social Theory of International Politics*, Cambridge: Cambridge University Press.

Wendt, Alexander and Daniel Friedheim (1995) 'Hierarchy Under Hierarchy: Informal Empire and the East German State', *International Organization*, 49:4 (Autumn), pp. 689–721.

Wight, Martin (1966) 'Why Is There No International Theory?' in Herbert Butterfield and Martin Wight (eds) *'Diplomatic Investigations' Essays in the Theory of International Politics*, London: Allen & Unwin Press, pp. 17–34.

Williams, William Appleman (1980) *Empire as a Way of Life: An Essay on the Causes and Character of America's Present Predicament along with a Few Thoughts about an Alternative*, New York: Oxford University Press.

Wolfers, Arnold (1962) *Discord and Collaboration: Essays in International Politics*, Balitimore: Johns Hopkins Press.

World Bank (2004) *World Development Report* 2004, New York: Oxford University Press.

Young, Oran (1972) 'The Actors in World Politics,' in James N. Rosenau, Vincent Davis, and Maurice A. East (eds) *The Analysis of International Politics*, New York: Free Press, pp. 125–44.

Zaidman, Louise Bruit Zaidman and Pauline Schmitt Pantel (1992) *Religion in the Ancient Greek City*, trans. Paul Cartledge, Cambridge: Cambridge University Press.

'Zapatistas in Cyberspace: A Guide to Analysis and Resources'. Available at: <http://www.eco.utexas.edu/faculty/Cleaver/zapsincyber.html>.

Zinnes, Dina (1980) 'Prerequisites for the Study of System Transformation,' in Ole R. Holsti, Randolph P. Siverson and Alexander L. George (eds) *Change in the International System*, Boulder, CO: Westview Press, pp. 1–21.

Index